BUSINESS AND ACCOUNTING IN EUROPE

Business and Accounting in Europe

Edited by

A. T. McLEAN

Heriot-Watt University, Edinburgh

SAXON HOUSE | LEXINGTON BOOKS

Published by

SAXON HOUSE, D. C. Heath Ltd.
Westmead, Farnborough, Hants, England

Jointly with

LEXINGTON BOOKS, D. C. Heath & Co.
Lexington, Mass. U.S.A.

ISBN 0 347 0 1001 6
LOC No. 73 373 0
Printed in The Netherlands by D. Reidel Book Manufacturers, Dordrecht

Contents

The Authors

A. T. McLean, M.B.A., C.A. (editor), lecturer in Accountancy and Finance at Heriot-Watt University, Edinburgh.
T. A. Lee, M.Sc., C.A., A.T.I.I., lecturer in the Department of Accounting and Business Method, University of Edinburgh.
T. D. Lynch, C.A., partner in Whinney Murray and Co., chartered accountants, Glasgow., Member of Council of The Institute of Fiscal Studies and a former Member of Council of The Institute of Chartered Accountants of Scotland.
R. H. Parker, B.Sc. (Econ.), F.C.A., Professor of Accountancy and Dean of the Faculty of Law at the University of Dundee.
R. Shirley, M.A., Esmée Fairbairn senior research fellow in Finance at Heriot-Watt University, Edinburgh.
J. R. Small, B.Sc. (Econ.), F.C.C.A., F.C.M.A., J. Dip. M.A., Professor of Accountancy and Finance and Dean of the Faculty of Economic and Social Studies at Heriot-Watt University, Edinburgh. Member of Council of the Association of Certified Accountants.

Preface

My colleague, Michael J. Mepham, was primarily responsible for setting in motion a train of thought which is now expressed in this book. His interest in Europe was stimulated at the annual conference of Teachers of Accountancy in Scottish Universities held in March 1972 at Aberfoyle, where he was no doubt impressed by the eloquence and erudition of those members who presented papers, or contributed to the general discussion, on company accounting in the European Economic Community and its relevance to accounting practice and financial reporting in the United Kingdom. As I and several of my colleagues at Heriot-Watt, Edinburgh, and Dundee Universities had some considerable interest in '*les affaires européennes*' it appeared that a nucleus of information was already at hand, although eventually it required reinforcement from Glasgow and Paris, which may be construed as stretching the 'auld alliance' somewhat.

The subject matter of the book is designed to describe and illustrate certain financial, fiscal, and accounting matters which require the consideration of industrialists and accountants following the admission of the U.K. as a new member state of the Community. This in turn requires appraisal of the regulation of corporate bodies. The title of the book covers an extremely wide field and I do not claim to have achieved an optimum coverage of 'business and accounting in Europe', but rather that I have identified and included specific areas which do require explanation and illustration sufficient to excite further thought.

Most of the chapters examine the Community situation relative to that of the U.K. In this respect reasonable knowledge of British accounting, fiscal, and commercial practice and company law is assumed, although some of the authors take some care in explaining the British position relative to its European or Community counterpart. (In most cases the word 'Europe' is treated by the authors as being synonomous with the words 'European Economic Community' although in some illustrations third countries in the Continent of Europe have been introduced for comparative purposes.) The book, therefore, is intended as an introduction to important aspects of European business and accounting for advanced students of accounting and allied subjects, and business executives and accountants.

Part I, 'The company in Europe', embraces matters which, sooner or later, will affect the administration, control, and nature of companies. Chapter 1, 'The EEC and company regulation', describes the operations of the Community institutions and the creation of directives and regulations which will strike at the very heart of company law in the U.K. The thin edge of the wedge in this case can be found in the European Communities Act, 1972. Chapter 2, 'Societas Europea' examines a proposal for a new type of supranational corporate enterprise designed to facilitate industrial concentration in the Community. Despite dissension and debate in the Chambers of Europe and scepticism in the City it would appear that the national governments regard it as being of the highest priority. Chapter 3, 'The supervisory board', describes the two-tier system of administration of many companies in the Community—a system which is virtually foreign to British company management and one which may well have important implications for industrial relations in the U.K.

Part II, 'Accounting practice and financial reporting', contains four chapters of significance to the accounting profession. Chapter 4, 'Public accountancy in the European Economic Community', was read as a paper at the annual conference of Teachers of Accountancy in Scottish Universities in 1972 and now appears in a revised and updated form. The content of this paper is not available in any other currently published source. Chapter 5, 'Harmonisation of company financial reporting' (based on an article originally published in *The Accountant's Magazine*, March 1972), contains an appreciation of a proposal to standardise company financial reporting in the Community.

Chapter 6, 'British accounting and the EEC', examines the relationship between British and European accounting. Chapter 7, 'Consolidation of company accounts in Europe',—was originally published as a paper presented at the 6th Congress of the European Federation of Financial Analysts Societies at Montreux, October 1970. I have included this paper, which illustrates European attitudes to consolidated accounts in the absence of a definitive statement by the European Commission, and deserves more publicity than it has otherwise received. It should, however, be noted that the intelligence provided by this paper represents information from only one section of the financial community.

Part III, 'Industrial and financial developments' embraces the fundamental aspects of economic integration, and describes developments from both historical and anticipated bases. Chapter 8, 'Industrial policy in the Community' examines the economic plans of the Commission, and in particular covers the essential aspects of economic cooperation and describes the role of the *groupement d'intérêt économique* (GIE) as a cooperative vehicle for companies. British businessmen reared under the yoke of restrictive trade practices statutes may be surprised by European attitudes to cooperation. Chapter 9, 'Mergers in Europe' (with particular reference to an enlarged EEC) explains the significance of industrial concentration and examines the economic impact of the multinational enterprise. Chapter 10, 'Competition policy in Britain and the Common Market', examines the British and Community methods of regulating monopolies and cartels while attempting to encourage cooperation. As one leading business journal recently pointed out—any executive with European responsibilities who has not yet studied Articles 85 and 86 of the Treaty of Rome is possibly heading for trouble. This chapter records the leading European cases of 'trust busting', the significance of which should not be lost on British executives. Chapter 11, 'Trends in European taxation', (originally read at the 20th Summer School of The Institute of Chartered Accountants of Scotland at St. Andrews University, and published in the Institute's magazine in September 1972) discusses the trend and reform of various types of taxes, both direct and indirect, in western Europe. Chapter 12, 'Business finance in Europe', concludes by describing the essential and important differences in company financing between Common Market countries and the U.K. and by noting the diversity of stock exchange characteristics.

This book stresses the change that is about to descend on those employed in industry, commerce, and accounting in Britain. Reservations have been experienced many, and indeed, one of the major obstacles to integration comes from those who fear the unknown and the change it must bring. This was well demonstrated by the not-quite 'Wellsian' panic which spread among British chartered accountants who, following an address by E.H.V. McDougall at the 20th Summer School of The Institute of Chartered Accountants of Scotland at St Andrews University in September 1972 (published in the October edition of the Institute's magazine), envisaged themselves as being unemployable as auditors of British companies as from 1 January 1973. Mr. McDougall, whose address was based on the results of a Commission working party on professional qualifications of auditors, pointed out that British qualifications did not meet European standards (one should not assume from this that they are inferior; indeed many would assert the opposite applies.) What many did not realise was that it will take years to harmonise matters such as professional qualifications, and in the meantime the U. K. delegations in the Community will advocate on behalf of the British accountancy profession. Chapter 1 indicates that change does not happen overnight. The rest of the book should, at least, remove the hazards of the unknown.

In conclusion I sincerely thank my fellow authors, T. A. Lee, T. D. Lynch, R. H. Parker, R. Shirley, and J. R. Small for their amiable agreement to contribute to this book. Without their help, publication would have been impossible.

I also gratefully acknowledge the permission of the Fédération Européenne des Associations d'analystes Financiers, 90 Avenue des Champs-Élysées, 75 Paris VIIIe to reproduce 'Consolidation of company accounts in Europe'.

Acknowledgment is likewise due to the Esmée Fairbairn Charitable Trust which provided a research grant for a study of industrial concentration in Europe, of which this book forms a part, and to Edoardo Volpi of the European Commission who kindly supplied much needed information at, usually, very short notice. In this respect acknowledgment is also due to the staff of the European Communities Library, 23 Chesham Street, London SW1X 8NH, for helpful advice.

Finally I record my grateful thanks to two colleagues: R. Shirley for providing efficient and essential translation assistance, and Mrs. H. M. MacDonald for typing much of the manuscript.

PART I

The Company in Europe

1 The EEC and Company Regulation

by A. T. McLEAN

The European Communities Act, which received the Royal Assent on 17 October 1972, provides for legislative changes which will enable the United Kingdom to comply with the obligations entailed by membership of the European Coal and Steel Community, the European Economic Community and the European Atomic Energy Community, and to exercise the rights of membership. This historical and unique document is, among other things, the first indication of change in British company law, and will be followed in due course by many other statutory instruments which will affect the whole being of companies and financial reporting in the United Kingdom. British businessmen and accountants must appreciate that the winds of change are liable to affect them more than anyone else in the U.K. and, for that reason, this paper sets out to demonstrate the operations of the relevant institutions of the European Economic Community and to appraise the meaning and effect of those first proposals which will eventually be imposed on companies both in the original Six—France, Germany, Italy, Holland, Belgium, and Luxembourg—and in the new members, Britain, Ireland, and Denmark.

The institutions of the Community

As the European Communities Act, 1972 indicates, there are three European Communities: the European Coal and Steel Community (ECSC), established on 10 August 1952 by the Treaty of Paris which was signed on 18 April 1951 and effectively pooled the Six's coal, steel and allied by-products in one market; the European Economic Community (EEC), established by the Treaty of Rome of 25 March 1957 and operational since 1 January 1958; and the European Atomic Energy Community (Euratom or EAEC), established by a second Treaty of Rome of 25 March 1957 which effectively pooled the Six's atomic energy industries.

After the 1957 Treaty of Rome, the three communities were governed by a single assembly or parliament accompanied by a single Court of Justice. Each community, however, was responsible to its own Council of Ministers and each was administered by its own Commission (or High Authority for the ECSC). This arrangement was revised on 1 July 1967, following the Treaty of Brussels of 8 April 1965, by merging the two Commissions and the High Authority and the three Councils into a single Commission and a single Council of Ministers which now exercise the same powers and responsibilities of their predecessors as determined by the original treaties.

This amalgamation of institutions can be viewed as part of a movement towards a future single European Community. In this respect the concept of a federal Europe, both politically and economically, is much favoured by many who currently are talking essentially about its economic advantages. At the annual conference of the Institute of Directors in the Albert Hall, London, on 9 November 1972, Dr Walter Hallstein, a former president of the European Commission, went so far as to say that not only was economic integration a step on the road to political integration and a preparation for political integration; it was already part of it. He also believed that Britain's great democratic tradition and unrivalled experience in world politics was contributing to taking the Community towards a federal system able to respond with one political voice while maintaining the separate identities of the member states.

At present the Communities are effectively administered and controlled by four institutions: The European Parliament, the European Court of Justice, the Council of Ministers, and the Commission.

The Parliament

Originally described as a parliamentary assembly, the European Parliament oversees the process of democracy in the Community, but has little real power. It examines the activities of the Commission and ensures that the interests of the Community are adequately represented. It must also be consulted on all major proposals under the Rome treaties before these are presented by the Commission to the Council of Ministers. Some proposals have in fact been altered by the Commission on Parliament's advice before presentation to the Council of Ministers. Parliament essentially has the role of the Community watchdog, making sure that the interests of the respective member states do not take precedence over the interests of the Community.

The European Parliament has the power to dismiss the Commission by a vote of censure with a two-thirds required majority. Shortly before the entry of the U.K. as a member state, a move was made to censure the outgoing Commission for failing to make immediate proposals to strengthen Parliament's control over the Market budget. But should the Commission be dissolved by Parliamentary action a curious situation would arise because the European Parliament has no power to appoint a new Commission—this is the responsibility of the member states and not of the Community.

The Parliament has no control over the Council of Ministers but the

Council invariably recognises its views when major proposals are being considered. Parliament's powers were increased in 1971, however, in respect of that part of the Community budget which deals with the functioning of the Community's institutions. From 1975 onwards Parliament will have complete control for this part of the Community budget. It has been recognised in the past that the democratic process in the Community required strengthening. The Community has now established itself, and there is an increasing need for decisions to be made more in the spirit of the Community than of the member states. Community power is thus likely to increase, and will require greater democratic control.

A working party under the chairmanship of Professor Georges Vedel[1] has examined the problem of enlarging the powers of the European Parliament, and the Vedel report proposed a two-stage plan to increase these powers. Firstly, it recommends that Parliament should be given the power of co-decision with the Council of Ministers on matters affecting the constitution of the Community and its relations, with other bodies, and should have the right to be consulted—with some delaying powers—on a range of other matters. Secondly, the consultative right would later be extended to a right of co-decision. It may be, however, that this proposal in the interests of democracy would slow the decision-making process even further.

The Parliament, which meets as an assembly on a regular basis in the chamber of the Council of Europe in Strasbourg, has 142 members chosen from the respective parliaments of the Six and will be enlarged from 1 January 1973 on the admission of the U.K., Ireland, and Denmark. Surprisingly, the deputies are grouped not by member state but by political affiliation, and thus we have groups consisting of Christian Democrats, Liberals, Socialists and Gaullists, with a sprinkling of Communists. Some of the thirty-six British parliamentarians entitled to sit in the Assembly may have difficulty in identifying their political associates.

The Court

The Court of Justice of the European Communities sits permanently in Luxembourg and is independant of the three other institutions. Prior to the enlargement of the Community to nine member states, the Court consisted of seven judges and two advocates—general, these latter as experts rather than prosecutors—sort of *amicus curiae* presenting impartial and reasoned opinion on individual cases before the Court's deliberation. Lord Mackenzie Stuart has been appointed as the U.K. judge and J. P. Warner nominated for a post as advocate—general. As these gentlemen are already aware, Court procedure is far removed from that of the U.K.

The Court sits in plenary session which requires a quorum of five judges, to hear cases submitted either by a member state or one of the institutions, or when a preliminary decision is required in the interpretation of the treaties or on the validity and interpretation of the regulations of any bodies set up by the Council of Ministers. Other cases brought by private or corporate persons may be heard by chambers of three or five judges. In any event there must always be an odd number of judges on the Bench and, unlike the House of Lords or the English and Scottish Courts of Appeal, the Court gives one judgment arrived at by simple majority in secret, and no dissenting judgments are heard.

The Court settles disputes between member states on Community affairs and between member states and the institutions of the Community. Appeals are heard concerning matters covered by the treaties and brought by a member state, the Commission, the Council of Ministers or by an individual. Member states, Community institutions, corporate and private persons are bound by the Court's rulings. All legal questions falling within the scope of the treaties concern the European Court.

Any national disputes involving a question of Community law may be referred to Luxembourg for an authoritative ruling. The Court, however, has no power to enforce its own decisions, nor is there a Community police force; execution of a judgment is thus the responsibility of the national courts of member states.

The Council

As an institution of the European Communities, the Council of Ministers is the only one whose members directly represent the governments of the member states. Membership of the other three institutions demands a complete allegiance to the Community. The members of the Council of Ministers hold ministerial appointments in the respective governments of the member states, and actual attendance at meetings of the Council varies with the nature and subject matter of agendas. Thus foreign ministers would attend meetings involving major problems of over-all policy, finance ministers those on economic questions, agriculture ministers for problems involving agriculture, and so on. As the occasion demands, more than one minister may represent a member state on the Council.

The Council of Ministers is the decision-making body for most matters covered by the treaties. A small number of exceptions apart, all decisions it makes are based on proposals emanating from the Commission. In this respect the Commission must initiate action: if no proposals are submitted to the Council it is effectively paralysed and the Community's progress is halted. However, in 1970, for example, the Council had to deal with 390 proposals and 376 memoranda and other documents. During this time the Council's work included the adoption of 249 regulations, 25 directives, and 71 decisions, together with the second medium-term economic programme.

Once a proposal has been made by the Commission, a dialogue ensues between it and the Council of Ministers, one body stating national viewpoints, the other declaring the interest of the Community. A majority decision by the Council of Ministers is required for most proposals, with exceptions defined by treaty when unanimity is required. For cases in which the majority rule applies, the Council either adopts by a majority the Commission's proposal as it stands, decides unanimously against the proposal, or it may come to no decision at all. No proposal can be amended by the Council. Thus a majority acceptance of the proposal is for the complete proposal. If the Council wants an amendment made to a proposal which the Commission refuses it must vote against it unanimously. By this method, smaller member states with less voting power need not be overruled by larger ones if the Commission is on the side of a smaller one. However, in the spirit of the Community, there is tacit agreement that is rarely used.

The Council of Ministers meets in Brussels and Luxembourg at intervals only, and the preparation and coordination of its work is delegated to a committee of permanent representatives in Brussels (usually known as 'coreper', its abbreviated French title), which consists of the ambassadors of the member states to the Community. Thus also, proposals and memoranda emanating from the Commission will be subject to scrutiny and discussion by 'coreper', or one of its many subcommittees, at regular weekly meetings.

The Commission

The Commission of the European Communities has a wide range of responsibilities defined by the treaties. Firstly, it can be viewed as the guardian of the treaties, ensuring that the provisions of the treaties and the decisions of the Community's institutions are properly implemented. Thus infringements of the treaties may be examined by the Commission and possibly referred to the Court of Justice for judgment. The Commission can be regarded as a watchdog or policeman for the Community. Secondly, the Commission has substantial executive powers directly invested by the treaties and by the Council of Ministers. These powers embrace the preparation of the implementing orders with respect to certain treaty provisions or Council enactments; the application of the treaties' rules to particular cases involving either member states or corporate bodies; the administration of Community funds, and the administration of the safeguard clauses in the treaties. The latter responsibility places the onus on the Commission if a requirement is waived under exceptional circumstances. Finally, the Commission is also the initiator of Community policy and advocate of the Community interest to the Council of Ministers.

Since 1 July 1970 the Commission has consisted of nine members, but will be re-created on the admission of the U.K., Ireland, and Denmark to the Community and will then total 13 members. Major member states—France, Germany, Italy, and the U.K.—will appoint two commissioners and the smaller member states—Belgium, Denmark, Holland, Ireland, and Luxembourg—will appoint one each. Two leading British politicians have been appointed to the Commission. Sir Christopher Soames, former ambassador to France, and George Thomson, former Labour M.P. for Dundee East, and holder of various ministerial posts in the 1964 Labour Government.

Members of the Commission are appointed by their respective governments for four-year renewable terms. The president and vice-president hold office for two-year renewable terms. The treaties require the Commissioners to perform their duties with complete independence and they may neither seek nor accept instructions from governments or any other interest. As Jean Rey, a former president of the Commission, once said: 'We are not only the clergy, we are also the prophets of Europe'.

Prior to the admission of the new member states in 1973 these 'eurocrats' had heavy responsibilities, each commissioner having been assigned to one or more Community activity. The members of the outgoing 1972 Commission had the following responsibilities:

President Sicco Mansholt: secretariat, legal service, spokesman's group, Security Office

Vice-President Raymond Barre: economic and financial affairs, Statistical Office

Vice-President Wilhelm Haferkamp: internal market and harmonisation of laws, energy, supply agency, safeguards and controls

Vice-President Carlo Scarascia Mugnozza: agriculture

Albert Coppé: social affairs, transport, credit and investments, personnel and administration, budgets, financial control

Jean-François Deniau: coordination of the enlargementnegotiations, development aid

Albert Borschette: competition, regional policy, press and information, dissemination of scientific information

Ralf Dahrendorf: external relations, external trade

Altiero Spinelli: industrial technological and scientific affairs, joint research centre

Indications at the time of writing, shortly before the creation of the new 1973 Commission under the presidency of François-Xavier Ortoli, of France, were that the Commission would continue the practice by which each commissioner is allocated a 'ministerial portfolio' covering a specific policy sector. It would not be correct, however, to assume that the new, enlarged Commission's workload was thus to be lightened because the meeting of Heads of State of the enlarged Community in Paris in October 1972 agreed a new and formidable programme covering economic and monetary union, regional policy, energy, overseas aid, social affairs, foreign policy, and the institutions of the Community itself. One Brussels eurocrat informed me that he had reached the melancholy conclusion that the commissioners' responsibilities would be greater than ever.[1a]

The Commission, with its headquarters in the new Berlaymont building on the Rue de la Loi, Brussels, has an administration divided into 20 directorates-general, each of which is responsible to a member of the Commission, and there is also a secretariat-general, a legal department, a statistical office, and a few special services. By the terms of the treaties, the operation of the commission is 'collegiate', i.e. the Commission itself must act as a body in adopting the various measures incumbent upon it by the treaties. No one member of the Commission can assume a degree of independence. Decisions are taken by simple majority vote of its members. The system also provides for procedural devices to ensure that the Commission is not inundated by excessive detail. Where members of the Commission have interlocking responsibilities, working parties have been set up to undertake essential groundwork.

In establishing policy, the Commission makes use of its own directorates-general, after consulting with political circles, civil servants, employers' and employees' organisations etc. Having agreed the main lines of its policy, the Commission has systematic recourse to expert groups from the member states for advice on detailed aspects of particular proposals. These expert groups serve only in an advisory capacity and in no way compromise their respective member states. The results of the various preparatory meetings are then laid before the Commission, which in turn agrees and frames its proposals for submission to the Council of Ministers.

Other institutional bodies

All major proposals presented to the Council of Ministers are examined by a large consultative body called the Economic and Social Committee and which comprises representatives of employers' organisations, trades unions, and other organised economic groups from the member states. The Committee's opinion must be obtained by the Council or Commission when dealing with matters such as the harmonisation laws, the free movement of workers, agricultural policy, and transport policy. The Committee makes no decisions but nevertheless exercised a strong influence on policy making.

Other Community organs embrace the *consultative committee* for the European Coal and Steel Community, which has a function similar to that of the Economic and Social Policy Committee, the *monetary committee*, the *short-term economic policy committee*, the *medium-term economic policy committee*, the *committee of central bank governors*, the *budgetary policy committee*, the *transport committee*, the *administrative commission for the social security of migrant workers*, the *scientific and technical committee*, and the *nuclear research consultative committee*. All these lesser organs advise the Commission on problems covered by their respective briefs.

Directives and company law harmonisation

In implementing the provisions of the Rome treaties, the Council of Ministers and the Commission issue regulations, directives, decisions, recommendations, and opinions. A clear distinction must be made in this case as the effect of each differs to some extent. Regulations are Community laws or statutes and are legally binding on all member states and have the same force as national laws. Directives are binding on those member states to which they are addressed, as regards the result to be achieved, but the national authorities are free to decide on the means of carrying them out. As an example, the European Communities Act, 1972 altered some aspects of British company law to comply with the Community's first directive under the programme of company law harmonisation. The distinction between a regulation on one hand and a directive on the other is significant and important. A regulation will have immediate effect whereas a directive will not become effective until the member state has taken steps to bring it into effect.

Decisions may be addressed either to a member state or to a corporate or private person and are binding in every respect on the party or parties named. Recommendations and opinions have no force of law and are not binding.

So far as harmonisation of company laws is concerned, an appraisal is required of the impact of directives promulgated by the Council following proposals made by the Commission. The harmonisation or approximation of company law is proceeding surely, if a little slowly; at the time of writing, five proposals have been made by the Commission, the first of which is now a directive under article 54(3) (g) of the Treaty of Rome which created the EEC. In addition one draft regulation is in the process of being appraised and this concerns a proposal for a statute for a supranational European company (see Chapter 2). The directives, one passed and the others proposed, therefore warrant some attention.

The realisation of a directive covers several stages. The Commission first consults with government officials from the member states and will obtain expert advice from special advisors drawn from them. If coordination in some respect of company law (for example) is deemed advisable the Commission will frame and submit its draft proposal to the Council of Ministers. At that stage the proposed directive is officially published for the first time. The Council in turn remits the draft to the Economic and Social Committee and to Parliament. On receiving opinions from the Committee and Parliament, the Council starts negotiations with national delegations and the ministers will debate the proposal themselves. Even at this stage it may be possible to effect some essential changes in the draft. Finally, the directive is addressed to whichever member state or states it was created for, and so published, in its final form.

The first directive of the Council

On 9 March 1968, the Council of the European Communities adopted its first directive on the approximation of company laws of member states which was addressed to all member states. In this respect the Council had, among other things, particular regard to Article 54(3) (g) of the Treaty of Rome which required the Council and the Commission to carry out duties devolving upon them under Article 54(1) and (2) in particular, by coordinating to the necessary extent the safeguards which, for the protection of the interests of the members and others and with a view to making such safeguards equivalent throughout the Community—are required by member states of companies or firms (companies or firms being taken to mean, by Article 58 of the treaty, companies or firms constituted under civil or commercial law, including cooperative societies and other legal persons governed by public or private law except for those which are non-profit making). The companies or firms referred to have differing titles which should not be confused. The companies are described as below.

For Germany
Die Aktiengesellschaft[2]
Die Kommanditgesellschaft auf Aktien[3]
Die Gesellschaft mit beschränkter Haftung[4]

For Belgium
De naamloze vennootschap or la société anonyme[2]
De commanditaire vennootschap op aandelen *or* la société en commandite par actions[3]
De personen vennootschap met beperkte aansprakelijkheid *or* la société de personnes à responsabilité limitée[4]

For France
La société anonyme[2]
La société en commandite par actions[3]

La société à responsabilité limitée[4]

For Italy
Società per azioni[2]
Società in accomandita per azioni[3]
Società a responsabilità limitata[4]

For Luxembourg
La société anonyme[2]
La société en commandite par actions[3]
La société à responsabilité limitée[4]

For the Netherlands
De naamloze vennootschap[2]
De commanditaire vennootschap op aandelen[3]
The Enlargement of the Powers of the European Parliament HMSO 1972. Equivalent to the Britisch public limited liability company. Partnerships limited by shares of which there is no British equivalent. Equivalent to the British private limited liability company.

The directive, therefore, applies also to the public and private limited company in the U.K. and Ireland and at least to the Aktieselskab (A/S) in Denmark.

The scope of the directive has been restricted to those entities which have the most important economic effect on the Community, i.e. those companies with status similar to British public and private limited companies; also the uniquely continental partnerships limited by shares and consist of one or more partners with unlimited liability, together with shareholders with limited liability. The directive has three main requirements, all of which are of particular interest to third parties in their relationships with companies.

Disclosure requirements

Companies are required to publish certain documents and information such as the memorandum and articles of association, including amendments thereto; particulars regarding directors; the company's annual return; winding up orders, notice of situation or change of registered office; notice of liquidation, etc. Companies must also publish their annual accounts, but the European equivalents of British private limited companies (e.g. the société à responsabilité limitée in France) are not obliged to publish their annual accounts until a directive is put into effect on the coordination of the contents of balance sheets and profit and loss accounts; this dispenses with the necessity to publish all or part of the said documents of such companies whose 'montant du bilan' is below a figure which will be fixed in the directive. The directive referred to, at the time of writing, is still at a draft stage: *Proposition d'une Quatrième Directive, presentée par la Commission au Conseil, le 10 Novembre 1971* (see also Chapter 5).

This draft fourth directive recognises that all private companies are not equal—some being more equal than others. This sensible provision recognises the fact that many private companies in the Community are as large as typical public companies. Three classes of private company are identified: (1) Those whose 'montant du bilan'[5] exceed 1 million U/A's[6], whose net turnover exceeds 2 million U/A's, and whose average number of employees exceeds 100, are classified with public company's for disclosure purposes, (2) Those with gross assets ranging from 100,001 to 1 million U/A's, with net turnover ranging from 200,001 to 2 million U/A's and average number of employees ranging from 21 to 100 may be exempted from disclosing turnover, (3) Those with gross assets of up to 100,000 U/A's, with net turnover of up to 200,000 U/A's and employees averaging up to 20 may be exempted from publishing the profit and loss account.

This provision for exemption from disclosure applies also to the Dutch 'closed stock company', a singular type of entity known only to the Dutch Commercial Code. When the directive was adopted, the Dutch had no equivalent to the 'private limited' type of company; the directive allows possible equivalent exemption from disclosure of accounts for the Besloten naamloze vennootschap (BNV) provided it fulfils certain conditions prescribed by the directive. The Dutch, however, fell into line with the rest of the member states by passing a new Act *de Aanpassingswet besloten vennootschap met beperkte aansprakelijkheid* on 3 May 1971 which created a private limited company called a Besloten Vennootschap met beperkte aansprakelijkheid (BV).

A uniform system of publication has also been adopted. A file in conjunction with a central register must be opened by each member state for each of the companies registered in that country, and all documents and information which are the subject of mandatory disclosure must be deposited in this file or entered in the register. The documents and information which require disclosure must be published in an official gazette stipulated by the member state.

Validity of commitments undertaken by the company

This section of the first directive is aimed at increasing the protection available to third parties. By publication of the documents and information as prescribed, third parties cannot be made to suffer because of any irregularity in the nomination of those who can legally commit the company. Member states may, however, provided that the company shall not be liable when transactions entered into by authorised officers of the company are outside the objects of the company if it proves that third parties knew that the transaction went beyond the objects, or could not be unaware of it. In this case, publication of the articles of association shall of itself be sufficient to constitute such proof. The limits on the powers of the authorised officers of the company arising under the company's articles or from a decision by the competent authorities may always be relied upon as against third parties provided they have been published.

Invalidation or nullity of the company

To protect the interests of third parties, the directive requires formal authentication of the constitutional documents (the memorandum and articles of association) of the company, but strictly limits the grounds on which invalidation may be pronounced, namely non-existence of or irregularity in the constitutional documents, illegal nature of the company's objects clause in the memorandum, incapacity of the subscribers, non-observance of provisions for minimum capital, and insufficient number of subscribers. Invalidation shall bring about the liquidation of the company, but invalidation shall not of itself affect the validity of any commitments entered into by the company, or the validity of those made with it, subject to the effects of liquidation.

The European Communities Act, 1972

Clause 9 of the Act is concerned with amendments to British company law necessary to comply with the provision of the first directive of the Council. Subsection 1 states:

> In favour of a person dealing with a company in good faith, any transaction decided on by the directors shall be deemed to be one which it is within the capacity of the company to enter into, and the power of the directors to bind the company shall be deemed to be free of any limitation under the memorandum or articles of association; and a party to a transaction so decided on shall not be bound to enquire as to the capacity of the company to enter into it or as to any such limitation on the powers of the directors, and shall be presumed to have acted in good faith unless the contrary is proved.

The objects clause in a company's memorandum of association defines the scope of the company's powers, the purpose of this being to inform the shareholders of the types of business their capital may be employed in and to inform third parties as to the nature of the company's powers. By the doctrine of *ultra vires*, a registered company cannot do anything beyond the powers (*ultra vires*) conferred on it by its constitutional documents or by a special

Act of Parliament. A contract made by the directors in the name of the company, but which happens to be outwith the scope of the company's objects is *ultra vires* the company, and so beyond the powers of the directors.

Third parties entering into a contract with a company, even though they are unaware of the objects of the company, are deemed by law to be aware of them because the company's memorandum, like most of the documents registered with the Registrar of Companies, is available for public inspection and, therefore, they cannot enforce a contract which is *ultra vires* the company. The onus rests clearly on the third party. The Jenkins Committee[7] was of the opinion that:

> A contract between a company and another party contracting in good faith should not be invalid as against the other party on the ground that it was *ultra vires* the company. In entering into such a contract the other party should be entitled to assume without investigation that the company is possessed of the necessary power; and should not by reason of his omission to investigate be deemed not to have acted in good faith, or be deprived of his right to enforce the contract on the ground that he had constructive notice of any limitation on the powers of the company, or on the powers of any director or other person to act on the company's behalf, imposed by its memorandum or articles.

The *ultra vires* rule was seen to be unfair in operation, but no change in the law was observed following the Jenkins Report.

Subsection 1 of Clause 9 now secures that a third party contracting in good faith with a company will be able to enforce an *ultra vires* contract against the company. The company, however, will still be bound by the *ultra vires* doctrine and will not be able to enforce the contract. The onus is now on the company to prove that the third party did not act in good faith.

Subsection 2 of Clause 9 states that:

> Where a contract purports to be made by a company, or by a person as agent for a company, at a time when the company has not been formed, then subject to any agreement to the contrary the contract shall have effect as a contract entered into by a person purporting to act for the company or as agent for it, and he shall be personally liable on the contract accordingly.

This subsection now partly satisfies a further recommendation of the Jenkins Committee.

> A company should be enabled unilaterally to adopt contracts which purport to be made on its behalf or in its name prior to incorporation; until the company does so adopt such contracts, the persons who pur-

ported to act for the company should be entitled to sue and be liable to be sued thereon.

Had this recommendation been recognised and adopted, the law, as laid down in Kelner *v.* Baxter (1866, L.R. 2 C.P., 174) and Newborne *v.* Sensolid (Great Britain) Ltd (1954, 1 Q.B., 45), would have been reversed. As it is, subsection 2 gives effect to the latter half of the Jenkins recommendation.

The remaining subsections are concerned, *inter alia*, with the publication in the London and Edinburgh *Gazette* of certain specified documents concerning incorporation, annual returns and winding-up orders, etc.; notification to the Registrar, of alterations to a company's memorandum or articles either by Act of Parliament or statutory instrument (anticipating perhaps possible changes following the adoption of future directives); and disclosure of certain details on company notepaper and invoices, namely (a) the place of registration of the company (i.e. London, Edinburgh, Belfast) and its registered number, (b) the address of its registered office, (c) in the case of a limited company exempt from the obligation to use the word 'limited' as part of its name, the fact that it is limited, and (d) if a company makes any reference on its stationery to its share capital (an unusual occurrence in the U.K.) the reference must relate to the paid-up share capital.

Such is the change in British company law as at 1 January 1973. Further alterations to the statutes will become necessary as and when future proposals for the harmonisation of the company laws of the member states are adopted as directives by the Council.

Proposals for future directives

The Commission's programme of company law harmonisation in the Community continued when they submitted on 9 March 1970 a proposal for a second directive designed to coordinate the guarantees required in respect of the founding of joint-stock companies and the maintenance and alteration of their capital. The proposal for the second directive, unlike the first, is designed specifically for the public type of limited company, e.g. the Aktiengesellschaft in Germany, and the société anonyme in France. Provision is made, however, for the exclusion in the meantime of investment trusts. The draft second directive provides for member states to prescribe that 'les statuts des sociétés' (the memoranda and articles of association of companies) contain the following information:

1. Form and name of the company.
2. Its centre of business.
3. Its objects.
4. Separately the amount of subscribed and authorised capital.

5. Classes of shares; if more than one, the number of shares subscribed, or to be issued, of each class and the nominal value of each share unless relevant national legislation permit shares of no par value; also the conditions limiting the transfer of shares.
6. The nature of shares, whether registered or bearer, and the provisions as to the conversion of bonds or debentures unless this matter is regulated by law.
7. The rules, unless they are provided by law, governing the formation and competence of those bodies of the company representing, administering, and supervising or controlling the company.
8. The life of the company in so far as it is not indeterminate.

In addition full particulars are required to be given as to the subscribers, the initial capital and formation costs. Provision is made for maintaining the company when the number of members falls below the legal minimum, i.e. dissolution is not automatic and the company has six months in which to regularise the situation before being liquidated by judicial process.

One requirement of the proposal which might be of particular interest to the British is that seeking a minimum capital of 25,000 unités de compte (units of account) which can vary by 10% either way to accommodate currency differences. This means that British public companies will require a minimum nominal capital of around £10,000. Although of little consequence to a public company, British company law does not require a minimum capital for formation, though Stock Exchange rules demand an over-all minimum market capitalisation of £250,000 for companies seeking a quotation. This contrasts with the minimum nominal capital requirements of the Aktiengesellschaft in Germany of D.M. 100,000 (£13,280 approx), the société anonyme in France of Fr 100,000 (£8,425 approx.), and società per azioni in Italy of lire 1 million (£727 approx.). Private limited companies in these countries have minimum capital requirements of about one half of those for public companies!

The second proposal is also concerned with the maintenance, increase, and recudtion of capital. The Commission submitted to the Council on 16 June 1970 a proposal for a third directive under Article 54(3) (g) of the Rome Treaty. This draft is designed to achieve coordination of the safeguards required in the case of mergers between public limited companies subject to the laws of one and the same member state. This does not embrace the problem of cross-frontier mergers which will be the subject of a separate agreement at a much later date under Article 220 of the Rome Treaty. Acceptance of this proposal as the third directive should, however, facilitate a solution to the problem of regulation of mergers between companies registered in different member states.

Legislation for corporate mergers is unique in some member states as well as in the U.K. where more emphasis is placed on extra-statutory control by the City Panel on Takeovers and Mergers. Adoption of this proposal by the Council might have interesting consequences in the conduct of mergers in the U.K. Some aspects of this proposal consisting of 24 articles or sections are as follows:

1. Managements are required to draw up a 'merger plan' giving specific information about the merger and which must be made available to the shareholders of the merging companies.
2. Mergers shall require the approval of the general meeting of each of the merging companies, with individual member states' rules on attendance and majority applying.
3. The management of each of the merging companies shall draw up a detailed report explaining and justifying the merger plan and, more particularly, the share exchange ratio from a legal and economic standpoint. In addition one or more approved experts for each of the merging companies shall check the merger plan and draw up a report for the shareholders. These experts may in fact be the company auditors, who must state in their report whether or not the share exchange ratio is sound. In this respect their statement must be supported by:
   (a) a comparison between the net assets of the two companies on the basis of their true values,
   (b) a comparison between the profitability of the two companies both from historical and future viewpoints,
   (c) the criteria applied to value net assets and profitability.
4. The managements of each of the merging companies are required to report to their employees, explaining and justifying the merger and the legal, economic, and social effects it will have on them.
5. Member states will be required to fix rules governing the rights of creditors and debenture holders to obtain security for their debts.
6. Members of boards of management and of supervision will be liable for any loss suffered by shareholders as a result of wilful or negligent acts committed in preparing or implementing the merger.
7. Experts responsible for the report to shareholders will also be liable if the shareholders suffer any loss through wilful or negligent acts committed by these experts in the performance of their duties.

Conclusion

Proposals for fourth and fifth directives have been submitted to the Council. The fourth proposal published on 10 November 1971 covers the accounting requirements of companies and is examined elsewhere by Professor R. H. Parker (see Chapter 5). The fifth proposal published on 27 September 1972 embraces the supervisory board, an 'organ' virtually unknown to the British, and is appraised elsewhere (see Chapter 3). Other proposals can be expected, from time to time, to cover the requirements for consolidated accounts, the competence and rights of the general meetings of companies, and liquidation, to name but a few. Once adopted, these directives will interfere deeply with the present modes of company regulation in the member states.

It should, however, be borne in mind that the process of Community law is slow: the Commission's original proposal for a first directive was submitted to the Council in 1964. Following opinions from the European Parliament, the Economic and Social Committee, and other groups it was revised in 1966 and finally adopted on 9 March 1968. The Economic and Social Committee have also criticised the Commission's piecemeal approach to their procedures of equivalence and it would appear that the second, third, and fourth drafts, at least, will be adopted at the same time. This is unlikely until late in 1974 at the earliest. It should also be noted that member states typically have 18 months from the adoption of a directive in which to amend their own national laws.

Apart from the first directive, all the published proposals are aimed at the public type of limited company. In view of the economic importance of the other types, we may expect the private company to receive the Commission's public attention in due course.

The winds of change are with us. Let us trust that a gale does not blow us off our feet!

Notes

1 The Enlargement of the Powers of the European Parliament (HMSO) 1972.

1a The 1973 Commission and their responsibilities are:

President François-Xavier Ortoli: General secretariat, legal service, spokesman's group, security office

Vice-President Wilhelm Haferkamp: economic and monetary affairs, including ECSC credit and investments

Vice-President Carlo Scarascia Mugnozza: relations with the European Parliament in conjunction with the Commission President, environmental policy, consumer protection, transport policy, press and information

Vice-President Sir Christopher Soames: external relations

Vice-President Patrick John Hillery: social policy

Vice-President Henri Simonet: taxation, financial institutions (banking and insurance), harmonisation of company law, energy policy, Euratom safeguards and control, Euratom supply agency

Jean-François Deniau: development aid and co-operation policy, community budgets, financial control

Altiero Spinelli: industrial and technological policy
Albert Borschette: competition, personnel and administration
Ralf Dahrendorf: research, science and education (includes external relations in the scientific, technical and nuclear sectors), dissemination of technical and scientific information, mutual recognition of diplomas, joint research centre, statistical office
George Thomson: regional policy
Petrus Josephus Lardinois: agriculture
Finn Olav Gundelach: internal market (includes removal of technical barriers to trade, right of establishment and freedom to supply services, harmonisation of economic legislation, European Company law), administration of customs union.

[2] Equivalent to the British public limited liability company.

[3] Partnerships limited by shares of which there is no British equivalent.

[4] Equivalent to the British private limited liability company.

[5] i.e. the amount of the balance, or balance sheet, and construed as the total of the assets or liabilities side of the balance sheet: a meaningful and comparable figure only in 'European' accounts.

[6] 1 million units of account, equalling approximately £ 400.000.

[7] Report of the company law Committee (Cmnd. 1749), 1962.

Bibliography

The first directive of the Council together with the proposals for the other four directives are (at time of writing) obtainable from the European Communities Press and Information Office, 23 Chesham Street, London SW1X 8NH. Some of these have not been officially translated into English.

Emile Noël, *How the European Communities Institutions Work*, European Communities Press and Information London, 1972.

European Community: The Facts European Communities Press and Information, London, 1971.

Richard Mayne, *The Institutions of the European Community*, Chatham House; P.E.P. London, 1968.

The Effect on Company Law of the United Kingdom entry into the European Common Market, Institute of Chartered Secretaries and Administrators. London, 1972.

The European Communities Act, H.M.S.O. 1972.

Charles de Hoghton (ed.), *The Company: Law, Structure and Reform in Eleven Countries*, P.E.P.; George Allen and Unwin 1970.

G. A. Zaphiriou, *European Business Law*, Sweet and Maxwell. 1970.

2 Societas Europea A Consideration of the Proposals for the European Company

by A. T. McLEAN

This paper[1] is based on an initial part of a study on industrial concentration in Europe under the direction of Professor J. R. Small, of Heriot-Watt University and financed by the Esmée Fairbairn Charitable Trust. The author acknowledges his indebtedness to those who kindly assisted him with his enquiries in Brussels.

Industrial concentration in Europe

The European Economic Community about ten years ago was starting to develop as a significant trading association with, at that time, nascent political inclinations. The idea of political and economic integration of a commercially debilitated Europe, where nationalism could be contained but with the safeguarding of legitimate national elements, is now coming to fruition, despite British and Scandinavian arguments for cooperation rather than integration. The signing of the Treaty of Rome in 1957 has been followed generally by outstanding and significant economic achievements. Commercial success, however, has been achieved not only by remarkable productivity but also by a painstaking and laborious harmonisation of national identities into a single economic unit comprising France, Germany, Italy, the Netherlands, Belgium and Luxembourg. This difficult and slow process of integration requires emphasis, for it is now almost 20 years since the establishment of the European Coal and Steel Community, which can be regarded as the precursor of the Common Market as we know it today. It was another five years before the European Economic Community, together with the European Atomic Energy Community, could be officially established in 1957, but in the interim we saw the failures of the European Defence Community and the European Political Community, which were certainly serious set backs for European visionaries.

Nevertheless, it is now apparent that the spirit of economic union has been established, but the problems of commercial integration are perhaps a little more difficult than many realise. Industrial concentration in the EEC has been influenced to a significant extent by the influx of American business; and the commercial challenge from Japan and, to some extent, from members of the European Free Trade Association has not been ignored. Despite the progress made since 1957, the economic growth of industrial enterprises within the Common Market has been restrained by conflicting commercial codes of the member states of the community. The purpose of this paper is to examine and comment on the work being carried out in Brussels in an attempt to further the progress of industrialisation in Europe.

The question of a pan-European limited company was first posed in 1959. Significant among those whose thoughts were concerned with the structure of company law within the newly or formed community was Prof. Dr Pieter Sanders, then Dean of the Faculty of Law in the University of Rotterdam. The idea was simple: create a commercial entity without any national identity save that it be of European origin, answerable only to the European Court and paying European taxes. The political implications are obvious, which explains why it has taken so long to deal effectively with a problem which has had an adverse effect on industrialisation in Europe.

The need for a European company can in all probability be related to industrial concentration in the United States, where concentration by merger and acquisition helped to create large industrial corporations capable of dominating to some extent many a country with a GNP less than the turnover figures of those concerns. American corporations present a significant challenge to any community, and the fragmentation of companies in the member states of the EEC did not help the commercial response to 'le défi américain'.

Admittedly, since the early 1960s the closing of the ranks in the community as well as in Britain has been noticeable, but significantly these business combinations tended to take place within member states rather than across national frontiers. In other words, European companies tended to grow within the confines of member states with an obvious limitation being placed on productive capacity, marketing capability, and sources of finance. The arguments for the creation of the European limited company are primarily based on the differences of company and fiscal statutes among member states, thereby making cross-frontier mergers difficult if not impossible. It is recognised that, while national companies may achieve significant dimensions within their respective member states, the creation of a pan-European company is the most reasonable method of achieving the necessary size to offset competition from overseas multinationals. The creation of pan-European supranational organisations, answerable not to any particular member state but to the European Court, would be an effective way to divorce national interests in respect of companies which may conflict with pan-European objectives.

At present, cross-frontier mergers are difficult because of national legal and fiscal barriers. Firstly, joint enterprisesbetween companies in two member states must recognise the commercial law of only one of those states. Thus one of the partners starts off at a disadvantage by being unfamiliar with the commercial statutes of another country, under which it must operate. Secondly, mergers between limited companies of different member states cannot be carried out directly but must take place by the creation of a relatively complicated system of subsidiary companies in each member state. The alternative in the case of a full amalgamation would be the liquidation of one of the companies party to the merger and the reconstitution of that company by the incorporation of its net assets within the other company. Obvious problems of delay, expense, and national prestige make this an unpopular method. Thirdly, there are significant difficulties inherent in the different types of contract law which exist within the community. This can be contrasted with the common law of contract applicable to all companies in the United States despite the lack of a common company law. Finally, possibly the most serious restraints to European industrial concentration are the existing fiscal barriers. The occurence of corporate mergers or takeovers within member states of the community inevitably results in the creation of liabilities to forms of capital gains taxes based on the difference between the book value of net assets acquired and the acquisition price of shares transferred. Some form of alleviation of such tax imposition on business combinations exists within member states; by deferral of tax in France and by waiving such tax in Belgium and Germany until the actual realisation of the assets by the absorbing company. Cross-frontier mergers, however, do not qualify for capital gains exemption. Similarly, foreign branches of companies tend to be penalised by double taxation on the re-routing of profits.

In order to alleviate such problems the harmonisation of company and fiscal laws within the community is well under way, but progress tends to be slow, though deliberate. The proposal for the formation of a supranational European company is seen as a way of establishing more quickly a suitable legal vehicle which will assist industrial concentration without conflicting with the major proposals concerning overall legal and fiscal integration.

So-called mergers which have already been consummated in Europe tend rather to be trading partnerships linked by some form of cross-holding of shares. The Agfa-Gevaert union, which is a classic example, was one such, of of West German and Belgian photographic companies combining to compete with the American Kodak company: it was effected by a series of cross-holdings. The Belgian organisation Gevaert has a 50% holding in both Gevaert-Agfa N.V. of Belgium and in Agfa-Gevaert GmbH of West Germany. The German company has corresponding holdings. This particular form of union was successful in achieving a remarkable managerial and political balance in the face of a common competitor.

Other multinationals such as Royal Dutch Shell, Unilever, Fokker-VFW, and Dunlop-Pirelli have achieved their own versions of combination. The trading and commercial effects of cooperation are usually of prime importance in such combinations, and fiscal and legal disadvantages tend to be of secondary importance. Sir Reay Geddes, for example, recently stated[2] that the combination of Dunlop and Pirelli had, among other advantages, the benefits of larger scale, economies in supply and production, the use of common services, and was better placed to raise finance for expansion. Against this could be measured the fiscal disadvantages of re-routing profits through parent companies. The concept of a European company was welcomed by Dunlop despite the fact they could not wait for it.

General provisions in the proposed statute for a Societas Europea

The dialogue among European professions and businesses concerning the need for a pan-European enterprise was appreciated by the Commission of the EEC, which in 1966 requested Professor Sanders and a small group of jurists from the member states to draft proposals for such an enterprise. The Sanders text of a draft statute was completed by the end of 1966. Not unnaturally the Sanders draft for a Societas Europea (S.E.) was in part in skeleton form, as substantially more discussion was necessary for various aspects of the proposed new law. Matters of employees' representation, fiscal provisions, and financial statement disclosure warranted much more examination. Working parties, thereafter, studied various aspects of the proposed statute, and in 1969 the EEC Commission took steps to prepare the draft for the proposed statute, which was unanimously accepted in 1970. The proposed statute is under consideration by the European Parliament and will eventually be presented to the Council of Ministers for a final decision. That the proposal will be accepted by the Council is a foregone conclusion (in the opinion of the author), but the specific content will certainly be changed from Professor Sanders's original draft. For example, the problem of group disclosure and consolidated accounting has still to be examined in detail though it is understood that discussions have been under way since autumn 1971. It would appear that the earliest expected date of ratification of the proposed statute would be sometime in 1973, although a 1974 forecast would not be considered unreasonable.

In its present form the proposed statute for the European Company can be likened to a British Companies Bill. There are, however, some noteworthy differences. The European Company proposal consists of 284 Articles (sections) contained within 14 titles (chapters) which embrace:

1. General provisions,
2. Formation
3. Capital—shares and the rights of shareholders—debentures,
4. Administrative organs,
5. Representation of employees in the European company,
6. Preparation of the annual accounts,
7. Groups of companies,
8. Alteration of company regulations,
9. Winding up, liquidation, insolvency, and similar procedures,
10. Conversion,
11. Merger,
12. Taxation,
13. Offences,
14. Final provisions.

There are no supplementary schedules to the proposed statute such as the 1948 Companies Act's Table A and Eighth Schedule regulating the internal management and accounting disclosure of British companies. Such matters are effectively dealt with under the 14 titles of the proposal.

The detailed requirements of the proposal are beyond the scope of this paper. Certain provisions, however, are worthy of comment, especially as increasing numbers of British accountants and businessmen will eventually be encountering European companies.

Typically, European companies shall be commercial companies with limited liability and an identifiable legal personality. The company, with the suffix S.E. after its name, shall be registered in the European Commercial Register at the Court of Justice of the European Communities. Registration requirements of the S.E. constitute a bureaucratic formality which is not unfamiliar in Britain. Formation requirements, however, are noteworthy. Firstly an S.E. can be created by any of the following methods:

1. By merger of existing companies within the EEC,
2. By formation as a holding company for existing companies within the EEC
3. By formation as a joint subsidiary.

An existing S.E. may, in addition, form an S.E. by merger or by formation of a holding company or of a joint subsidiary with other S.E.s or with companies incorporated under the national law of a member state. A subsidiary in the form of an S.E. may also be created by an established S.E. Individuals may not, therefore create S.E.s, although they may eventually become share holders either by transfer of shares or by an increase in capital. Companies in the EEC permitted to establish S.E.s are of the public limited company type;

sociétés anonymes, Aktiengesellschaften, società per azioni, or naamloze vennootschappen. European private companies—sociétés à responsabilité limitée, Gesellschaften mit beschränkter Haftung, società a responsabilità limitata—are not permitted to found S.E.s.

Secondly, a minimum capital is specified for the S.E., the amount of which depends on the method of formation of the company. In the case of formation by merger or by formation of a holding company the minimum capital shall be 500,000 units of account; in the case of formation of a joint subsidiary 250,000 units of account: and in the case of formation of a subsidiary by an established S.E. 100,000 units of account. The expression 'unit of account', quaint in any language, is the established currency unit used for all EEC matters. The value of such currency is related to a gold standard and in fact is the equivalent of one U.S. dollar. The explicit justification for the minimum capital requirement is that such constituted companies will be multinational in character and therefore require substantial assets to facilitate credit rating. It is recognised, however, that in the case of formation of a subsidiary the capital requirements need not be so rigorous as for a merger or holding company. My personal understanding of the necessity for such relatively high minimum capital requirements, despite the fact that the Commission sets lower requirements than those proposed by Professor Sanders, is that relatively few S.E.s will be formed in the first instance, on the assumption that small organisations will not be prepared to subscribe to these standards. On this basis it is thought that the passage of the proposed statute through the European Parliament and the Council of Ministers should be more smooth. If the S.E. were to be immediately available to all companies within the community, then greater attention would require to be paid to the important differences in commercial and fiscal laws in the member states, which would necessitate a much more lengthy appraisal of the proposal.

The share capital of the S.E. may be divided into different classes which can be of different nominal values, but shares of no par value are not permitted, on the basis that a functional relationship must exist between a share, as the embodiment of the rights of the shareholder, and the capital of the company specified in its regulations. Shares may carry different rights in respect of distribution of profits and assets of the company, but promises to pay or payment of fixed interest are prohibited. The issue of shares carrying no voting rights is subject to certain limitations because, as with shares carrying multiple voting rights, which are prohibited, they involve the danger that the functional relationship between capital subscribed and the right to vote may be undermined. Thus the issue of non-voting shares is permissible only up to an over-all nominal value equal to one-half of the capital of the company. Shares can be in bearer or registered form, and indeed an S.E. should be able to issue different classes of shares in bearer and registered form. This provision has already caused some problems in Italy, for instance, where by royal decree in the early 1940s the issue of bearer shares was prohibited for most of the country. In this respect Italy was the odd man out in the EEC, where bearer shares are more widely used than registered shares, but apparently the influence of company law harmonisation has brought Italy into line with the rest of the member states. The use of bearer shares underlines the importance placed on the publication of all notices concerning the S.E. in the Official Gazette of the European Communities, in the official bulletins of company publications in the member state in which the S.E. has its registered office, and in a daily newspaper circulating in that state. These publications are known as 'company journals'.

Debentures and convertible debentures may be issued by an S.E., and the body of debenture holders will be represented in its relationship with the company by a person initially appointed by the company. No security is specified in the proposed statute for the debenture holders and indeed the British method of security by floating charge is unknown in continental Europe.

The S.E. shall be administered by a board of management (which must consist of individuals and not of companies or other unnatural persons) exercising its functions under the control of a supervisory board which appoints the members of the board of management to office and can dismiss such members where serious grounds justify such action. Each member of the board of management will be under a contractual relationship with the company through the supervisory board, and no member of the supervisory board may be a member of the board of management. Certain acts by the board of management shall be subject to prior authorisation by the supervisory board, namely:

1. Closure or transfer of the undertaking or of substantial parts thereof.
2. Substantial curtailment or extension of the activities of the undertaking.
3. Substantial organisational changes within the undertaking.
4. Establishment or termination of long-term cooperation with other undertakings.

In addition, the S.E.'s regulations (equivalent to the British Articles of Association) may specify necessary collaboration between the two boards for certain acts by the board of management. The rights of third parties are protected if prior authorisation is not obtained from the supervisory board where necessary, but the board of management exposes itself to an action by the supervisory board for damages or dismissal of one or more of its members. Authorisation by the supervisory board, however, does not relieve the board of management from ultimate liability in the event of improper action.

Members of the supervisory board are appointed by the general meeting of the S.E. for a period, prescribed by the proposed statute, of not more than five years. The board of management is required to report regularly on the administration of the company and its subsidiaries or divisions to the supervisory board, which has a right of inspection of all company books and documents. Otherwise, members of the supervisory board will not be concerned with the day-to-day administration of the company. Nevertheless they shall be jointly and severally liable to the company for any failure to observe the provisions of both the statute for the European company and the company's own regulations unless they can prove that no fault can be attributed to them.

It is generally recognised in the member states of the EEC that an employee has both a *de facto* and *de jure* relationship with his firm, and this is recognised by each country's laws even although they differ in content. The principle involved, that employees of a company must be enabled to unite in defence of their interests within the undertaking and to share in the making of certain decisions, caused some considerable difficulty to Professor Sanders and his colleagues in the first draft of the proposed statute. At that time France and Germany were the two countries in the community which permitted employee representation in the management of limited. companies, but the method employed in each of these states differed substantially; German law allowed full participation of the employees by permitting them to elect one-third of the supervisory committee, who had the same powers and functions as the shareholders' representatives, whereas the French law provided for employee representation at directors' meetings by two nominees who had no voting rights. Professor Sanders envisaged two possible solutions to the dilemma of employee representation:

1. The statute should contain comprehensive codetermination rules of its own.
2. The statute should contain rules adapted to those of the existing national systems.

In the case of the co-determination system (1) he felt such a proposition beyond his capabilities as a jurist, although he envisaged some such solution as this on the European level being arrived at by the combined efforts of legal experts and union representatives of the member states. Under these circumstances he advocated solution (2) and in doing so devised a practical but rather cumbersome method of establishing a degree of employee participation based on the proportions of S.E. employees who worked in France and Germany and related this to the participation rules of the respective countries.

Meanwhile, national laws have been in a state of flux with regard to employee representation, and after further deliberation, as envisaged by Professor Sanders, the Commission proposed three types of legal machinery for regulating the representation of employees within the management structure and for facilitating the regulation of conditions of employment remuneration within the European Company.

1. The European Works Council, representing the employees in each establishment of the undertaking.
2. Representation of employees on the supervisory board of the European Company.
3. The possibility of concluding collective agreement between the European Company and the unions represented within the undertaking.

It is proposed that a European works council be formed in every European company having establishments in more than one of the member states. In the case of a European Company being situated in only one member state the national law of that state shall apply. Uniformity is thus assured where an S.E. operates in more than one member state but no special provision in the proposed statute would be required if only one country was involved. Normally, organs of employee representation formed in the establishments of an S.E. pursuant to national laws shall continue in existence with the same functions and powers as are conferred upon them under that law. The numbers of representatives appointed to the European Works Council will depend upon the number of employees in each establishment of the S.E. and each employee so elected to serve receives certain protections and guarantees by the statute in respect of his normal employment, emoluments and time required to carry out his duties. Expenses, including the cost of expert advice to the Works Council, shall be borne by the S.E., and within limits the board of management shall make all necessary information available to the Works Council. The statute provides for regular discussion between the board of management and the European Works Council, who shall also receive quarterly reports on the general operational developments of the company, the same communications and documents as the shareholders and the adopted annual accounts and management report. Decisions concerning general aspects of employee welfare, including recruitment, promotion and dismissal of employees, industrial safety and holiday schedules can be made by the board of management only with the agreement of the European Works Council. In addition the latter must also be consulted before decisions are made by management concerning job evaluation and wage rates per job or for piecework. In general, where employees' interests are concerned, the proposed statute requires consultation by the board of management with the European Works Council. Where disputes arise between the board of management and the European Works Council provision is made for settlement by arbitration.

Employees shall also be represented on the supervisory board, one member being appointed for every two appointed by the general meeting, although the company's regulations may provide for a higher degree of employee representation. It is possible, and this is not uncommon in certain companies in member states, that employees may not wish representation on the supervisory board, and under these circumstances the proposed statute provides for the normal functioning of that board.

The proposed statute, in addition to establishing the concept of the European Works Council and determining the employees' rights of representation on the supervisory board, also provides that conditions of employment may be regulated by collective agreement made between the S.E. and the trade unions represented in its establishments. In this respect the S.E. is not to be restricted to making collective agrreements on a national basis.

Accounting provisions in the proposed statute for a Societas Europea

The accounting and disclosure requirements of the S.E. were only sketchily outlined by Professor Sanders and his committee, the intention being that further appraisal of financial requirements was essential but outwith the scope of their remit. Substantial work on accounting requirements was later undertaken by a study group (Groupe d'Etudes Droit des Sociétés des Experts Comptables de la C.E.E.), under the chairmanship of Wirtschaftsprüfer Dr Wilhelm Elmendorff, which drew up proposals for the harmonisation of the accounting requirements of the member states under Article 54(3)(*g*) of the Treaty of Rome. The proposed requirements for accounting and disclosure by the S.E. are largely in line with the proposed directives under the harmonisation rules but in some respects go beyond the national requirements, on the basis that European companies should disclose a wide range of information and that the requirements should deny the opportunity for evasion so far as the preparation of accounts is concerned.

The annual accounts of the S.E. shall comprise the balance sheet, the profit and loss account and the notes on the accounts, which shall be drawn up in accordance with regular and proper accounting principles and shall be presented clearly and accurately. Subject to the provisions on valuation and classification, they shall reflect as true and fair a view as possible of the company's assets, liabilities, financial position, and results. It should be noted that banks and insurance companies are exempted from the accounting requirements of the S.E. and they shall comply with the law of the member state from which they are managed.

Classification of items in the balance sheet and profit and loss account is prescribed and emphasised, although variations may be permitted where the special nature of an S. E.warrants this and this fact is disclosed. The balance sheet may be drawn up in the horizontal or in the 'narrative' (vertical or columnar) form. No agreement has yet been reached on the method of presentation of the so-called 'narrative' form, possibly because of a certain dialogue between the Dutch and German interests. The horizontal form of presentation is, however, prescribed as-follows.

The following items shall be shown on the assets side:

Costs of formation

Fixed assets

I. Intangible assets:
   1. Research and development costs,
   2. Concessions, patents, licences, trade-marks, and similar rights which:
      (a) were acquired for consideration and are not to be included under 3, or
      (b) were created by the company itself,
   3. 'Derivativer Firmenwert', goodwill, 'fonds de commerce', 'avviamento',
   4. Work in progress and pre-payments on account of intangible assets.

II. Tangible assets:
   1. Land and buildings,
   2. Industrial plant and machinery,
   3. Other plant and industrial and commercial equipment,
   4. Plant under construction and pre-payments on account of tangible assets.

III. Investments and other financial assets:
   1. Investments other than those included under III-2,
   2. Holdings in associated companies,
   3. Securities representing financial assets other than those included under III-1 and 2,
   4. Claims on companies in which the S.E. holds an investment,
   5. Claims on associated companies,
   6. Other claims.

Current assets

I. Stocks:
   1. Raw materials and auxiliary materials, including fuel,
   2. Products in course of manufacture, including rejects,
   3. Finished products and goods for resale,
   4. Pre-payment on account of stocks.

II. Debtors:

(Amounts becoming due and payable within one year shall be shown separately in each case.)

1. Debtors (trade),
2. Debtors (undertakings in which the S.E. holds an investment),
3. Debtors (associated companies),
4. Miscellaneous.

III. Securities forming part of current assets and other liquid assets:

1. Bills of exchange,
2. Other securities forming part of current assets except cheques included under 3,
3. Balances with banks and in post office current accounts, cheques, and cash.

Pre-payments

Aggregate loss transferred from profit and loss account

The following items shall be shown on the liabilities side:

Share capital

Different classes of shares, if any, shall be shown separately, stating the nominal amount of each share.

Reserves

1. Balance on share premium account.
2. Reserves arising on revaluation.
3. Reserves for intangible assets.
4. Statutory reserves.
5. Free reserves.

Depreciation not shown on the assets side

1. Depreciation of costs of formation.
2. Depreciation of intangible assets.
3. Depreciation of tangible assets.
4. Depreciation of investments and other financial assets. (Items included under 2 to 4 should be broken down in the same way as the corresponding assets.)

Provisions for depreciation where the provision is not shown on the assets side

1. Of intangible assets.
2. Of tangible assets.
3. Of investments and other financial assets. (Items included under 1 to 3 should be broken down in the same way as the corresponding assets.)

Provisions for contingencies and charges

1. Pensions and similar commitments.
2. Taxation (provision for future taxation being shown separately).
3. Miscellaneous.

Creditors

(In respect of each of the following headings, debts becoming due and payable within one year, and fully secured debts shall be shown separately.)
1. Loans (convertible loans being shown spearately).
2. Bank borrowings.
3. Prepayments on orders received.
4. Suppliers of goods and services.
5. Bills of exchange.
6. Creditors (companies in which the S.E. holds an investment).
7. Creditors (associated companies).
8. Miscellaneous.

Accruals

Aggregate profit transferred from profit and loss account

The balance sheet or notes thereon will also require to show contingent liabilities on bills of exchange issued and negotiated, indemnities, guarantees and similar commitments, together with any financial obligations incurred for an amount exceeding 100,000 units of account and for a term exceeding one year. Liabilities incurred towards associated companies are to be shown separately. In order to show clearly the company's financial position it has been thought desirable to state separately any obligations, such as those arising under leasing agreements, incurred for a term exceeding one year.

The profit and loss account of an S.E. can be presented in any one of the four different methods prescribed by the proposed statute. These differ not only in presentation (double-sided or columnar) but also in the method and classification of income and expenditure. One alternative is to give the total expenditure for the year broken down, according to kind, against which is shown turnover, plus goods and services produced during the year, but unsold at the year end, and adjusted for the corresponding opening stock balance. The other method is to break down expenditure according to the operations in respect of which it was incurred and to relate the cost of sales to the resultant turnover. The necessity to specify these several methods arises from the diversity of practices existing within the member states, and it is thought by the Commission that some latitude as to the method of presentation would be desirable. The most widely used method in member states of presentation of the profit and loss account is as follows:

I. Trading results (excluding income and expenditure, if any, included under II):

1. Net turnover.
2. Changes in stocks of finished and semi-finished products.
3. Other goods and services supplied by the undertaking to itself.
4. Other trading income arising out of the operations of the undertaking.
5. Raw materials and auxiliary materials including fuel.
6. Labour costs.
7. Depreciation of costs of formation.
8. Depreciation and provisions for depreciation of intangible and tangible assets.
9. Other trading costs.
10. Trading profit or loss.

II Financial results:

11. Income arising under agreements requiring transfer of profits, whether relating to the whole or a part of the profits, income from associated undertakings being shown separately.
12. Income from trade investments, other than income shown under 11, income from associated undertakings being shown separately.
13. Income from other securities held and from claims forming part of the financial assets, income from associated undertakings being shown separately.
14. Other interest and similar income, that from associated companies being shown separately.
15. Expenditure arising from absorption of losses.
16. Depreciation and provisions for depreciation of investments and other fixed financial assets.
17. Interest and similar charges, those arising in respect of associated undertakings being shown separately.
18. Financial profit or loss.

III Non-recurring income and expenditure:
- 19. Non-recurring income.
- 20. Non-recurring expenditure.
- 21. Balance of non-recurring items.
- 22. Subtotal.

IV Taxation:
- 23. Taxation of profits
  - (a) current,
  - (b) future.
- 24. Other taxes not included under I, II, or III above.
- 25. Subtotal.

V Set-off or transfer of profit or loss:
- 26. Income arising as a result of set-off of losses.
- 27. Profits transferred under agreement requiring transfer of profits, whether relating to the whole or a part of the profits.

VI Profit for the year/loss for the year.

VII Profit or loss brought forward from the previous year.
- 28. Subtotal.

VIII Changes in reserves:
- 29. Withdrawals from reserves.
- 30. Appropriation of profit for the year to reserves.

IX Profit/loss to balance sheet.

The other columnar method of presentation detailed in the proposed statute is 'more advanced from a business management point of view and should therefore be admitted with an eye to the future'. This futuristic method of presentation in fact differs only in the content of the 'Trading result' as below.

1. Net turnover,
2. Production costs of goods and services supplied (including depreciation and provisions for depreciation),
3. Gross trading profit,
4. Distribution costs (including depreciation and provisions for depreciation),
5. General administration expenses (including depreciation and provisions for depreciation),
6. Other trading income,
7. Trading profit or loss.

The former and apparently most widely used method of presenting the trading results in member states is favoured, firstly, because the breaking down of expenditure according to kind creates no problem of analysing trading costs by operations, and secondly, because it is possible to arrive at the value of the total production of the undertaking, which is one yardstick of its profitability. The latter method is favoured by some because the separation of expenditure according to the kind of operation in many cases is more compatible with the cost accounting system used by undertakings than is a breakdown of costs according to kind and so affords an insight into their cost structure. Similar items are also grouped together, which is seen to be advantageous. One disadvantage of this latter method is that it is impossible to ascertain actual output achieved in an accounting period and where production processes last a long time, e.g. contract work, there could be undesirable fluctuations in published results.

British accountants may well look askance at some aspects of the specimen balance sheet and profit and loss account, but in reality the information requirements of the S.E. can be said to be of a substantially higher standard than previously existed in some of the European member states. Differences of presentation are less important than information content, though many may dislike seeing depreciation of assets listed on the liabilities side of the balance sheet. In this respect it is interesting to note that the proposed statute provides for the inclusion in depreciation of all losses in value definitively sustained as at the date of the balance sheet, and that provisions for depreciation shall be the adjusting items for losses in value of assets which have not yet definitively been sustained but which are to be expected in the light of prudent valuation. The distinction between depreciation and provision for depreciation will depend largely on the judgment of those who prepare and certify the accounts.

The valuation of items in the annual accounts is a matter of some importance which is recognised in the proposed statute, companies having the option of using either the historical cost method or the replacement cost method. Arguments for each method are recognised by the proposed statute which, however, does not attempt to prescribe the rules for the replacement cost method in any detail on the grounds that consultations on this subject are still far from complete. The *caveat* of the true and fair view is nevertheless repeated for the benefit of those who decide to apply the replacement cost method, and undertakings using this method must transfer to revaluation reserve the differences arising between historical cost and valuation. The reserve may be written back only to the extent that it is no longer required for the purpose of replacement of assets, as would be the case if replacement costs declined or the undertaking reduced its production activities. Any differences arising through revaluation must be shown separately in the notes on the accounts. Depreciation and provisions for depreciation shall be calculated annually on the basis of the replacement cost arrived at for the year in question.

The content of the notes on the accounts is also prescribed and includes information relating to principles of valuation; details of investments held by the S.E. where the percentage holding is 10% or more; details of investments in the capital of the S.E. exceeding 10% of the S.E.'s capital; group relationships; details of associated companies; turnover broken down according to products, operations and markets; details of the labour force; emoluments paid to the board of management and supervisory board; and value added tax and other taxes comprised in the trading results, financial results and non-recurring income and expenditure. Some of this information has still to be reflected in accounts of companies in the member states.

The regulations contained in the proposed statute relating to the preparation of group accounts are concerned mainly with small matters of detail and refrain from specifying methods of consolidation. This contrasts strangely with the detail and clarity of expression evident elsewhere in the draft. Group accounting still remains something of a phenomenon in the member states, and I understand that there will be much more discussion and consultation on this subject before the proposals become law.

The audit of the accounts is naturally provided for in the proposals. Persons who are suitably qualified and experienced, and authorised in a member state to act as auditors of the annual accounts of limited companies whose shares are quoted on a stock exchange, shall be eligible for appointment as auditor by the general meeting of the S.E. An auditor may not be removed by the general meeting save where there are serious grounds for so doing.

The remaining provisions contained in the proposed statute are of a non-accounting nature, and relate to groups, alteration of companies' regulations, liquidation, mergers, and taxation. Of these the most crucial will be the eventual regulations on taxation.

Other steps towards harmonisation

The creation of the S.E. is not intended as a step towards replacing national companies but is designed more as a vehicle to assist the concentration of European industry by facilitating cross-frontier mergers. This is one method of effecting a form of harmonisation of national commercial and fiscal laws, by removing the national influence and jurisdiction from the S.E. Another path towards the unification of national laws in the EEC is being pursued in a fashion somewhat parallel to that of the S.E. By utilising Article 54(3) (*g*) of the Treaty of Rome, which stipulates that the safeguards which member states require of companies, to protect the interests of members and of third parties shall be coordinated with a view to making them equivalent, the

Council of Ministers on the recommendation of the Commission issues directives to member states, as opposed to the uniform legislation required, for example, for the establishment of the S.E.[3]

Tax harmonisation in the EEC is nowhere near completion, and the proposed statute for the S.E. does little more than indicate the general fiscal problems which will arise: (a) when an S.E. is formed, (b) during the company's lifetime, and (c) in deciding its domicile for tax purposes.

Firstly, the formation of a European company raises the problem of indirect taxation on the raising of capital, and, as S.E.s must not receive preferential treatment compared with national companies, the S.E. will accordingly suffer a rate of capital duty between 1 and 2%. Where an S.E. is created by merger of companies from different member states, the proposed statute refers to the provisions of the Commission's proposed directive concerning the common system of taxation applicable in the case of mergers; divisions and contributions of assets would take place between corporations of different member states which, in general, rules that no form of capital gains tax may be imposed by any member state on the consummation of a corporate merger across national frontiers. It would appear that the adoption of the articles of the proposed directive on international mergers by the proposed statute is highly probable, as the S.E. may well be in existence before national laws are harmonised, and without the removal of the existing barriers to cross-frontier mergers the S.E. will be a highly ineffective aid to industrial concentration.

The taxation problems affecting the formation of European companies are likewise compounded by the existing difficulties of double taxation of profits by member states, and the domicile of companies will be critical without complete harmonisation. A further proposed directive by the Commission concerning the common system of taxation applicable in the case of parent corporations and subsidiaries of different member states has been recognised, the articles of which may be adopted by the proposed statute under the previously mentioned circumstances in order to prevent double taxation of profits transferred by a subsidiary company to a parent company. As far as the domicile of the S.E. is concerned the use of letterbox registered offices is discouraged, and its domicile for tax purposes will largely be determined by its centre of effective management of operations.

I have discussed taxation only in general terms, but the difficulties of harmonisation are immense and cannot be overemphasised. Despite the urgency, expert opinion has it that satisfactory harmonisation will take many years to achieve. The maxim of *festina lente* seems appropriate.

Conclusion

The recent decision of the British Parliament to join the European Economic Community can be viewed by British accountants and businessmen as an indication of future changes in, *inter alia*, company law in the U.K. The existing disparity between British company law and the proposed statute for the European company is substantial. The most obvious differences between British and European company law to be tackled by jurists would be the British lack of minimum capital requirements and the absence of the supervisory board and works council in Britain; the latter of course embraces substantial differences in industrial law. Britain does not recognise bearer shares and in this respect the more sophisticated British capital markets compared with those existing in Europe constitutes an important difference between the two systems. The floating charge does not exist as a protection for creditors in the European system and serious disparities arise in the field of taxation. The European rejection of the no par value share will also be viewed with disfavour in certain British quarters. The present directives being proposed by the European Commission would apply to the U.K. on entry into the Common Market and the first directive under Article 54(3) (g) of the Treaty of Rome which, *inter alia*, is concerned with the validity of commitments entered into by officers of a company would immediately affect the British *ultra vires* rule.

Had the British Parliament rejected the entry terms for admission to the Common Market the existing problems of industrial participation would have remained the same since companies in non-Member States appear not to have the right to form S.E.s within the EEC. Professor Sanders was quite explicit in his preliminary text when he provided for the formation of an S.E. by 'Stock Corporations which are established in a State which is not a member of the European Economic Community and which have been engaged in economic activities for the last three fiscal years prior to the application to record the S.E.' Such provision is not even implied in the text of the Commission's draft statute, and the right to create S.E.s is apparently restricted to the public companies of the member states.

The European legislators are not unfamiliar with the statutes and conventions of other nations, but nevertheless one is left with the impression that the activity in Brussels tends to be somewhat divorced from the rest of the world. For example, Dr Elmendorff's study group on company accounting requirements is quite familiar with accounting trends and techniques elsewhere, and though one has to acknowledge the quality of the end product of their deliberations, solutions and proposals are definitely European orientated and not a little introverted. It is also understood that the roles of British extra-statutory institutions affecting the interests of society, such as the Stock Exchange Regulations and the City Code, have received little acknowledgement in the European supranational proposals. Admittedly the structure of share ownership in Europe is different from that of the U.K. and the U.S.A., but nevertheless there is a trend towards greater direct public participation in European industry. British entry into the European Economic Community may in fact act as a stimulus to pan-European investment and accordingly there must be a greater European acceptance of British institutions affecting industrial concentration. However, as one spokesman for the EEC in Brussels told me, 'We will cross this bridge when we come to it'. Some bridge—some crossing!

Notes

[1] First published in *The Accountant's Magazine,* December 1971.

[2] Sir Reay Geddes: 'Towards the European Company of the Future', European Review, Summer 1971.

[3] Reference in this section of the original article, to the draft directives issued by the Commission has been deleted as this is covered in greater detail in Chapter 1—Ed.

Bibliography

Pieter Sanders, *European Stock Corporation*, Commerce Clearing House Inc.

Proposed Statute for the European Company—Supplement to Bulletin 8—1970, of the European Communities, H.M.S.O.

Proposal for a Third Directive on Mergers Between Joint-Stock Companies—Supplement to Bulletin 5—1970, of the European Communities, H.M.S.O.

Charles de Hoghton (Ed.), *The Company*, P.E.P., George Allen and Unwin.

Robert R. Pennington, *Companies in the Common Market*, Oyez Publications.

Dennis Thomson, *The Proposal for a European Company*, Chatham House, P.E.P.

Christopher Layton, *Cross Frontier Mergers in Europe*, Bath University Press.

La Politique Industrielle De La Communauté—Memorandum de la Commision au Conseil, Office Des Publications Officielles Des Communautés Européennes, Luxembourg.

Horst Kaminski, 'The European Limited Company Statute', *Journal U.E.C.* April 1971.

Wilhelm Elmendorff, 'Co-ordination of the legal accounting requirements in the various countries of the European Economic Community—Further results of the discussions within the "Groupe d'Etudes Droit des Sociétés des Experts Comptables de la C.E.E." on accounting in a Group and in private limited companies', *Journal U.E.C.* 1 January 1971.

The E.E.C. Proposed Directives on Mergers and Take-Overs and Parent-Subsidiary Relationships, International Bureau of Fiscal Documentation.

Robert O. Prinsky, 'Commission submits draft Eurocompanies Law', *European Community*, August/September 1970.

Richard Shepherd, 'Dunlop-Pirelli Link-Up', *European Community*, April 1970.

Sir Reay Geddes, 'Towards the European Company of the Future', *European Review*, Summer 1971.

'Company Law, E.F.T.A. Studies the Case for a Supranational Company', *E.F.T.A. Bulletin*, September/October 1970.

Heinz Haller, 'Tax Harmonization', *European Community*, February 1971.

B. D. Barton, 'The Proposal for a European Company,' *Accountancy*, April 1971.
J. T. Brown, 'European Business—The Legal Framework', *The Accountant*, 15 July 1971.
Guy Bernard, 'Reflections on a European Type of Company', The *Accountant's Magazine*, September 1963.
Y. Scholten, 'The European Company', *Common Market Law Review*, 1967/68 Vol. V.
Per V. A. Hanner, 'Towards a "Nordic Companies Act"', *Journal U.E.C.* 1 April 1971.

3 The Supervisory Board

by R. SHIRLEY

For some years, questions have been raised about the role of the company and its social and economic function. In theory, the purpose of the company has traditionally been simple: the maximisation of profit for the shareholder. While companies were small there was a much closer alliance between management and shareholders, so this purpose was more likely to be observed. As companies grew in size, and shareholders became individually less prominent, a divergence of interest between them and management arose. Management, quite naturally, might develop special interests of their own, such as transforming their jobs into sinecures, or extending their empires. Other interests, too, came into focus: the special and vital relationship of employees to a company, and the less specific, but no less important, interest of the public at large.

These matters will be brought to a head with entry of the U.K. into the European Economic Community, and with the harmonisation of company law which it entails. The Supervisory board is the means by which the purpose of the company in this country might be radically transformed. In essence, this organ of the company—as it functions now in West Germany, and as proposed in the context of European company law—is a body interposed between the shareholders and the executive board, and its function, as the name indicates, is to direct and control the board of management.

There are two elements in the Supervisory Board, one representing the shareholders, and the other the workers. Although in most cases the workers are numerically weaker in their representation, forming only one third, the Supervisory Board is really the creation of the trade union movement in Germany, and was designed as an organ of worker's participation in the direction of the company. Workers' participation is a concept of long lineage in Germany. The word commonly used is *co-determination* (Mitbestimmung), which we use interchangeably with *participation*.

The idea was put forward in the mid-nineteenth century but was not embodied in law until the Workers' Protection Law of 1891, which provided for representation of the workers' interest in the direction of the company. This law had little effect in practice, but it did provide a precedent and source of ideas. In 1920 the German Industrial Council Law required the establishment of workers' councils in all firms with more than 20 employees. This law was repealed in 1934, but after the war the development of co-determination resumed its course, and resulted in the enactment of two laws.

The first, in 1951, was concerned with the coal, iron, and steel industries. This was the Co-determination Law providing for representation of the workers on both the Supervisory and the Management Boards of the firms in question. The second was the Industrial Constitution Law of 1952, which required workers' representation on the Supervisory Boards (but not management boards) of all public companies other than those covered by the 1951 law.

In the coal, iron, and steel industries, workers' representation on the Supervisory Board was set at 50% of the board membership, the other 50% being elected by the shareholders; in other firms the participation was one-third workers' and two-thirds shareholders' representatives. The workers' representatives are elected directly by the workers in the firm.

The value of supervisory boards in German industry, and of workers' representation on them, is hard to determine. One commentator[1] asserts: 'The supervisory board has ceased to be the supervisory instrument of the owners and has become a parliament built into the AG, an organ which preserves the balance of opposing politico-economic interests'. This is exactly what one might expect, and it tends to be confirmed by a recent case involving the Volkswagen company.

Volkswagenwerke AG was state owned until 1960 when it was transformed into a joint-stock company. The shares had restricted voting rights to ensure widespread control. Besides this, the state maintained a proprietary interest in the form of a 20% share participation by the State of Lower Saxony, and 16% by the Bonn Government; a public-interest foundation had 4%, and the remaining 60% was taken up by the public. The Supervisory Board of 21 members had seven workers' representatives (the statutory third) and four representatives of the two Governments.

In 1968 the Supervisory Board appointed a new executive chairman, Kurt Lotz, despite the opposition of some members of the Management Board. The new chairman's subsequent career was marked by increasing opposition, due in part to an unpopular decision to expand the range of models, and consequently to involve the company in heavy investment. He also incurred the hostility of the workers by opposing their choice of personnel director for the Management Board. His opposition was to no avail since, although workers' representatives on the supervisory board have in general the same rights and power as those of the shareholders, they have what amounts to the privilege of appointing the personnel director; such an appointment, besides requiring a majority of the board as a whole, must also be approved by a majority of the workers' representatives.

Another point of friction appeared to be the replacement of the Christian Democrat Government (whom Lotz supported) by the Social Democrats in 1970. The Social Democrats are roughly equivalent to the British Labour

Party, and are therefore more favourable to co-determination. Lotz was regarded as an opponent of this concept, and thus incurred the disfavour of the representatives of the new government, as well as the workers. Because of these various pressures he resigned 'by mutual agreement' in 1971[2].

While some of the other five original members of the EEC provide for Supervisory Boards, in none are they compulsory ,as in Germany. Both Belgium and the Netherlands are proposing to introduce compulsory Supervisory Boards, possibly in anticipation of Community company law which might impose the Supervisory Board on public limited companies in the interests of harmonisation. Norway, which until the referendum of September 1972 looked like becoming a member of the Community, had drafted a law providing compulsory Supervisory Boards which was almost identical in form and function with that proposed for Community companies.

A fundamental principle of the EEC is to create a 'system in which competition be not distorted'. It follows that company law should be harmonised in order to ensure that no legal obstacles stand in the way of competition between companies of different member states. This is a highly complex matter, and many problems have still to be resolved before full harmonisation can be achieved. One such problem concerns the supervisory board. To achieve harmonisation, Germany would have to abandon the compulsory Supervisory Board, or the other member states would have to accept it. However, two recent developments strongly indicate that the Community is moving towards adoption. These are the proposal for a European Company, or Societas Europea, and the proposed fifth directive on the coordination of the structure of public limited companies.

Societas Europea

In 1970 the Commission for the European Communities published a proposed statute for the European Company. The preamble to this statute sets out a justifying argument, and states that the achievement of economic union presupposes 'a reorganisation of the factors of production and distribution on a Community scale in order to ensure that the enlarged market will operate similarly to a domestic market'. European undertakings, extending to several member states are subject to a particular national legal framework, which 'no longer corresponds to the economic framework within which they are to develop if the Community is to achieve its purpose'. Therefore, to achieve both legal and economic unity, a new entity, the European Company, will be required. This will be formed 'side by side with companies governed by one or other national law' and will be 'subject only to a specific legal system that is directly applicable to all the Member States, thereby freeing this form of company from any legal tie to any particular country'.

No doubt, in devising a system, those who framed the European Company proposal tried to abstract the best from each body of national company law. And in the matter of the administrative structure they opted in favour of the German compulsory two-tier system, even to the extent of adopting workers' representation in the same one-in-three ratio.

Composition of the Supervisory Board of the European Company

Two-thirds of the members of the Supervisory Board are appointed by the general meeting of the shareholders, and one-third by the employees; the number of members must thus be a multiple of three, in fact, ranging up to 21, in proportion to the capitalisation. Once appointed, the Supervisory Board is empowered to appoint the Management Board and to designate its chairman. In appointing their representatives, the shareholders are advised to choose members for their 'personal qualities and dynamic character'. The period of appointment is no more than five years, and the remuneration is laid down in the articles of association, or decided by the general meeting. Dismissal of shareholders' representatives is also in the hands of the general meeting, and there is no mention of grounds or compensation. However, the unwieldy method of securing this dismissal is probably a fair quarantee of justice to the member.

The election of the workers' representatives is much more complex, since pains are taken to avoid dominance by one nationality. The system is that the election should be by list, that is, the choice will not be between several individual candidates but between groups, who must be voted for as a complete slate; each list will contain as many names as there are workers' vacancies and the candidates on the list should be in the same proportion with respect to their nationality as the various nationalities occur among the firm's employees. Considering that the workers' places on the board can be only seven at the maximum, and may well be something less than that, it is obvious that the nationality ratio rule will call for a good deal of compromise.

Another complexity in the election of the workers' representatives is that it should be through the medium of recognised workers' organisations, i.e. by a form of electoral college. The organisations are specified in Article 102 of the proposed statute. For the six founding members of the Community they comprise officially recognised workers' bodies set up by statute according to the various national laws.

What if the workers refuse to participate in the supervision of the company? Provision is made for this in Article 138(1): 'Employees shall not be represented on the Supervisory Board if not less than two-thirds of the employees so decide'. In such a case the Supervisory Board shall function without the workers' representatives, and the rules relating to the quorum (half the members) and the voting majority (51% of members present), shall apply to the numbers actually appointed.

Powers of the Supervisory Board of the European Company

The purpose of the Supervisory Board is to exercise permanent control over the management of the company. This is primarily achieved by its power to appoint and dismiss the Management Board. Not only does the Supervisory Board appoint the Management Board, it also has the right to appoint the chairman, the vice-chairman, and the personnel and industrial relations director. This last power indicates how closely the German model has been followed. Power of dismissal of its appointees lies with the Supervisory Board. The dismissal must be on serious grounds, and there is right of appeal to the European Court. However, even if the appellant wins his case he cannot be reinstated. The best he can do is obtain damages. No matter how unjust his dismissal, he must, in the interests of harmony, remain dismissed.

To aid the Supervisory Board in its task it has unlimited rights of inspection and control over all company activities. It is entitled to a quarterly report from management on the administration of the company, and of its subsidiaries and divisions. It has also the right to be informed immediately of all events coming to managements' attention that might have a substantial influence on the position of the company. Certain important matters require the authorisation of the Supervisory Board before the board of management may act. These are:

1. Closure or transfer of the undertaking or substantial parts of it.
2. Substantial curtailment or extension.
3. Substantial organisational changes.
4. Establishment or termination of long-term cooperation with others.

On these same matters the board of management is required to consult the Company Works Council before taking action. Further, the Supervisory Board may not authorise such actions until it has heard the opinion of the works council. It is not, however, obliged to follow this opinion.

Certain sanctions and constraints are applicable to members of the Supervisory Board. Thus they may not, without the authorisation of the board as a whole, engage in an agreement to which the company is a party, and in which they have an interest. They are jointly and severally liable for failure to observe the articles of association of the company, and for wrongful acts. If they deal in company shares, the shares must be registered or, if in bearer form, lodged with a bank; notice of ownership of the shares shall be given to the European Commercial Register, and any profit made in dealing with shares of the company within a period of six months must be handed over to the company.

European Works Council

A works council is an employees' representative body. The European Works Council has an important bearing on the administration of the company, and therefore on the Supervisory Board. Its establishment is compulsory for the European Company, which is obliged to pay its operating expenses (including even the hire of expert consultants); assure that its elected members are not dismissed from their normal employment during their term of office and for three years after they cease to be members; allow them all the time off that the councillors think necessary to fulfil their duties, yet pay them the wages and bonuses which they would be entitled to if they were full-time workers; the company must also provide the council with a quarterly report as well as all information received by shareholders.

The European Works Council is responsible for representing the interests of the employees of the company, and its agreement is necessary on matters relating to employment conditions, such as wage rates, hours of work, and dismissal procedures. As mentioned above, the Works Council is entitled to consultation before action is taken on matters such as closure and substantial organisational changes. Between the Works Council, employee representation on the Supervisory Board, and the normal management of collective agreements, it will be seen that great scope is provided in the European Company proposal to cater for the interests of the labour force.

The proposed fifth directive

In September 1972 the European Commission published a proposal for a fifth directive on the structure of companies to be constituted in accordance with a common Community law. Whereas the transformation into the European Company would be voluntary, the new structure proposed in the fifth directive would be compulsory for all public limited companies.

The Supervisory Boards envisaged by the two proposals are similar. Both provide for two-thirds representation for shareholders, and one-third for workers. Both are charged with the appointment of the board of management and specifically with the appointment of the director of personnel. The list of four special concerns of the Supervisory Board—closure or transfer, curtailment or extension, organisational changes, and cooperation—is identical for both.

The draft fifth directive goes into much less detail than the European Company proposal, for example, it does not discuss the possibility of the workers' refusing to participate, nor does it lay down regulations about share dealing on the part of members. However, it expressly limits to 10 the number of supervisory board memberships that one person can hold, while the European Company proposal simply requires that the consent of the whole board be obtained for the assumption of membership in another board. Although the provision of the draft fifth directive would in general apply to all public limited companies, the two-tier structure of Supervisory Board and Management Board would be compulsory only for those companies employing 500 or more. Precise figures are not available, but a reasonable estimate indicates that, excluding government employees and those in nationalised industries, over 60% of the U.K. work force would be engaged in companies with compulsory Supervisory Boards.

An important, indeed radical difference is introduced, however. Article 4(2) of the draft fifth directive provides for the appointment of representatives of other than the shareholders and workers. 'The laws of member states may provide for the appointment of a portion of the members of the Supervisory Board who are not appointed as laid down in the preceding paragraph, from competent bodies other than the general meeting.' This is a literal translation from the original French and is admittedly not translucent. But an appendix makes it clear that what is contemplated is additional representation of other interests: 'Finally, the laws of member states may provide that some members of the Supervisory Board be appointed neither by the general meeting nor by the workers. One thinks particularly of representatives of the public interest'.

This is a radical development in the concept of the supervisory board. Originally its purpose was to provide a means of workers' participation; this involved, as a necessary counterweight, the representation of the shareholders. Now, scope is provided for the recognition of yet other interests, and in particular that of the public. These other interests may be represented by members appointed by the government. But being government appointees might these not represent the interest of the government itself? If so, this provision could be a means by which national legislation could either dilute or strengthen workers' representation on the Supervisory Board. Indeed, this may well be a 'concealed' objective of the provision, for the imposition of a Supervisory Board with workers' representation is the main obstacle to the acceptance of the directive. If governments are allowed to participate they could largely overcome this objection.

Value of the Supervisory Board

The value of the Supervisory Board has yet to be proved. At present the concept has only been introduced on a large scale in West Germany, and even there, no two periods of 'normality' have elapsed, one with the regime of the supervisory board, and one without, that can be compared. From the beginning of the century until the establishment of the Supervisory Board in

1951/52, the German economy has been distorted by preparations for war, the waging of war, and recovery from war, as well as by a bout of punitive inflation and massive unemployment. Undoubtedly, however, the Federal Republic's high growth rate since the war is closely related to the country's relative freedon from industrial strife. And this peace and cooperation relates, either as cause or effect (and probably a bit of both), to co-determination.

From a general and philosophical standpoint the evaluation of the Supervisory Board becomes more complex still. If the board is seen as a means of achieving the purpose of the company, such purpose must then be examined and defined. The obvious and pristine purpose of the company is to make money for the shareholders. But later, as companies grew in size, and shareholders were further removed from management, the enhancement of the power, prestige, and wealth of the board of directors became a second aim. This second purpose has never been written into articles of association, but it is nevertheless real. A third purpose, which in recent times has become very prominent, is the advancement of the interest of the employees. A fourth is the public interest. A fifth purpose, can also be distinguished: the company itself—a sort of company nationalism springs from a sense of community and pride felt by many shareholders, managers, and workers. Rolls-Royce Ltd exemplified this, and there are undoubtedly many other companies that evoke in some degree the moral involvement of their employees and shareholders.

For this study of the Supervisory Board I shall confine attention to the three fundamental purposes of the company—those of the shareholders, the workers, and the public.

Interest of the shareholder

There are many occasions for incompetence or bad judgment, or even simple complacency, on the part of the management board, to impair a company's performance. But even more, there is strong reason to believe that the special interest of management in advancing itself (the second purpose in our list) has done harm to many companies and their shareholders. I refer in particular to mergers and takeovers. These are always presented as being good for both sides but there is room for serious doubt. The likelihood is that in many cases the board of the dominant company, even unknown to themselves, are motivated by personal ambition. The same consideration applies to abortive takeovers: often, these have been aborted because of a spirited, if not violent defence by the threatened board; would it not really have been in the *shareholders'* interest to accede to the takeover?

This might be illustrated by the P & O case. In August 1972 a bid for Bovis Ltd was announced by the board of the Peninsular and Oriental Steam Navigation Co. Ltd. The bid was worth £170 million at the time, and as far as the public and the shareholders knew it had strong backing from both boards. Two weeks after the announcement Lord Inchcape, a member of the P & O board, announced strong opposition to the bid. It was then revealed that the P & O board was seriously divided. Six of the executive directors were opposed to the move, but had not made their disagreement public because, according to the financial editor of the *Sunday Times* (27 August), 'they are worried about their jobs'. Lord Inchcape let it be known that the decision to make the bid was finally swayed by Lord Poole and Adam Harris, who, interestingly, besides being directors of P & O, are also directors of Lazard Brothers, financial advisers to both P & O and Bovis. One of the dissenting P & O directors, Denys Brown, explains his apparently late realisation of the disadvantage of the takeover as a movement from 'shock through hesitation to rejection': the shock was occasioned by the speed of the decision, made in the face of doubt expressed by several members, and by the fact that the decision was reached without the P & O board having seen the Bovis balance sheet.

Here, we have a situation in which a decision of the utmost importance was made with evidently inadequate consideration. Dissenters from the decision did not see fit to reveal their dissent for personal (though understandable) reasons, and the decision was strongly influenced by two board members, the Lazard directors, who had strong extraneous reasons for supporting it. The battle was waged by means of full-page advertisements placed in the press by each faction, and which consisted merely of loud exhortations containing little in the way of reasoned arguments. The situation became even more tangled when a £232 million takeover bid was made for P & O by the Inchcape Co Ltd whose chairman is the same Lord Inchcape who made the original, if tardy objection to taking over Bovis. Eventually the shareholders of P & O rejected the bid for Bovis, and its chief proponent, the chairman of P & O resigned. Lazards also resigned as financial adviser to both companies.

Would a Supervisory Board have avoided such a situation? It would certainly have introduced a beneficial delay into the proceedings and would have required the supporters of the takeover to prove their case. And, provided that there were no Lazard directors on the Supervisory Board, it would have been more likely to reach an unbiased conclusion, or rather, a conclusion biased towards the interest of the P & O shareholders. The Bovis Supervisory Board would be fulfilling the same duty on behalf of the Bovis shareholders. This presupposes that it would be possible to elect a Supervisory Board who would have no personal gain or loss from a merger except as shareholders. This would not be easy and would involve certain constraints.

A central question is: 'What type of people should the general meeting appoint to the supervisory board?' We might start on this problem by referring to an existing board, that of AKZO NV, the giant Dutch chemical concern. Among its present or recent members are an ex-Prime Minister and an ex-Minister for War of the Netherlands. Another member was simultaneously chairman of the supervisory board of Deutsche Bank AG, chairman of the management board of the Reconstruction Loan Corporation, and a member of the supervisory or management boards of 25 other companies, including Deutsche Shell AG, Deutsche Lufthansa AG, Badische Anilin- und Soda-Fabrik AG and Siemens AG.

Yet another was, during the term of his membership, President of Otto Wolff AG, president of the Association of German Chambers of Commerce and a member of the boards of 16 industrial or insurance companies.

When the draft fifth directive with its 10-board limitation finally passes into law, it is evident that many members of existing boards will have to resign from some of them.

Another question is whether there will be enough suitable people available for the several thousands of supervisory boards that will be called into existence in Britain. The draft fifth directive anticipates no difficulty here. Already boards have a complement of 'active' and 'passive' directors, i.e. executive and non-executive; it will be sufficient simply to allocate these between the two new boards, the executives going to the board of management, and the non-executives to the Supervisory Board. But this is much too facile. We need to examine more precisely what qualities are needed by a shareholders' representative to ensure the selection of the right person. I discern four basic conditions that should be fulfilled.

1. Common interest: the member should himself be a shareholder and his holding should comprise a sufficient proportion of his own wealth or income to involve him substantially in the fortunes of the company. What this proportion ought to be is a matter for debate, but for present purposes let us suggest 10%.
2. No contrary interest: a shareholder in two companies might have a strong interest in one taking over the other; as a member of the dominent company he will gain a net advantage, even though his fellow shareholders in the second company might suffer a loss. As a member of the Supervisory Board of each he has plainly a common interest with the shareholders of the first company, but a contrary interest relative to the second. Conflict of this nature could be resolved by requiring the member to resign one of his appointments. Alternatively, the restrictions on share ownership and dealing, as proposed for members of the Supervisory Board of the European Company, might be used to this end.
3. Expertise: the board member should have expert knowledge of at least one facet of the business. Retired employees, especially ex-members of the management board, would be likely to serve the Supervisory Board well, though the danger of fossilisation must be avoided.

4. Sufficiency of time: the board member should have enough time to accomplish his duties, which would embrace more than merely attending board meetings. The draft fifth directive sets a limit of 10 memberships, evidently with this in mind. Even 10 active memberships seems rather a lot, though they could possibly be encompassed if the member were particularly accomplished and energetic. But there could be other demands on a member's time such as salaried employment or consultancy, and a more general limitation would be required.

Besides these considerations 'personal qualities and dynamic character' as suggested for the European Company would be desirable.

Workers' representation

It is now many years since employers believed that their sole duty to their workers was to pay them a subsistence wage for the hours they worked. It has come to be accepted that employers are obliged to protect the worker even from his own inadvertence near dangerous machinery, to help provide a pension and sickness benefit, to contribute to unemployment insurance and to give reasonable notice of dismissal. Since 1965, provision is even made, in virtue of the Redundancy Payments Act of that year, for compensation for the loss of a worker's job.

A new concept in the theory of labour relations is now being advanced to the effect that instead of paying for redundancy, redundancy should be avoided; that it is the company's duty, having induced the worker to invest some of his life in his job, to protect that investment, even if it means extraordinary effort, and costs more than the job produces. An organ of some kind is needed to consult with the board of management in such industrial relations matters, but should this be a body with supervisory powers and, since supervision entails sanctions, with the ultimate power to dismiss the management? The idea of workers empowered to dismiss the boss is far from absurd in itself, but it leads to absurdity when we think of it in conjunction with the ultimate power of the shareholders to dismiss the management, either in general meeting or through a Supervisory Board. There cannot be two final authorities.

The problem is not really resolved by having substantial workers' representation on the Supervisory Board. Given that the workers' and the shareholders' interests are often in conflict, one side will tend habitually to override the other, or the body will tend to develop into a regulator of 'opposing politico-economic interests', to quote Wurdinger again.

While there has been no official union pronouncement on the matter, there appears to be a general reluctance to become embroiled in the control and management of companies. This at first sight seems strange. Why should the employees of a firm not seize the opportunity of participating in its direction, and so establish some degree of control by the workers? The answer may be in part that they recognise that their forte is producing the goods, and that quite other skills than they happen to have learned are required to finance and organise the production, and finally to sell it. A further explanation, however, is that union leaders realise that workers' representatives on the Supervisory Board would be their rivals, who would receive constant publicity within the firm, and the credit for any advantages gained. Union leaders are already beset by the problem of their authority leaking away to the shop floor, and would hardly tolerate another leakage into the board room.

As it is, the unions are free to comment on any matter affecting the company, and enjoy wide publicity in doing so. Clive Jenkins, secretary of the Association of Scientific, Technical and Managerial Staffs publically supported the P & O/Bovis merger on behalf of his members. His grounds were that the old management was inefficient and that introduction of new blood from Bovis would be to the workers' benefit.

Another consideration is that the British trades unions are largely craft unions, i.e. their members tend to belong to a particular trade, so that any one company is likely to contain several different unions representing electricians, engineers, carpenters, clerks, transport workers, and so on. A difficult problem would arise in devising workers' representation on a single Supervisory Board so that the various unions themselves would be satisfactorily represented—a similar problem to the representation of nationalities among workers in the European Company. In Germany, on the other hand, the unions fit neatly into the Supervisory Board, for they are *industrial unions* (Industriegewerkschaften), comprising all the workers in a particular industry or company. Thus there are no problems of demarcation, no membership raids, and no disputes about differentials.

What the situation would be if a Community company had, say, its German workers actively participating on its Supervisory Board, while its British workers did not, would make interesting speculation. Would the Germans become the unofficial representatives of the British employees?

All things considered, the interest of the workers—an interest that is certainly more intimate than that of the shareholders'—will probably be much better served by concentrating representation and rights of consultation in the Works Council. This body, after all, is a kind of specific Supervisory Board which has its own ultimate sanction of calling a strike, or to put it another way, of dismissing the company.

The public interest

Pollution, inflation, exports, quality of goods and services, employment and congestion are all matters of public interest on which the company has direct bearing. All of these are regulated by the government in a general way. The Export Guarantees Acts, 1945/67, the Prices and Incomes Act, 1966 (now repealed), and the Restrictive Trades Practices Act, 1959, are legislative manifestations of the public interest in the running of companies. But simply because an Act of Parliament is far too blunt an instrument to probe with proper accuracy into a company's affairs, it is far from certain that these and other acts achieve their purpose. It would be well if the members of the Supervisory Board could be relied on to keep the public interest in mind as they concerned themselves with the shareholders' interest. But this is more than we should expect. If companies are to be induced positively to serve the public interest, what is required is a public appointee on the Supervisory Board. His position would be as observer and adviser, without ruling power, to induce the company to conform to the spirit of the public interest law rather than merely the letter. The beginnings of such a system can be seen in the nationalised industries where there is direct contact with the government on pricing, employment, and so on. If in the nationalised industries why not in the larger joint-stock companies? The proposed fifth directive also provides scope for this.

The impact of the supervisory board on U.K. industry

The proposed statute for the European Company has not yet been adopted by the EEC Council, and it may be that the U.K. will be able to influence its final form. It is unlikely, however, that major changes will be accepted, considering that the draft statute has been three years in the making, and has the implicit approval of the Commission. In particular, it is virtually certain that the provision for the Supervisory Board will remain, for it will have the backing of West Germany, where it is already compulsory under national law.

What will the effect of this be on the British business scene? I consider that the European Company will eventually prove to be a serious, even overwhelming competitor with traditional British companies, such as to force them to convert to the European form. I believe this principally because the European Community was designed in the first instance to enhance competition, and the European Company designed specifically to operate within it. We have, as it were, a sudden change of climate, to which the pre-existing species are ill adapted, and at the same time the instant evolution of a new species perfectly adapted to it because it was created by it.

The ratification of the statute for the European Company seems virtually certain. 'That the proposal will be accepted by the Council is a foregone conclusion...'[3]. This may be likely before the end of 1974, i.e. within two years. Whether or not U.K. companies will voluntarily convert to the form of the European Company, eventually they will have to adapt themselves to the harmonised company law of the Community. This harmonisation may be long delayed, but nevertheless will be implemented. Then the question will be not whether to institute a Supervisory Board, but what form will it take and who will be on it?

Management in our one-board system might be assumed to oppose the idea of a supervisory body being set above them. Little has been said about it so far, but one can imagine grumbles about interference, rigidity, and destruction of initiative. Need it be so? Some management boards might, on the contrary, be relieved that the formulation of over-all policy, and responsibility for it, be taken off their shoulders. They would then be able to concentrate all their skills on running the company within well-defined guidelines. Less of their energy would be taken up with formulating and paying for an anti-pollution policy, in coping with Government injunctions on inflation, in encompassing mergers, or fighting them off. The executive directors of P & O might have been glad of a supervisory board.

The fact that the Supervisory Board has not been brilliantly successful in Germany can be ascribed to the schizophrenic character of such a body. A more integral concern, representing only one interest—that of the shareholders—would have a much greater chance of success. It seems probable that the trade unions in the U.K. (unless they change their character) will contribute to this desirable homogeneity by refusing to participate. Thus the Supervisory Board will have changed from its original German concept of being a means of workers' control, which is a contradiction in a capitalist society, to being a means of shareholders' control. If the workers want control, let them buy shares.

It would be desirable, however, to accord substantial recognition at a high level to the two other great interests embodied in the company. This, I suggest, could be achieved by giving a seat on the Supervisory Board to one workers' representative and to one representative of the public. These members would be too few usually to affect the voting, but they would serve a necessary purpose as advisers both to the board and their superiors who appoint them. By this means the unions could participate without incurring responsibility (or running the risk of creating rival leadership), and the public could have their ombudsman right at the centre of decision. The essential unity of the Supervisory Board could thus be maintained, and an instrument created that will keep the company more positively motivated by the interests it should serve, and resolve the conflicts that negate them.

Notes

[1] Wurdinger, *Aktienrecht* in Zaphiriou, op cit.
[2] Fortune, March 1972.
[3] See Chapter 2.

Bibliography

Proposition d'un Statut des Sociétés Anonymes Européennes, Commission of the European Communities. Brussels 1970.

Proposition d'une Cinquième Directive, Commission of the European Communities. Brussels 1972.

Helga Grebing, *History of the German Labour Movement*, Oswald Wolff, 1969.

Charles de Hoghton (Ed.), *The Company*, P.E.P., George Allen and Unwin. London 1970.

G. A. Zaphiriou, *European Business Law*, Sweet and Maxwell. London 1970.

Campbell Balfour *Industrial Relations in the Common Market*, Routledge, 1972.

PART II

Accounting Practice and Financial Reporting

4 Public Accountancy in the EEC

by T. A. LEE

This empirical study of public accountancy standards in the EEC, outlines what these standards are at present in the countries concerned, and indicates some of the main problems facing accountants attempting to harmonise standards. It is based on first-hand data supplied by officials of many of the public accountancy bodies in the EEC. The author gratefully acknowledges his thanks to the officials of the accountancy bodies concerned who spent so much time supplying required information.

Britain's entry

Since 1969, when President Pompidou of France stated that his country had no objection in principle to the entry of Britain into the EEC, the British public has been bombarded continually with comment on the implications of entry on trade, industry, finance, agriculture, fisheries, and other economic, political and social matters. So far as accountancy is concerned, the debate has been understandably less public but no less intense. However, it was not until 1971 that a regular public commentary on the accountancy implications of EEC membership began to appear in the British accountancy press. This relative lack of interest is surprising, considering the economic implications to Britain of EEC membership, and there is little doubt that it has tended to leave the 'average' British accountant with no more than the vague impression that accountancy on the Continent is somewhat different from that in Britain, the United States, or Australasia, and that, in general, continental European accountancy standards may be lower than those of the latter countries. The purpose of this essay is to inquire into existing EEC public accountancy standards,[1] with particular regard to a function which is widely recognised throughout the developed business world—that is, auditing (auditing is an acceptable function existing in some form or another in every EEC country); also to pose some of the problems which may well concern investors and accountants in Europe in the years to come.

Britain and Europe—existing accountancy contacts

For many years Britain has had a somewhat limited, but important accountancy contact with the continent of Europe. In 1951 several leading European accountants formed the Union Européenne des Experts Comptables, Economiques et Financiers [UEC] to harmonise and coordinate European public accountancy bodies in light of the then EEC proposals. This federation of bodies includes members from most of the western European countries (including Britain), and therefore embraces EEC and non-EEC countries. Through congresses, research committees, and its official publication, the *Journal UEC*, it provides a forum for debate on the state of accounting practices in the various countries. Its long-term aim is European unity of accounting thought and method. Britain has contributed greatly to UEC, and in so doing, British representatives have acquired a valuable knowledge of European standards and practices. This long-standing 'foot in the door' will be of undoubted benefit when Britain is formally integrated into the EEC, but whether it has had much impact on the 'average' British practitioner is debatable.

One further contact with Europe, though much less formal than the above, has been the extensive network of British-based professional accountancy firms and offices established in most of the major western European cities. However, as British or American standards undoubtedly will have played a large part in the development of accountancy practices in these firms (because many of their clients are British or American controlled), it seems unlikely that such relationships will have given British-based practitioners much idea of the over-all standards and practices adopted by European accountancy practitioners.

These exceptions apart, it has been hard for the British accountant to gain ready access to material on European accountancy standards, the language problem being a major barrier. The following sections outline some facts about individual countries which the writer has been able to obtain directly from officials of the main public accountancy bodies in the countries concerned, as well as from an initial survey of the existing literature.

European public accountancy—some preliminary facts

The subject of this paper was suggested to the writer some time ago, within the context of company auditing. However, it is difficult to discuss the latter topic without looking more widely at the over-all subject of public accountancy and the related subject of financial reporting. The countries surveyed include the six original members of the EEC, and Denmark (which was included as a potential member of the EEC). Before dealing with each of these countries, it is interesting to look at the relative size and importance of public accountancy in them, contrasting this with the British position. The figures in Appendix 1 to this chapter represent the most recently computed official membership numbers relating to European public accountancy bodies which are most similar in nature and function to the British Chartered and Certified bodies.[2]

The countries listed have in total approximately 121,000 professionally qualified accountants, of which something like 63% belong to Britain and Ireland. Looking at this situation more closely from the EEC viewpoint, Britain and Ireland with an approximate population of 60 million (1969 figures) have 76,000 professionally qualified accountants belonging to the Chartered and Certified bodies, i.e. approximately one for every 800 of population). In the original Community of Six, there are approximately 188 million people with 44,000 professionally qualified accountants (i.e. approximately one for every 4,300 of population). Therefore, although public accountancy exists in all the countries studied, its size, nature, and rate of development are in many instances not directly comparable with the situation in Britain, e.g. West Germany has a highly developed and intensely industrialised economy and yet has just over 3,000 professionally qualified accountants—little more than Ireland whose economy is far less developed and industrialised. Certainly, the lack of development of the accountancy profession in terms of numbers is a common characteristic of all existing EEC countries. With the exception of Holland, the lack of growth of the accountancy bodies in the EEC has, until recently, retarded the development of its accounting and auditing standards. The reason for this over-all lack of development is difficult to explain without a long and extensive socio-economic study, but the following are some of the more obvious points.[3]

1. In continental Europe there have not been the same highly developed and extensive capital markets as have existed in Britain and the United States. There has not therefore been the same degree of public interest in corporate activities, and this effectively has tended to minimise the need for investor protection and, similarly, the need for accounting information for stewardship and investment decision-making purposes. The related need for a sophisticated audit function has been equally minimised (assuming that there is such a correlation between capital markets, investor protection, and the audit function). Recognition but minimisation of the audit function in this way must inevitably have limited the development of the accountancy profession in Europe until relatively recently.

2. The facts outlined in (1) have meant that corporate financial reporting has not been developed in continental Europe in the same way as, for example, in Britain. Because of a lack of public interest, there has not been the continuous pressure to improve standards. The main influencing factor has tended to be taxation which has, until recently, encouraged maximum con-

servatism in valuation (in certain European countries, such as Sweden, secret reserves being encouraged by statutory provisions[4]), with a consequential lack of emphasis on reporting a 'true and fair' view of corporate activity. Because 'fair' reporting has not been widely recognised, the need for public accountants competent to examine and judge such reports has again apparently been lacking until fairly recent times.

3. There appears to be a traditional emphasis in continental Europe on the form rather than the substance of financial reports. This can be seen in: (a) The legal provisions, existing in many European countries, which demand that businesses keep and maintain accurate books and records—even stipulating the types of books which must be kept, as well as the type of book-keeping entries which must be made in specific circumstances—yet making no mention of valuation problems. (Examples of this record-keeping emphasis can still be seen in the Commercial Code in Belgium, the Plan Comptable in France, and the Civil Code in Italy.[5]) (b) The somewhat inflexible reliance on uniform *pro forma* financial statements for reporting purposes.[6]

Arguably, this de-emphasising of the judgmental aspects of accountancy, and the corresponding emphasising of mechanical book-keeping procedures, would not create a large demand for highly skilled and qualified professional accountants. At the most, it demands highly trained book-keepers for accounting purposes, and suitably experienced persons (who need not be accountants) to audit or 'supervise' the book-keeping process. (Until recently, France provided a classic example of this situation.[7]) On the other hand, in continental European countries where a less rigid approach has been taken to financial accounting, the use of professionally qualified accountants as auditors has been evident for a long time, e.g. in Holland and Germany.

4. The significant time lag between the development of a sophisticated industrial and investment community in Britain and the corresponding development in mainland Europe—much there occurring since World War II—has meant that a highly qualified and trained accountancy profession was required in Britain long before it was as widely needed in continental Europe. Appendix 4.2 gives some idea of this time gap, and the 'head start' of the British profession, by showing the dates at which the existing main public accountancy bodies were formed in each of the countries studied. These dates, of course, do not preclude the fact that an unregulated profession of accountants may have existed previously, as for example in Britain.[8]

European public accountancy—a review

This section analyses public accountancy in the various EEC countries in more detail. The emphasis is mainly on the auditing aspects, but will comment on other aspects of the over-all professional function as and when appropriate. The amount of detail given in each section varies from country to country, certain of the public accountancy bodies approached giving more information than others.

Belgium

The organised public accountancy profession in Belgium is very small indeed for a country of its size, the number of professionally qualified accountants amounting to no more than about 1,700. The main public accountancy body is the Collège National des Experts Comptables de Belgique which has just over 1,500 members, of which about 100 are also members of the other main Belgian body, the Institut des Réviseurs d'Entreprises. The Collège was formed in 1950 as part of an over-all strategy to organise the Belgian accountancy profession. Originally, 26 separate bodies associated themselves with the Collège, but now there are only 21 such members, of which the main one is the Ordre des Experts Comptables et Comptables Brevetés de Belgique.

Collège members are engaged in all major public accountancy activities, i.e. auditing, taxation, accounting, book-keeping, and business consultancy. How many are engaged in each category is unknown, although approximately 100—those who are also Institut members—are involved in statutory company audits (see below). The educational requirements of the Collège include the holding of an economics or commerce degree or an approved accounting and book-keeping diploma, and the passing of a professional examination at the end of a five-year training period with a member of the Collège. The Collège has a published code of ethics for its members, and occasionally publishes guidance statements on accounting and auditing problems. However, details of these statements were not made available to the writer.

The Institut des Réviseurs d'Entreprises was formed by law in 1953 in a further attempt to organise the accountancy profession. It has a specialised function, and its 200 or so members are mainly concerned in audits of companies which are legally required to appoint a réviseur d'entreprises. Its present entrance requirements are similar to those of the Collège mentioned above. No further details were made available about its members' activities, except that they are rather strictly limited to auditing by the Royal Decree of 16 March 1957.

The Belgian Commercial Code requires most types of company to appoint one or more commissaire réviseurs (statutory examiners). Once appointed, the examiner has an unlimited right of access and surveillance of company operations. However, in practice, his examination resembles a conventional if limited audit, including the checking of financial statements with underlying books and records. A shareholder can be appointed as a statutory examiner. All public companies, insurance companies, and stock exchange quoted companies are legally required to be audited by a member of the Institut des Réviseurs d'Entreprises. It is therefore to be assumed, in these situations, that auditing is along conventional lines. It must also be further assumed that some of the other audits are also conducted by public accountants; no information is available on these points.

From information supplied to the writer, the generally accepted audit objectives relevant to companies in Belgium include giving an opinion on information credibility, checking the financial statements with accounting records, verifying the accuracy of these records, and detecting fraud. Again from information supplied, internal control review, statistical sampling, debtors confirmations, and attendance at stock-takings are all widely used in Belgian auditing. These, together with the statements on objectives, must be interpreted, however, as applying more to audits conducted by réviseurs d'entreprises than to all audits conducted by commissaires réviseurs.

There is no standard form of audit report in Belgium, though most confirm generally that the accounting records have been checked, that they agree with the financial statements, and, after examination of these statements, that it is proposed that they should be adopted by the shareholders.

Denmark

Denmark has a small, but highly organised public accountancy profession, with about 1,000 members at present. The only major public accountancy body is the Foreningen af Statsautoriserede Revisorer, formed in 1912, and having 971 members who are all State-authorised public accountants (only a few State-authorised public accountants are not members of the Foringen). The work of these accountants covers auditing, taxation, accounting and book-keeping, as well as consultancy, and approximately 870 Foreningen members are actively engaged in auditing. In order to become State-authorised public accountants, and thus be eligible for membership, candidates must be economics or business administration graduates, have passed the State-authorised public accountants' examinations administered by the Ministry of Commerce, and have completed three years' practical training with State-authorised public accountants. The Foreningen issues guidance statements for its members on auditing and accounting topics (several are being prepared at present) and also has a formal code of professional ethics.

Although all Danish companies are required to be audited, only stock exchange quoted companies and banking and insurance companies are legally required to appoint a State-authorised public accountant as auditor. The generally accepted objectives of company audits are stated as including giving an opinion on information credibility, verifying the legal conformity of financial statements, checking these statements with the underlying accounting records, and verifying the accuracy of these records. Detection of fraud is not given as an objective.

Internal control review, debtors confirmations, and attendance at physical stock-takings are said to be widely used by auditors, but statistical sampling techniques are not. The only standard form of audit report is a simple statement that the financial statements have been audited by a State-authorised public accountant, but a new exposure draft has just been issued by the Foreningen suggesting that the audit report should also state an opinion along conventional British and American lines.

France[9]

France has one of the largest organised public accountancy professions in the EEC, with a total membership between 13,000 and 14,000 approximately. The main body is the Ordre des Experts Comptables et des Comptables Agréés, with 10,059 fully qualified members and 2,561 student members. The Ordre was formed by the Government in 1945, and its membership consists of two classes of accountants—experts comptables or auditors (3,568 in number) and comptables agréés or commercial and industrial accountants (6,491 in number). The activities of Ordre members therefore include auditing, taxation, accounting, and consultancy, with just over 3,500 members, who are members of the Compagnie Nationale mentioned below, being engaged in audits.

To become a member of the Ordre the candidate must hold the diplôme d'expertise comptable, having passed three sets of professional examinations, presented a thesis on an approved accounting topic, and had three years practical experience with a qualified *expert comptable*. There are certain examination exemptions for candidates who are university graduates. The Ordre has a formal code of professional ethics, and has published many guidance statements on auditing, accounting, and consultancy topics for the benefit of its members.

The other main public accountancy body in France is the Compagnie Nationale des Commissaires aux Comptes. It was formed by law in 1970, to improve and regularise company auditing, all companies in France being legally required to appoint a commissaire aux comptes or statutory auditor. The Compagnie has 6,300 members at present, of which approximately half are members of the Ordre mentioned above. Because of the nature of the Compagnie, its members are mainly concerned with company auditing. Its membership requirements are that candidates should be qualified *experts comptables* or have had at least 15 years' practical experience in accounting or finance (reduced to a minimum of 10 years for candidates holding certain school certificates), together with three years' experience in the employ of a member of the Compagnie (waived if the candidate is an *expert comptable*). The Compagnie does not therefore administer any examinations as a prerequisite to membership. A code of professional ethics, as well as several guidance statements on auditing, have been published by the Compagnie, the latter statements mainly concerning auditor responsibility and the duty of care.

There is one other public accountancy body in France which deserves mention—the Institut Français des Experts Comptables. This is an association, formed in 1962 to represent the specific activities and problems of *experts comptable*, and comprising a partnership of the Compagnie Nationale des Experts Comptables, the Chambre Nationale des Diplômés Experts Comptables and the Union Professionnelle des Sociétés Fiduciévres d'Expertise Comptable. It has 2,700 members of which 1,900 are members of the aforementioned Ordre. Institut members are required to hold the diplôme d'expertise comptable, are subject to a formal code of ethics, and receive occasional guidance statements on accounting and auditing.

Recent changes in French company law have greatly altered the audit function. Prior to 1966, the company auditor or commissaire aux comptes was only required to have a professional competence and was not required to be a professionally qualified accountant. However, due to the Decrees of 24 July 1966 and 23 March 1967, all companies (similar to those under the jurisdiction of the Companies Acts 1948 and 1967 in Britain) are required to be audited by approved commissaires aux comptes. Through the entrance provisions of the Compagnie Nationale des Commissaires aux Comptes, the latter are required to be experienced and trained in accounting and auditing. Auditors are legally prohibited, by the Decree of 12 August 1969, from having any family, personal or financial relationship with client companies; they must give their opinion on the financial statements within six months of the relevant year-end; they have a right to obtain information from third parties; they can 'intervene' if the shareholders are not being treated equitably; and they have a duty to disclose to the public prosecutor any 'unlawful happenings' concerning client company affairs.

Company audit objectives are said to be the giving of an opinion on information credibility, ensuring the legal conformity of financial statements, checking these statements with the underlying accounting records, verifying the accuracy of these records, and only to a limited extent, the detection of fraud. Again from information received, internal control reviews and statistical sampling techniques are stated to be widely used by auditors. On the other hand, debtors' confirmations and attendances at physical stock-takings are said to be used to a limited extent only.

So far as the company audit report is concerned, there is no standard form, although commissaires aux comptes are legally required to give an opinion on accounting information in terms of its 'regularity' and 'sincerity'—approximating to the British 'true and fair' view opinion. The following is a suggested standard form issued by the Ordre des Experts Comptables et des Comptables Agréés: 'Our examination, conducted in conformity with auditing standards and the principles of due care which were considered by us as necessary, has resulted in our opinion that the inventory, trading account, profi. and loss account and balance sheet presented to you are regular and sincere't

Holland[10]

The Netherlands has one of the best organised and most advanced public accountancy professions in the world, despite a membership of only 3,200 qualified public accountants. A formal profession was instituted in 1895 with the founding of the Nederlands Instituut van Accountants. In 1919 and 1935 there were minor amalgamations of the Instituut with other bodies but in 1962 the accountancy profession was regulated for the first time by law through the provisions of the Registeraccountants Act, 1962. This Act was intended to legally protect the title of *Registeraccountant*, and to bring the existing public accountancy bodies into one body. Thus, the main ones, the Nederlands Instituut and the Vereniging van Academisch Gevormde Accountants, amalgamated in 1967 to form the Nederlands Instituut van Registeraccountants. Approximately 50%, or 1,600 members, of the Instituut are in public practice involved in auditing, taxation, and consultancy. The remaining members are either employed in government, industry or the universities.

Candidates for membership of the Instituut are expected to qualify either as university graduates in business economics (a process which normally takes five or six years) or by passing the Instituut's professional examinations in mathematics, economics, law, auditing, and management (which usually take 11 or 12 years to complete). There are no practical experience requirements for membership, though most applicants have several years' experience by the time that they qualify for membership. The Instituut has a formal code of professional ethics which, *inter alia*, forbids members having financial interests in client companies, having a family relationship with managers of client companies, or from being a director or officer of a client company. It also publishes relatively frequent guidance statements on highly specialised auditing topics as well as on accounting and financial reporting topics.

All Dutch companies which are legally required to file their annual financial statements with the trade registrar are also legally required to have these statements, and the underlying accounting records, audited. The audit must be conducted by a *Registeraccountant* or by a suitably qualified foreign accountant approved by the Ministry of Economic Affairs. The companies concerned include all public companies, banking and insurance companies, and private companies with assets or share capital of stipulated amounts.

The main audit objective is stated to be the giving of an opinion of information credibility; supporting aims are the verification of the legal conformity of financial statements, checking the agreement of these statements with the underlying accounting records, verifying the accuracy of the records, and also, the detection of fraud, to a limited extent only. Internal control review, statistical sampling techniques, and attendance of the auditor at physical stock-takings are said to be widely used in Holland. Debtors' confirmations, on the other hand, are not used, confirmation of the receipt against the balance due being regarded as sufficient verification.

There is no standard form of audit report as yet in the Netherlands, but recently the Instituut issued an exposure draft to its members containing the following suggested outline: 'We have audited the annual accounts of.... In our opinion the Balance Sheet and the Profit and Loss Account together with the explanatory notes present fairly and systematically the size and composition of the capital at ... and the result for the year ...'

Italy

Italy has the largest public accountancy profession in the EEC. However, most of its 22,000 members are employed in industrial or commercial accountancy rather than public accountancy. The main Italian public accountancy body is the Ordine dei Dottori Commercialisti, with approximately 14,000 members. It was founded in 1924 ,but obtained its present structure in 1929 when it amalgamated its membership with that of the then Collegio dei Ragionieri. The Collegio continued as a separate body despite this, and now constititutes the Collegio dei Ragionieri e Periti Commerciali (see below). The Consiglio Nazionale dei Dottori Commercialisti is the administrative body for the Ordine, which is comprised of a separate Ordini for each of the provinces in Italy.

Members of the Ordine are engaged in auditing, tax, accounting, and consultancy. Auditing, however, is not as formal or as rigorous as in other EEC countries, and although all members of the Ordine are qualified to audit, few of them do (the relevant number is not known). Most are either concerned with taxation or commercial or industrial accounting. Membership of the Ordine depends on the candidate having a degree in economics and commerce, and having passed a State examination in accounting practice. There are no practical experience requirements for membership. The Ordine does not issue guidance statements nor does it have a formal code of ethics, although several provincial Ordini have issued their own codes.

A similar situation to the above exists with the Collegio dei Ragionieri e

Periti Commerciali, the other main public accountancy body in Italy. Like the Ordine, it is based on regional Collegi with a central administrative body. Its membership requirements include the passing of its professional examinations in accounting and law, together with two years' practical experience with a Collegio member. Most of the members are concerned with commercial and industrial accountancy, although a few (probably between 300 and 350) are involved in auditing, tax and consultancy. The Collegio issues no guidance statements and has no formal code of ethics.

The Italian Civil Code requires all limited companies and certain other types to have a Collegio Sindacale or Board of Auditors. Such a board is composed of three or five persons, depending on the size of company. One of the members (two if the company has issued capital of more than 50 million lire) must be on an official list of auditors maintained by the Ministry of Justice. However, there is no requirement that such registered auditors need to be public accountants, five years' experience as an auditor or as an accountant or manager of a company with issued capital of more than 50 million lire is regarded as sufficient qualification. For the remaining members of the Collegio Sindacale there is not even this limited experience requirement. No auditor, however, is permitted to be a manager or director of the company concerned, but there is no regulation preventing shareholders from being appointed to the Collegio Sindacale.

In the information supplied to the writer, it is stated that the generally accepted audit objectives in Italy include giving an opinion on information credibility, verifying the legal conformity of financial statements, checking the agreement of these statements with the underlying accounting records, verifying the accuracy of these records, and detecting fraud. However, although these may apply in some way to most audits of Italian companies, the more general objectives are ensuring that the book-keeping systems and accounting valuations used are in accordance with the provisions of the Civil Code, and verifying that management's activities are not *ultra vires* the rules of the company.

Again from information supplied, the audit techniques of internal control review, statistical sampling, and attendance at physical stock-takings are widely used by Italian auditors. Because of the informal nature of auditing in most companies, it must be assumed that these techniques are mainly applied by public accountants engaged on audits of very large companies.

There is no standard form of audit report in Italy, but the following points are normally incorporated into those produced: (a) that financial statements comply with legal requirements, (b) these statements are in agreement with the accounting records, (c) any variations made are in accordance with legal requirements, (d) internal records have been periodically reviewed and found to be sound, (e) attendance has been made at all meetings of directors and shareholders.

Luxembourg

Not surprisingly, Luxembourg has the smallest public accountancy profession in the EEC, with 27 members. The only body is the Ordre des Experts Comptables Luxembourgeois, founded in 1951. The main activities include auditing, taxation, and accounting. Consultancy does not appear to form part of the professional work, but auditing is a major part. Entry into the Ordre depends on the candidate having an economics or business degree and three years' practical experience with a member of the Ordre. There are no professional examinations. The Ordre has a code of ethics, but does not issue guidance statements to its members.

All companies in Luxembourg are required to appoint an auditor, although they are not required to be audited by a professionally qualified accountant. Several of the companies concerned, however, must be presumed to be audited by members of the Ordre. From information supplied, the following comprise the generally accepted objectives of auditing in Luxembourg: giving an opinion on information credibility, verifying the legal conformity of financial statements, checking that these statements agree with the underlying accounting records, verifying the accuracy of these records, and detecting fraud. No information was made available regarding the relative priorities attributable to these objectives. So far as techniques are concerned, the most widely used are stated to be internal control review and statistical sampling. There is no standard form of audit report.

West Germany[11]

Germany has a well-regulated if rather small public accountancy profession. The membership of a little more than 3,000 has been somewhat restricted over the years due to the number of accounting assistants which professionally qualified accountants are allowed to employ. The German Company Law of 1931 stipulated that all public companies be audited by a public accountant and, as a consequence, 1932 saw the introduction of such a person—the *Wirtschaftsprüfer*. In that year, the Institut der Wirtschaftprüfer in Deutschland was formed, although previously, public accountants, called Vereidigte Buchprüfer, had existed. Membership of the Institut is voluntary, and its aims are to advance the profession, protect the interests of Wirtschaftsprüfer, and educate future Wirtschaftsprüfer.

Any qualified Wirtschaftsprüfer (either individually or as a partnership) can join the Institut, and approximately 90% have done so; this means that there are between 300 and 400 Wirtschaftsprüfer who have not. However, the Wirtschaftsprüferordnung of 24 July 1971 created the Wirtschaftsprüfer-kammer (Chamber of Accountants) to administer the affairs of the accountancy profession, and every Wirtschaftsprüfer is legally required to register with the Kammer. Although the latter body is legally responsible for professional standards and education, it successfully co-operates with the Institut and has delegated its responsibility for education to that body. Members of the Institut are engaged in auditing, tax, accounting, and consultancy, and it is estimated that, on average, one-third of their work is taken up with auditing, and one-third with tax.

Some 96% of Wirtschaftsprüfer join the Institut as university graduates (in economics, commerce, or law), having passed the Institut's examinations and completed six years' practical experience, of which four must be with a public accountant. The remaining 4% of members qualify in the same way, with the exception that the requirement of 10 years of prior accountancy experience is substituted for the university degree. The Institut has published a code of professional ethics (which restricts members to accountancy employment) and has issued guidance statements on most accountancy subjects including auditing. These statements are mandatory, and Wirtschaftsprüfer must adhere to them unless they can justify any departure.

It should also be mentioned that there are two other classes of public accountant in Germany in addition to the Wirtschaftsprüfer—the Steuerberater (tax advisor) and Steuerbevollmächtigte (tax assistant). As the names imply, their occupation involves taxation matters. For the Steuerberater, educational requirements are just as onerous as for the Wirtschaftsprüfer, though for the Steuerbevollmächtigte they are far less demanding.

The German Public Companies Act, 1965 requires all public companies to appoint a Wirtschaftsprüfer as auditor. In addition the same provision applies from 1971 onwards to certain private companies, partnerships, and sole traders of over a certain size. The auditor is appointed by the shareholders, and is required to attend their meetings and those of the supervisory board. The audit report is addressed to the board, and in this way, the auditor effectively acknowledges a wider responsibility than merely to the shareholders. The standard form of audit report is prescribed by the 1965 Act as follows: 'According to our audit work made in conformity with our professional duties, the accounting, the annual financial statements and the report of the board of managment comply with German law and the company's statutes.' There is also a long-form report, similar to the British or American management letter, which is regularly issued to the supervisory board, describing weaknesses in internal control, accounting procedures, etc.

The over-all aim of auditing in Germany, therefore, is to ensure that financial statements comply with legal provisions, that accounting principles used are acceptable, and the valuation bases adopted legal. The review of internal control is a commonly used audit technique, but statistical sampling, debtors' confirmations, and attendances at physical stock-takings are techniques which are only used if they are thought to be useful in the specific circumstances.

Summary

It is useful at this point to stop and reflect on the various situations described in the foregoing sections. Appendices 4.3 to 4.9 attempt to compare certain key points applicable to each of the seven EEC countries surveyed. They reveal that situations, conditions and standards vary from country to country, and that they are at variance to a certain extent with those in Britain. However, what they can never reveal is the absolute quality of public accountancy in each contry. Nevertheless, it does not seem unduly cautious to say that, generally speaking, the standards in the existing EEC countries have risen considerably over the last few years, as witnessed by the recent reforms in France and West Germany. As is the case throughout Europe, the so-called 'veil of secrecy' is being lifted off corporate affairs, particularly with a greater disclosure of financial accounting information.[12] Less and less emphasis is being given to the traditional continental practice of maintaining secret reserves, and there is also a definite movement towards improving the over-all quality of the company audit function.

Indeed, public accountancy in most of the EEC looks remarkably similar to that of the U.K. and apparently smashes the traditional image of Europe as a 'back water' of accountancy. This process should accelerate in the future for, as both Bedford and Murphy[13] have pointed out, there should be a beneficial flow of accounting thought between countries as trade follows flag, and the accountancy profession follows trade. The main benefit of this flow is that it tends to improve local accounting, and in extreme cases, may help to found it. However, when looking at Europe, there are distinct barriers which tend to minimise this effect, e.g. the significant language and cultural differences. It is, fairly obvious, however, that when Britain plays a bigger economic and social part in European affairs, it may well have a considerable and beneficial influence on European accountancy. It is also fairly obvious that there may well be attendant problems. The next section sets out to identify some of these.

Britain's entry into the EEC—some identifiable problems

Increasing finance and investment

It is a well-known fact of economic life that business enterprises, when seeking new markets and new customers, can outgrow their countries of origin. Thus trade expands, foreign subsidiaries are formed, quotations are sought on foreign stock exchanges, finance is raised in foreign money markets —effectively the company 'goes international'. Britains entry into Europe is likely to mean: (a) a significant increase in British investment in Europe by both private and institutional investors, (b) a significant increase in the number of British companies with European subsidiaries or associates. Both situations create accountancy problems for the British investor. In the first instance, he will receive accounting information direct from the European companies concerned; in the second, such information will be received indirectly as part of the information of the group of companies as a whole. In both cases, and particularly in the first, there are bound to be questions about the quality of the information, and the underlying financial accounting and auditing standards applied in its production.

As reported accounting information, describing the profitability and financial position of companies, is regarded generally as a vital means of investor protection, it is important that the investor should have confidence in its quality and credibility. If he does not, it becomes meaningless and potentially dangerous to him if he uses it. Knowledge, however superficial, of the underlying accounting and auditing standards is vital to this confidence. The latter is easier to maintain when the standards are of the investor's own country; it is more difficult when they are those of a foreign country. When reviewing and analysing foreign accounting information, the investor must ask basic questions such as: What standards were adopted? How do they differ from those of my own country? What sort of effect would any significant difference in standards from the British norm have on the information reported? These are not new questions, and the overall problem has occupied a large part of international accounting literature.[14] However, they deserve some further attention in the context of this paper.

The British investor investing in European companies

The main accounting and reporting problems facing potential investors in Europe include the following:

1. *Language.* Although some European companies translate their reports into English, they are the exception rather than the rule. And even the use of translation, with its attendant difficulties, could well prove misleading to the British investor unless reports in English become more widespread.

2. *Accounting practices.* Apart from the inevitable flexibility due to the number of alternative methods available and the personal judgments involved in accounting, there are also difficulties for investors when faced with differing accounting treatments of matters such as secret reserves, depreciation of fixed assets, revaluation of assets, taxation, goodwill amortisation, and so on. Such variation in practice tends to create doubt about the quality and reliability of reported figures. EEC efforts at accounting harmonisation are, how-

ever, aimed at minimising this particular problem. They will be described in a later section.

3. *Accounting disclosure.* Disclosure requirements in Europe vary from country to country, some disclosing far less than regarded as normal in Britain. The British investor may not get as much information, therefore, as he is accustomed to; EEC harmonisation may well alleviate this problem, however. An obvious example of the problem is the consolidation of financial statements, Germany being the only existing EEC country which legally requires companies to produce consolidated statements, though several others have a limited voluntary system. These comments are also subject to the present EEC harmonisation proposals.

4. *Auditing standards.* Investors will also be faced with the problem of finding out what standards have been applied in the audit of accounting information from certain European countries, as the credibility of the audit and auditor very much determine the credibility of the information. What are the professional qualifications of the auditor? What tests did he apply to the information? What has he verified? What meaning is to be taken from the wording of his report? Questions such as these must be of concern to investors—particularly, institutional investors—if they are going to have any confidence in the information supplied to them. So far, there are no finalised EEC harmonisation auditing standards.

These then are some of the problems looming on the horizon for British investors receiving European accounting information. It is a situation which does not affect the individual British accounting practitioner directly because he is not involved in the accounting, auditing, or reporting concerned. Nevertheless, the accountancy profession in Britain, through its representatives on the EEC and UEC bodies, must be concerned that EEC standards are at least at a level comparable that to known and accepted by the investor in Britain. Failure to do this would be a negation of the profession's function to maintain and improve accountancy standards for the benefit of the community. As Murphy reports,[15] the largest international accountancy firms have for some years been attempting to do this through the use of international firms which develop international professional accountancy policy, as well as through the use, by such firms, of internal 'quality controllers' to ensure uniformity of auditing practice, at the highest level, throughout their foreign offices. Such isolated action, however, can only be of limited use.

British companies with European subsidiaries or associates

This clearly is a problem facing the individual British accountancy practitioner today. In his capacity as a holding company auditor responsible for auditing consolidated financial statements containing subsidiary company and/or associated company information, he may well have to judge and give an opinion on accounting information of continental European origin. The problem is not great so long as the 'foreign' information has been prepared on bases of British origin, and so long as it has been audited by persons subject to British auditing standards, as in the case of a branch office of a British accountancy firm which is administered by British personnel. However, there will be occasions when the accounting and auditing of a foreign subsidairy or associate will be the responsibility of local accountants subject to local standards. The problems will then be those of judging the quality of standards applied in producing and verifying the relevant information, of whether these standards differ from those normally applied in Britain, and if so, of whether these differences materially affect the over-all quality of the total information describing the activities and affairs of the group as a whole.

These problems are not new, particularly from the auditing point of view, and in recent years, have been discussed in British, American and continental European writings.[16] Essentially, they concern decisions on the nature and degree of checking necessary to satisfy the holding company auditor as to the quality of the audited information of a foreign subsidiary or associate. In other words, answers must be obtained to questions such as: Who conducted the audit? What are his professional qualifications? What audit techniques did he use? What has he verified and what has he not verified? What accounting bases underlie the reported information? How do these compare with accepted British bases? It is this situation, in which the 'home-based' auditor cannot assume the quality of the 'local' accounting information, that British auditors may find themselves in increasingly in the future.

Apart from the legal and technical question of whether the principal auditor should have access to information from and working papers of the other auditor; or the question of whether he should re-audit the subsidiary or associated company's financial statements if he is not satisfied with the quality of the relevant information and/or related audit, it is apparent that British accountants—both industrial and practising—will require to become much more familiar with continental European accounting, reporting, and auditing standards than they have been hitherto.

Increasing mobility of labour

One of the essential features and provisions of the Treaty of Rome is that there should be complete mobility of labour within the EEC. In addition, the treaty also provides for the harmonisation of national laws and for the liberalisation of the professions. Eventually therefore, there should be no restrictions to prevent accountants of one member state working as such in others. This, theoretically, could mean the waiving of any national restrictions regarding qualifications, nationality, and training. The philosophy of professional liberalisation has created the need to harmonise commercial laws and standards, and thus, the need to know what accountancy standards exist presently in the EEC member countries.

Integration of this sort cannot take place overnight; it can only happen after long and serious discussion and debate between all those concerned. However, movement of professional accountants within EEC countries is likely to be minimal in the short term, if not in the long term, due to language difficulties; cultural barriers; a lack of adequate knowledge of the various economic, fiscal, business and accountancy standards in each country; the relative smallness of the qualified accountancy professions in most of the existing EEC countries, which are at present having to cope with a growing local demand for their services; and the extremely slow process of removing national restrictions and formulating harmonisation laws. To the credit of continental European accountants, attempts made so far at EEC accountancy harmonisation have witnessed great efforts to bring existing continental European standards up to the British or American level. This process should help enormously in the eventual production of truly European accountancy standards.

European attempts at harmonisation and uniformity

Because of the liberalism of the Treaty of Rome, coupled with the attendant increase in international investment, finance and business, it is clear that there must be a recognisable flow of accounting thought within at least the EEC countries in order to ensure a higher standard and a greater uniformity of over-all accountancy practice. As Bedford suggests,[17] this is a long-term educational and training process. However, one or two points about accountancy harmonisation in general, and uniformity in particular, are appropriate here. There are three main schools of thought:

1. Those who regard uniformity between nations as unnecessary and even dangerous.[18] They question the need for uniformity, Jennings,[19] for example, stating that variations in practice between nations are no more serious or extensive than those existing within nations; and Trigg[20] stating that uniformity can lead to lack of individuality and independence. They advocate an international exchange of ideas and adoption of those practices which are the best possible in the circumstances, this being essentially a matter of individual judgment. Their argument may be best summed up in the words of Trigg[21]: 'I venture to suggest that the profession throughout the world is looking for unity, but in looking for unity it is not necessarily looking for uniformity. In my mind uniformity is a step backwards and unity is a step forwards.'
2. Those who favour a situation tending towards absolute uniformity, both nationally and internationally, including uniform accounting principles, audit-

ing standards, and reporting practices.[22] Advocates of this approach claim that such uniformity aids investment judgments, improves shareholder protection, simplifies the work of the auditor, makes life easier for non-accounting managers when changing jobs, and generally assists greater corporate comparability in information terms. Not surprisingly, support for this idea comes mainly from accountants in countries which have, or are experiencing a good deal of uniformity in financial accounting and reporting.

3. Those who advocate a flexible uniformity—i.e. a continual attempt to reduce the degree of variation from one country to another—which should not result in a rigid set of accounting, auditing and reporting rules to be followed by accountants, auditors and managers in all countries of the world. For this reason, Stamp[23] has advocated an international harmonisation of standards rather than procedures, the former tending to prevail internationally while the latter vary according to the local environment; Mueller[24] has suggested that uniformity should be national rather than international, and that finacial statements should retain their national individuality and reflect the environment they evolve from; and Deering[25] has suggested limited reductions in the current flexible situation, e.g. in the area of accounting terminology.

Of the above three alternatives, the last seems to be the most persuasive and sensible, in recognising the problem of variation, yet appreciating that only a limited harmonisation of standards and practices can eventually be achieved. With this in mind, the next section looks at the efforts which have so far been made at harmonisation in Europe, and particularly in the EEC.

Firstly, looking at Europe in the broadest sense, there are the activities of the UEC (including both EEC and non-EEC members) which hopes to create a truly European accountancy profession. So far, it has produced little in the way of concrete proposals for harmony, though several conferences have been held and several committees meet regularly to discuss contentious and common problems. The main efforts at harmony have come, presumably due to the provisions of the Treaty of Rome, from members of the EEC. In 1965, a wish was first expressed by the existing EEC members that there should be some co-ordination of legal accounting requirements in the Community. For this reason a study group (Groupe d'Etudes Droit des Sociétés des Experts Comptables de la CEE) was formed to see if certain minimum uniform legal accounting requirements could be produced for companies in the Community.

Although much of the early discussions concerned accounting valuations, consolidated financial statements and auditing, the eventual effort has concerned a standard lay-out for company financial statements.[26] So far as auditing in general is concerned the group's draft proposals include, *inter alia*, the following suggestions: (a) that the auditor should be an independent accountant, with qualifications similar to those required by the law of his own country, (b) that he should ascertain that financial statements comply with legal and company requirements and with normal financial accounting procedures, (c) that in addition to his report to the shareholders, he should report to the company's Supervisory Board on the outcome of his examination, including any matters which may imperil the company's existence, and any acts by the directors contrary to legal or company regulations.[27] At the time of writing there have been four proposed company law Directives stemming from the work of this study group but little or nothing, however, has directly encompassed the nature of the company audit function, or the rights and duties of the auditor.

One last factor should be mentioned on the subject of harmonisation—the European Company or Societas Europea (see Chapter 2), first proposed by Professor Sanders of the Netherlands in 1959.[28] A proposed statute has now gone to the European Parliament and like a full British Companies Bill, deals with all aspects of company activity including financial reporting and auditing. Financial statements are to be 'in accordance with regular and proper accounting principles' and a 'true and fair' view must be given. Accounting classifications are fully described, and there is an option to use historical or replacement cost as the measuring basis. The auditor has to be qualified to audit a public company in his own country. Generally the standards are high but, at the time of writing, are still being debated.

Conclusion

Britain stands at the brink of an exciting venture into Europe—an example of economic co-operation on a massive scale. Accountants are going to be an essential part of this co-operative effort, and should have a much deeper knowledge of public accountancy standards in the EEC than hitherto. It is also apparent that Europe is fast catching up with U.K. and American standards, and that it is now somewhat dangerous to assume that Britain is many years in advance of Europe in this field. Indeed, it is not unreasonable to think that Europe has a lot to teach Britain.

Notes

[1] The term public accountancy will be used throughout this essay, and is intended to cover all accountancy activities conducted by professionally qualified accountants. It does not therefore include the activities of industrial or commercial accountants who nevertheless are professionally qualified accountants, i.e. members of the accountancy profession. It is thought to be a term acceptable to both British and European readers.

[2] There are one or two other bodies in France and West Germany but,

because of their limited or specialised objectives, and because of pressure of space, they have been omitted from the detailed survey material in the Appendices. However, they are covered to a limited extent in the appropriate narrative sections of this essay.

3 Certain of these points have also been made by numerous writers over the years, but more recently by P. Raymond Hinton, 'How is Europe to find its accounting principles?' *Accountancy Age*, 8 October 1971, pp. 14–15; and Nigel Latham-Sharp, 'International Variations in Presentation and Certification of Accounts', *Paper*' 1971 Institute of Chartered Accountants in England and Wales summer conference on the growing challenge of world business.

4 For a view of the changing attitudes towards the question of gross undervaluation in European financial reports, see Per V.A. Hanner, 'The Rise, Decline—and Ultimate Fall?—of the Hidden Reserve', *Journal UEC*, January 1969, pp. 1–5.

5 More emphasis in certain countries is being given to this problem and to the substance of financial reports in recent times; for example, in the German Public Companies Act 1965 and in the proposals for Nordic company law reform. See Per V.A. Hanner, 'Towards a "Nordic Companies Act": a Report on the Company Law Reform in Denmark, Finland, Norway and Sweden', *Journal UEC*, January 1971, pp. 19–25.

6 The concept of uniform accounting is generally attributed to Eugen Schmalenbach of Germany who, in 1929, published *The Model Chart of Accounts* advocating nationwide uniformity in accounting in order to increase comparability of financial results. Such was the appeal of this concept that in 1937 a Decree in Germany made uniformity compulsory. For a more detailed account of uniform accounting, see Gerhard G. Meuller, *International Accounting*, Macmillan, 1967, pp. 88–114.

7 It should be noted, however, that in France use of professionally qualified accountants as auditors is required for limited companies, following the company law reform of 24 July 1966 and 12 August 1969.

8 For example, Alexander Heriot of Edinburgh, *c.* 1700; George Watson of Edinburgh, *c.* 1700; James Kerr of Glasgow, *c.* 1800; James McClelland of Glasgow, *c.* 1820. These are examples of early Scottish professional accountants. Further details can be found in Richard Brown, *A History of Accounting and Accountants*, Jack, 1905.

9 More details can be obtained from the following sources: (a) André Henrot, 'The Revision of Company Law in France as it Concerns the Audit of Company Accounts', *Journal UEC*, October 1968, pp. 226–227; and (b) J. Wisner, 'The Amendment of the Law relating to Statutory Audits of the Accounts of French Companies', *Journal UEC*, July 1970, pp. 148–152.

10 More details can be obtained from: (a) Arie L. de Bruyne, 'Statutory Regulation of the Accountancy Profession in The Netherlands', *Journal UEC*

October 1967, pp. 239–243; (b) A.B. Frielink, 'The Auditor's Function and the Organisation of the Accounting System', *Journal UEC*, October 1968, pp. 240–245; (c) P.C. Louwers, 'Statistical Sampling and the Auditor', *Journal UEC*, July 1969, pp. 136–144; and (d) K. Kruisbrink, 'The International Harmonisation of Auditing Standards and Procedures', *Paper*, 9th International Congress of Accountants, Paris, 1967.

[11] More details can be obtained from: (a) Rudolph J. Niehus, 'Stock Corporation Law Reform in Germany and the Public Accountant,' *The International Journal of Accounting*, Spring 1966, pp. 25–41; and (b) W. Dober, 'On the Significance and Minimum Content of the Audit Certificate with Reference to a Company's Economic and Financial Position', *Journal UEC*, January 1970, pp. 30–32.

[12] See, for example, 'Lifting Corporate Curtains', *Fortune*, March 1966; and Robert Ball, 'The Declining Art of Concealing the Figures', *Fortune*, September 1967 (both in Kenneth B. Berg, Gerhard G. Mueller, and Lauren M. Walker (eds.), *Readings in International Accounting*, Houghton Mifflin, 1969, pp. 11–14 and 15–26, respectively); and Henk C. Treffers, 'The Changing Nature of the European Accounting Profession', *The International Journal of Accounting*, Fall 1967, pp. 43–54.

[13] Norton M. Bedford, 'The International Flow of Accounting Thought', *The International Journal of Accounting*, Spring 1966, pp. 46–51; and Mary E. Murphy, *Advanced Public Accounting Practice*, Irwin, 1966, pp. 505–531 (*passim*).

[14] See, for example, Alvin R. Jennings, 'International Standards of Accounting and Auditing', *Journal of Accountancy*, September 1962, pp. 36–42; Frank T. Weston, 'International Accounting and Reporting Problems', *The Arthur Young Journal*, Summer 1965 (in Berg, Mueller and Walker, op cit, pp. 52–66); John W. Queenan, 'Problems in International Auditing', *The New York Certified Public Accountant*, July 1966 (in Berg, Mueller and Walker, op cit, pp. 67–76); and C. C. Bowles, 'International Accounting—A Challenge for Ingenuity', *The International Journal of Accounting*, Fall 1968, pp. 83–97.

[15] Murphy, op cit, pp. 513–521.

[16] See, for example, 'Subsidiaries not Audited by Us; a Dissenting View', *Accountancy*, April 1966, pp. 223–227; David Flint, 'Audit of Group Accounts (Reliance on Other Auditors)', *The Accountant's Magazine*, August 1967, pp. 366–378; Accountants International Study Group, *Using the Work and Report of Another Auditor*, 1969; AICPA, 'Using the Work and Reports of Other Auditors', *Statement on Auditing Procedure No. 45*, 1971; F. van Amerongen, 'Using the Work and Report of Another Auditor', *Journal UEC*, July 1971, pp. 141–147; and R. Goerdeler, 'Using the Results of Other Auditors' Auditing', *Journal UEC*, July 1971, pp. 162–167.

[17] Norton M. Bedford, 'The International Flow of Accounting Thought', *The International Journal of Accounting*, Spring 1966 (in Berg, Mueller and Walker, op cit, pp. 46–51).

[18] See, for example, Alvin R. Jennings, 'International Standards of Accounting and Auditing', *Journal of Accountancy*, September 1962, pp. 36–42; F. E. Trigg, 'The International Harmonisation of Auditing Standards and Procedures', *The Chartered Accountant in Australia*, October 1967, pp. 303–314; and H. B. Dhondy, 'International Harmonisation of Auditing Standards and Procedures', *The Chartered Accountant* (India), December 1967, pp. 305–315.

[19] Jennings, op cit, p. 689.

[20] Trigg, op cit, p. 304.

[21] ibid.

[22] See, for example, Karl Käfer, 'European National Uniform Charts of Accounts', *The International Journal of Accounting*, Fall 1965, pp. 67–83; Joseph Loore, 'The Utility of Normalisation for Accountancy and Auditing' (in Berg, Mueller and Walker, op cit, pp. 173–184); and Uno Lönnqvist, 'Some Aspects on the Way in Which the Need for Harmonisation of Auditing Standards and Procedures Could be Met', *Paper*, 9th International Congress of Accountants, Paris, 1967.

[23] Edward Stamp, 'The International Harmonisation of Auditing Standards and Procedures—Some General Considerations', *Paper*, 9th International Congress of Accountants, Paris, 1967, pp. 1–2.

[24] Gerhard G. Mueller, *International Accounting*, Macmillan, 1967, pp. 160–164 (*passim*).

[25] John J. Deering, 'The Need for Developing International Terminology and Uniform Accounting Practices' (in Berg, Mueller and Walker, op cit, pp. 192–199).

[26] See Wilhelm Elmendorff, 'Coordination of the Legal Accounting Requirements in the Various Countries of the European Economic Community', *Journal UEC*, October 1967, pp. 232–239.

[27] W. Schattinga, 'The Harmonisation of European Practices in the Presentation of External Financial Accounts', *The Accountant's Magazine*, April 1971, pp. 165–172.

[28] See B. D. Barton, 'The Proposal for a European Company', *Accountancy*, April 1971, pp. 189–191 (for a brief look at the proposals); and A. T. McLean 'Societas Europea: A Consideration of the Proposals for the European Company', *The Accountant's Magazine*, December 1971, pp. 631–640 (for an in-depth study); (See also Chapter 2).

Appendix 4.1

Membership of European public accountancy bodies

Country	Main public accountancy bodies	Membership numbers	As at
Belgium	Collège national des experts comptables de Belgique [1]	1,560	31.12.71
	Institut des réviseurs d'entreprises [2]	220 [6]	31.12.71
Denmark	Foreningen af statsautoriserede Revisorer	971	15.5.72
France	Compagnie nationale des commissaires aux comptes	6,300 [6]	1.1.72
	Ordre des experts comptables et des comptables agréés [3]	10,059	31.12.71
Holland	Nederlands instituut van register accountants	3,200	21.7.72
Italy	Collegio dei ragionieri e periti commerciali	8,000 [6]	31.12.71
	Ordine dei dottori commercialisti [4]	14,000 [6]	13.7.72
Luxembourg	Ordre des experts comptables Luxembourgeois	27	1.6.72
West Germany	Institut der Wirtschaftsprüfer [5]	3,005	1.7.72
Britain	The Association of Certified and Corporate Accountants	13,681	1.1.72
	The Institute of Chartered Accountants in England and Wales	51,659	1.1.72
	The Institute of Chartered Accountants in Ireland	2,387	31.8.71
	The Institute of Chartered Accountants of Scotland	8,680	31.12.71

Notes

[1] The Collège was formed by an amalgamation of 26 small public accountancy bodies, of which 21 are still in existence. The largest is the Ordre des Experts Comptables et Comptables Brevetés de Belgique which accounts for approximately 38% of the membership of the Collège; 168 members of the Collège are, however, honorary members.

[2] Approximately one half of the membership of the Institut also belongs to the Collège National des Experts Comptables de Belgique.

[3] Approximately 3,500 members of the Ordre are members of the Compagnie Nationale des Commissaires aux Comptes.

[4] Very few members of the Ordine are members of the Collegio de Ragionieri e Periti Commerciali.

[5] This figure includes 358 extraordinary and honorary members.

[6] Approximate figures only made available.

Appendix 4.2

Formation dates of European public accountancy bodies

Country	Body	Date
Belgium	Collège national des experts comptables de Belgique	1950[1]
	Institut des réviseurs d'entreprises	1953[2]
Denmark	Foreningen af statsautoriserede Revisorer	1912
France	Compagnie nationale des commissaires aux comptes	1970[3]
	Ordre des experts comptables et des comptables agréés	1945[4]
Holland	Nederlands instituut van registeraccountants	1895[5] [1967]
Italy	Collegio dei ragionieri e periti commerciali	1929[6]
	Ordine dei dottori commercialisti	1924[6] [1929]
Luxembourg	Ordre des experts comptables Luxembourgeois	1951
West Germany	Institut der Wirtschaftsprüfer	1932
Britain	The Association of Certified and Corporate Accountants	1891[7] [1904]
	The Institute of Chartered Accountants in England and Wales	1870[8] [1880]
	The Institute of Chartered Accountants in Ireland	1888
	The Institute of Chartered Accountants of Scotland	1854[9] [1951]

Notes

[1] The Collége was formed by an amalgamation of 26 small accountancy bodies throughout Belgium. It was therefore a federation of all the then main accountancy bodies, 21 of which are still in existence today. The largest one is the Ordre des Experts Comptables et Comptables Brevetés de Belgique.

[2] The Institut was created by law in an attempt to regulate the then profession of accountancy in Belgium. Its members audit the financial statements of those companies which are legally required to appoint a member of the Institut as auditor.

[3] The Compagnie was formed as a result of *Decree No. 69-810* (12 August 1969) which was introduced by the French Government to regulate and organise that part of public accountancy activity concerned with the audit of companies.

[4] The Ordre was established by the French Government; membership is composed of public accountants of two types—commercial and industrial (comptables agréés) and auditors (experts comptables).

[5] In 1895 the Nederlands Instituut van Accountants was formed but, as a result of the Registered Accountants Act, 1962, it and the Vereniging van

Academisch Gevormde Accountants amalgamated in 1967 to form the Nederlands Instituut van Registeraccountants.

[6] Formed in 1924, the Ordine dei Dottori Commercialisti amalgamated its membership in 1929 with the membership of the Collegio dei Ragionieri, thus establishing a much larger Ordine as the primary public accountancy body in Italy. The Collegio then became the Collegio dei Ragionieri e Periti Commerciali.

[7] The Association (formed 1904) incorporates the Corporation of Accountants (founded 1891), the Institution of Certified Public Accountants (founded 1903) and the London Association of Certified Accountants (founded 1904).

[8] The Incorporated Society of Liverpool Accountants was formed in January 1870, followed by the Institute of Accountants in London (November 1870), the Manchester Institute of Accountants (February 1871), the Society of Accountants in England (January 1873) and the Sheffield Institute of Accountants (March 1877). These bodies were granted a Royal Charter, and in May 1880 formed the Institute of Chartered Accountants in England and Wales.

[9] The Society of Accountants in Edinburgh was formed on 31 January 1853 but its Royal Charter was not granted until 23 October 1854. The Institute of Accountants and Actuaries in Glasgow (granted a Royal Charter, 15 March 1855) and the Society of Accountants in Aberdeen (granted a Royal Charter, 18 March 1867) joined with the Edinburgh Society to form the Institute of Chartered Accountants of Scotland in 1951.

Appendix 4.3

Main work of members of European public accountancy bodies

Country	Public accountancy body	Auditing	Taxation matters	Business accountancy	Business consultancy
Belgium	Collège national des experts comptables de Belgique	*	*	*	*
	Institut des réviseurs d'entreprises	*			
Denmark	Foreningen af statsautoriserede Revisorer	*	*	*	*
France	Compagnie nationale des commissaires aux comptes	*		*	
	Ordre des experts comptables et des comptables agréés	*	*	*	*
Holland	Nederlands instituut van registeraccountants	*	*		*
Italy	Collegio dei ragionieri e periti commerciali	*	*	*	*
	Ordine dei dottori commercialisti	*	*	*	*
Luxembourg	Ordre des experts comptables Luxembourgeois	*	*	*	
West Germany	Institut der Wirtschaftsprüfer	*	*	*	*

Note:

This table was prepared from information supplied from the public accountancy bodies concerned. Few were able to give information regarding the percentages of the total public accountancy activity relevant to each of the above four activities. Where estimates were given, these have been commented on in the appropriate text.

Appendix 4.4

Members of European public accountancy bodies who are qualified to audit, and who actually conduct audits

Country	Public accountancy body	Total members	Those qualified to audit	Those conducting audits
Belgium	Collège national des experts comptables de Belgique	1,560	110 [1]	110 [1]
	Institut des réviseurs d'entreprises	220 [3]	220 [3]	220 [3]
Denmark	Foreningen af statsautoriserede Revisorer	971	870	870
France	Compagnie nationale des commissaires aux comptes	6,300 [3]	6,300 [2, 3]	6,000 [2, 3]
	Ordre des experts comptables et des comptables agréés	10,059	10,059	3,568 [2]
Holland	Nederlands instituut van registeraccountants	3,200	3,200	1,600 [3]
Italy	Collegio dei ragionieri e periti commerciali	8,000 [3]	8,000 [3]	unknown
	Ordine dei dottori commercialisti	14,000 [3]	14,000 [3]	unknown
Luxembourg	Ordre des experts comptables Luxembourgeois	27	27	27
West Germany	Institut der Wirtschaftsprüfer	3,005	2,647	2,647

Notes:

[1] Approximately 110 members of the Collège are members of the Institut and audit companies legally requiring audit by Institut members. However, no details were given about the numbers of Collège members who may audit companies not legally required to be audited by Institut members.

[2] Just over 3,500 members of the Compagnie are also members of the Ordre.

[3] Approximate figures only made available.

Appendix 4.5

A comparative study of membership requirements for European public accountancy bodies

Country	Public accountancy body	Normal age of entry	Educational requirements	Practical experience requirements
Belgium	Collège national des experts comptables de Belgique [1]	30	Candidates must hold a commercial or economics degree or an approved diploma in book-keeping sciences; professional examinations must be passed at the end of a period of articles.	A five - year period of articles with a member of the Collège.
	Institut des réviseurs d'entreprises [2]	—	—	—
Denmark	Foreningen af statsautoriserede Revisorer [3]	32	A five - year degree course in economics and business administration (equivalent to an LSE masters degree); a pass in the final examination of the State examination board under the supervision of the Ministry of Commerce.	Three years' practical training with a State-authorised public accountant. Usually this lasts between three and five years.
France	Compagnie nationale des commissaires aux comptes [4]	25	Qualification as an *expert comptable;* or 15 years' practical experience in accounting, finance, etc; or 10 years' practical experience plus certain school certificates.	Three years' practical training; waived if the candidate is an *expert comptable.*

	Ordre des experts comptables et des comptables agréés	25	Must hold the diplôme d'expertise comptable based on examination and the submission of an accounting thesis.	Three years' practical training with a member of the Ordre.
Holland	Nederlands instituut van registeraccountants [5]	30–35	By holding a business economics degree (equivalent to an LSE masters degree); by passing the Instituut's examinations.	There are no practical experience requirements, but most candidates do have experience on admission to the Instituut.
Italy	Collegio dei ragionieri e periti commerciali	25	By passing the examinations of the Collegio.	Two years' practical experience with a member of the Collegio.
	ordine dei dottori commercialisti	25	Must hold a university degree in economics and commere (equivalent to an LSE masters degree), and have passed a State examination in accounting practice	No practical experience requirements.
Luxembourg	Ordre des experts comptables Luxembourgeois	30	Must hold a university degree in business management or or economics.	Three years' practical experience, of which two must be with an *expert comptable*.
West Germany	Institut der Wirtschaftsprüfer [6]	30–35	Must hold a university degree in commerce, economics or law (or have ten years' experience with a Wirtschaftsprüfer) and have passed the Institut's examinations.	Six years' practical experience, of which four must be in public accountancy.

Notes:

1 Details can be found in *Reglements*, CNECB, pp. 12–19.

2 No specific details were made available, but it appears reasonable to assume similar membership requirements to those of the Collège.

3 Full details can be found in a statement of the Foreningen, *The Danish State-Authorised Public Accountant's Profession* (English version).

4 Details have been taken from *Decret No. 69-810 du 12 Août 1969: portant règlement d'administration publique et relatif à l'organisation de la profession et au statut professionnel des commissaires aux comptes de sociétés*, pp. 4–5.

5 Recent changes in the Instituut's educational programme can be found in its March 1972 publication, *Change of Structure of Accountancy Education* (English version).

6 Details can be found in *Die Wirtschaftsprüferordnung*, 24 July 1961, paragraphs 5–11.

Appendix 4.6

Publications of European public accountancy bodies

Country	Public accountancy body	Issuance of guidance or recommendation statements [1]	Existence of formal code of ethics
Belgium	Collège national des experts comptables de Belgique	Yes [2]	Yes [3]
	Institut des réviseurs d'entreprises [2]		
Denmark	Foreningen af statsautoriserede Revisorer	Yes [4]	Yes
France	Compagnie national des commissaires aux comptes	Yes [5]	Yes
	Ordre des experts comptables et des comptables agréés	Yes [6]	Yes
Holland	Nederlands instituut van registeraccountants	Yes [7]	Yes
Italy	Collegio dei ragionieri e periti commerciali	No	No
	Ordine dei dottori commercialisti	No	No
Luxembourg	Ordre des experts comptables Luxembourgeois	No	Yes
West Germany	Institut der Wirtschaftsprüfer	Yes [8]	Yes [9]

Notes:

[1] With the exception of Germany, such statements when issued are non-mandatory on the members of the public accountancy bodies concerned.

[2] No details made available.

[3] Contained in *Reglements*, CNECB, pp. 22–29. This includes sections on professional integrity, independence, incompatible occupations, and publicity.

[4] The subjects of these statements include financial reporting, auditing principles, internal control, and the auditor's report.

[5] See *Recommendations Relatives aux Diligences*, 1971, which contains guidance statements for auditors regarding the degree of care to be exercised in the audit function. It includes sections on the auditor's freedom to audit, his personal obligations, his relationship and duties towards shareholders and management, and the form of his audit report. It also includes sections on the main principles of accounting which he may come across during his audits.

[6] See, for example, *L'Exercise du Commissariat aux Comptes—dans le Cadre*

de la Nouvelle Législation des Sociétés Commerciales, published by the Ordre in 1970. This publication, in two volumes, describes the company audit function in the light of recent company law changes. It covers all aspects of auditing including the appointment and dismissal of the auditor, his relationship with management, shareholders and third parties, his legal and professional responsibilities, as well as audit verification techniques including internal control review. *Le Conseil de Gestion—Le Rôle des Membres de l'Ordre*, published in 1966, explains in three volumes the management consultancy function.

In addition, the Ordre has a regular series of guidance statements issued for members' use. The series is called *Recommendations à l'Usage des Membres de l'Ordre*, and is divided into five main parts: (a) *Information du Public*, containing advice on the form and contents of published financial statements, (b) *Gestion d'Entreprise*, the first statement of which deals with costing terminology, (c) *Cas Particuliers*, dealing with miscellaneous topics such as accounting for leasing operations, (d) *Révision Comptable*, containing advice on specific auditing problems such as direct confirmations, the control of stock and work in progress, and auditing standards in general, (e) *Principles Comptables*, describing problem areas of accounting, such as provisions, tax on value added, amortisation of fixed assets, revaluation of fixed assets, contingent liabilities, inventories and funds statements.

[7] These include guidance on topics such as use of the work and reports of foreign auditors; auditing computerised accounting systems; hidden reserves; deferred taxation; the auditor's responsibility with regard to fraud, and the public accountant's role in business. No English version is available at present.

[8] These include statements on the general principles of accounting, financial reporting, and auditing.

[9] The professional duties expected of the Wirtscharfsprüfer are laid down in Section II, 'Conscientiousness', *Berufsrichtlinien*, as required by Section 57(1) of *Die Wirtschartsprüferordnung*, 1971.

Appendix 4.7

European audit requirements

Country	Requirement for audit	Comments
Belgium	All public companies, insurance companies, and companies quoted on the stock exchange are required to be audited.	The auditor must be a member of the Institut des Réviseurs d'Entreprises.
Denmark	All companies are required to be audited.	The audit must be conducted by a State-authorised public accountant in the case of stock exchange companies, banks and insurance companies.
France	All companies are required to be audited.	The audit must be conducted by a registered commissaire aux comptes.
Holland	All public and certain private companies requiring to file their annual financial statements with the trade registrar are required to be audited.	The audit, in these instances, is required to be conducted by a *Registeraccountant*.
Italy	Certain types of companies are required to have a board of auditors.	The auditors are not required to be public accountants.
Luxembourg	All companies are required to be audited.	Audits are not required to be conducted by a public accountant.
West Germany	All public companies, insurance companies, and certain private companies are required to be audited.	Such audits are required to be conducted by a Wirtschaftsprüfer.

Appendix 4.8

Generally accepted European audit objectives

	Belgium	Denmark	France	Holland	Italy	Luxembourg	West Germany
Assessing and giving an opinion on the credibility of financial statements	*	*	*	*	*	*	*
Verifying the financial statements conform with legal requirements		*	*	*	*	*	*
Verifying the financial statements are in agreement with the underlying accounting records	*	*	*	*	*	*	*
Verifying the accuracy of the accounting records	*	*	*	*	*	*	*
Detecting fraud	*		*[1]	*[2]	*	*	*

Note:

[1] i.e. irregularities in the administation of the company.
[2] Only to the limited extent accepted in Britain, i.e. when checking for potential weaknesses in the system of internal control.

This table was prepared from information supplied by the public accountancy bodies concerned. All recognised the 'credibility' objective as primary to each of the others listed, as applicable. Few of the bodies gave sufficient information to judge the order of priorities in each of the countries. However, where this was made available, appropriate comments have been made in the relevant sections of the essay. In the other cases, the emphasis in objectives has had to be deduced from information from all available sources. The objectives listed, therefore, are in no way in any order of importance.

Appendix 4.9

Widely used European audit practices

	Internal control review and analysis	Statistical sampling techniques	Debtors confirmations	Attendance at physical stock-takings
Belgium	*	*	*	*
Denmark	*		*	*[1]
France	*	*	*[1]	*[1]
Holland	*	*		*
Italy	*	*		*
Luxembourg	*	*		
West Germany	*	*[1]	*[3]	*[3]

Note:

[1] Only to a limited extent.

[2] Recommended to be used if auditor regards it as useful for verification purposes—no information available regarding actual usage.

This table was prepared from information supplied by the public accountancy bodies concerned. However, there is some doubt in the writer's mind as to the extent of utilisation of the techniques concerned in the cases of Belgium and Italy particularly.

5 Harmonisation of Company Financial Reporting

The European Economic Community's first directive on company law, issued on 9th March, 1968 and incorporated into British legislation by Clause 9 of the European Communities Act, 1972 deals *inter alia* with publicity and contains the provision that

(1) Member states shall take the necessary measures to ensure the compulsory publication by companies of the following documents and particulars at least: (f) the balance sheet and profit and loss account for each financial period.[1]

No details were given as to what the contents of the balance sheet and profit and loss account should be. A study group under the chairmanship of Dr W. Elmendorff of the German Federal Republic prepared and published a draft directive on these matters in 1969.[2] On this draft are based the proposed fourth directive and also the accounting provisions of the proposed statute for a European company. All are firmly based on present practice within the Community, with little attention paid to practice outside, e.g. in the U.K.

The reasons for harmonising financial reporting are set out in an explanatory note to the proposed fourth directive:

> At the present moment considerable differences exist in the member states as regards the legal requirements governing both the structure and content of companies' annual accounts. The particulars that the companies have to furnish are plainly at variance, both qualitatively and quantitatively, from one country to another.
>
> This situation may be prejudicial to the fusion of national markets into a common market operating as an internal market. The idea of the Common Market implies that all companies having the same legal form can work in the Community under comparable legal conditions. It is a question of equality of opportunity as regards the law. Otherwise competition in the different member states between companies having the same legal form will continue to be distorted artificially.
>
> Persons who intend to establish relations with companies in other member states, or who have already done so, have the greatest interest in being able to obtain sufficient and comparable information concerning the assets, financial position, and results of such companies. At present the annual accounts of companies established in different member states are far from being comparable, partly because the nomenclature

in use in the different member states for the items in balance sheets and profit and loss accounts is often totally different. In most cases the reader of a balance sheet, while being quite familiar with the structure of the accounts and the terminology employed in his own country, is not able to analyse the annual accounts of companies in other member states. These circumstances might be enough to stop anyone from taking the risk of forming commercial ties with these companies.

The differences that exist between national laws as regards presentation of accounts can also provide a reason for companies—in choosing where they will establish themselves—to choose a country where the requirements in this matter are not stringent.

Finally, these differences may also be prejudicial to the rational orientation of capital investment in the Community to the extent that investors are not in possession of sufficient comparable information to take their decisions in full knowledge of the facts. This is particularly true as regards purchase of shares in companies in other member states.[3]

Disclosure requirements

Standards of disclosure are in general higher in Britain than on the continent. With two exceptions, however, the requirements of the proposed fourth directive are reasonably in line with current British practice. The first is that the directive applies only to single companies not to groups of companies. It has indeed been announced that consolidated accounts will be dealt with in a later directive but to deal with them separately in this manner is unsatisfactory and no doubt reflects the still undeveloped state of consolidation accounting in most EEC countries. The Study Group of Accountants in the European Economic Community has suggested that a directive dealing with group accounts be brought into force at the same time as the proposed fourth directive.[4]

The second exception is that the detailed disclosure requirements of the proposed fourth directive apply to companies in varying degrees, depending in effect on whether they are large, medium or small private (my terms, *not* those of the directive). Small private companies are private companies with total assets of not more than 100,000 units of account, net turnover of not more than 200,000 units of account, and an average labour force during the accounting period of not more than 20 persons. Medium companies (which may be public or private) are those with total assets of not more than one million units of account, net turnover of not more than two million units of account, and an average labour force of not more than 100 persons. All other commercial and industrial companies are large. Banks and insurance companies are not covered by the proposal.

Small private companies need not be required to publish a profit and loss account at all, and only an abridged form of balance sheet. Medium companies can be exempted, if a member state so wishes, from some of the disclosure provisions relating to the profit and loss account. Further details are given later. Large companies are subject to all requirements of the directive.

The distinction made between 'small private', 'medium', and 'large' can be criticised, and I would myself prefer the suggestion made by the Institute of Chartered Accountants in England and Wales that there be a distinction between 'proprietary' companies and 'stewardship' companies.

Underlying philosophy

The overriding requirement of company financial reporting in Britain is the showing of a 'true and fair view' (s. 149, Companies Act, 1948) and all the details of the Second Schedule of the Companies Act, 1967 are subordinate to this. The proposal, however, works the other way round. After stating that the annual accounts are to include the balance sheet, the profit and loss account and the notes thereto, and are to be drawn up in accordance with regular and proper accounting principles it is stated (Article 2(3)) that the annual accounts, *in the context of the provisions regarding the valuation of assets and liabilities and the lay-out of accounts*, shall reflect as *accurately* as possible the company's assets, liabilities, financial position and results (italics added).[5]

This is a most unsatisfactory section. An alternative and more satisfactory wording has been suggested by the Study Group of Accountants in the EEC:

> The annual accounts shall provide a true and fair view[6] of the assets and liabilities, financial position and results of the company. They should be presented with clarity and conform with the special provisions of this directive dealing with valuation and form of presentation.

Even in the new text it remains unclear what the position is should the special provisions referred to be thought incompatible with a true and fair view.

General principles of accounting

A list of general accounting principles to be followed is set out in Article 28 of the proposal:

1. Methods of valuation cannot be changed from one period to another.
2. Only profits realised (*réalisés*) at the date of the balance sheet can be recorded but account must be taken of all risks foreseeable at that date.
3. Account must be taken of any losses not known at the balance sheet date but which come to light before its completion and which arose during the period to which the accounts relate.

4. Account must be taken of any losses in value (*dépréciations*) whether the company makes a profit or a loss during the period.
5. Assets and liabilities must be valued separately.
6. The closing balance sheet of one period must correspond with the opening balance sheet of the next.

Most of the above are covered by the ideas of consistency and prudence set forth in Statement of Accounting Practice No. 2.[7]

Rules of valuation and income measurement

Much less palatable to British accountants are the detailed set of rules prescribed in Articles 32 to 39 of the proposal. These follow the traditional historical cost modified by conservatism basis of accounting and include the following:

1. If national legislation permits the showing of preliminary expenses, research and development costs and purchased goodwill as assets, they must be written off over a period of not longer than five years. To the extent that preliminary expenses and research and development costs are not completely written off, profits may not be distributed unless the company has free reserves at least equal to the unamortised expenses and costs.

2. Fixed assets must be valued at acquisition price or production cost, and depreciation written off each year calculated according to a plan based on the rules of good management (*les règles d'une bonne gestion:* the corresponding section in the draft European Company statute refers to *les règles d'une comptabilité regulière et sincère*).

Fixed assets can be written down further, however, if it is anticipated that the reduction in value will be permanent. Valuation adjustments (*corrections de valeur*) of this kind must be shown separately in the profit and loss account or in the notes and shall cease to apply when the reasons for them no longer exist (in contrast to the German Companies Act, 1965, s. 155). Where the value of fixed assets has been adjusted in order to take advantage of tax legislation, the amount of the adjustment must be shown in the notes.

Production cost is to be calculated by adding to the purchase price of raw materials and supplies, the manufacturing costs directly attributable to the product in question. A reasonable proportion of indirect manufacturing costs can be added to the extent that they relate to the period of manufacture. Distribution costs may not be included. Member states may authorise the inclusion in production cost of interest on capital borrowed or on own capital used to the extent that it relates to the period of manufacture. If interest is included the amount must be shown in the notes.

3. Fixed assets, raw materials and supplies which are constantly being replaced and whose total value is relatively small may be shown at a fixed

quantity and value if variations in the quantity, value and composition thereof are negligible.

4. Current assets are to be valued at acquisition price of cost of production. There is no express statement, as there is in Article 186 of the draft European Company statute, of the lower of cost or market rule, but reference is made not only to valuation adjustments as for fixed assets, but also to member states having the power to authorise exceptional valuation adjustments if they are necessary, upon a reasonable commercial assessment, to avoid the writing down of the assets in the near future. The amount of such adjustments must be shown separately in the profit and loss account or in the notes. As in the case of fixed assets, a valuation adjustment must be written back when the reasons for it no longer exist and the amount of any adjustments for tax purposes must be shown in the notes.

The cost of stocks may be calculated according to the weighted average, FIFO or LIFO methods or by a similar method.

5. Where the amount to be repaid on a debt exceeds the original amount borrowed, the difference may be shown as an asset and the amount indicated separately in the balance sheet or in the notes. It must be written off over a period not longer than the currency of the debt.

6. Provisions for contingencies and charges must not exceed in amount the sums which a reasonable businessman would consider necessary. Details of the item 'other provisions' must be given if material.

Dutch influence has, however, led to very important exceptions being allowed in Articles 30 and 31 of the directive. The former, for example, permits member states to authorise the use of replacement cost for depreciable fixed assets and stocks, the differences between historical cost and replacement cost being transferred to two separate revaluation reserves. Details and justification must be given in the notes. Such reserves may be capitalised. Any amounts transferred which are no longer necessary for the purpose of replacement of the assets concerned must be written back, added to the profit for the year or deducted from the loss for the year, and shown as a separate item in the profit and loss account. Apart from this and capitalisation, the revaluation reserves, once created, cannot be touched.

Neither Articles 32 to 39 nor Articles 30 and 31, are wholly satisfactory from a British viewpoint. The experiment of an Accounting Standards Steering Committee is working well and few, I imagine, would like to see its authority severely circumscribed by legislation of the kind just described. We could perhaps press either for the inclusion of a more flexible set of rules based on current British practice, or we could put forward the suggestion made by, among others, Professor Edward Stamp, that the rulemaking be delegated to the accountancy profession.[8] One wonders, however, how acceptable the latter would be to other members of the Community.

Structure and contents of published financial statements

Following mainly German law and practice the proposal sets out a number of prescribed forms for the balance sheet and profit and loss account. British practice is, of course, quite different. The second Schedule of the Companies Act, 1967 prescribes what has to be disclosed but does not contain any model financial statements. It is interesting to note, however, that a model balance sheet was annexed to Table B of the Companies Act, 1856 (later Table A of the Companies Act, 1862).[9] The adoption of such models, if they were not too inflexible, could lead to greater comparability and make it easier for the layman to understand published financial statements. The prescribed forms set out in the proposed directive, however, have many weaknesses.

The balance sheet is of two types only: an account form and a statement form. The former is reproduced in the translation in Appendix A to this chapter. Contingent liabilities, if not included in the balance sheet itself, must be shown as a note following the balance sheet, or in the notes to the accounts. Small private companies, as previously defined, can be exempted from publishing any items except those preceded by letters or Roman numerals.

There is not much latitude for departing from the prescribed forms of presentation. Only the following are allowed (they apply also to the profit and loss account):

1. A more detailed subdivision of the items preceded by Arabic numerals.
2. In exceptional cases, a different lay-out necessitated by the special nature of the company is admissible for the items preceded by Arabic numerals; an 'equivalent view' must still be given and explanations provided in the notes.
3. Member states can authorise a regrouping of items preceded by Arabic numerals, where they are of secondary interest in relation to the objects of Article 2(3).

Comparative figures for the preceding period must be given for both the balance sheet and the profit and loss account.

A number of items in the prescribed balance sheet are contrary to best practice in Britain, e.g. (a) The showing of unpaid capital as an asset, (b) A classification of debtors and creditors which makes it awkward to calculate working capital, (c) Permitting valuation adjustments to be shown on the capital and liabilities side, (d) The lack of some significant sub-totals, e.g. for total shareholders' funds.

In addition, some items have no counterparts in Britain, e.g. own shares (treasury stock) held by the company; and legal reserves. (In Germany, for example, section 150 of the Companies Act, 1965 prescribes that one-twentieth of each year's profit must be credited to a legal reserve until the reserve equals 10% of the share capital or such higher percentage as the articles of association may provide.)

There are special provisions dealing with certain balance sheet items. Article 12, for example, makes obligatory the 'gross method' of showing details of fixed assets in balance sheets, i.e. disclosing the original cost and the accumulated depreciation, as distinct from the 'net method' used, for instance, in Germany.

The profit and loss account is of four types, depending on whether it is in account or statement form and whether the classification is 'natural' or 'functional'. The statement form with natural classification is reproduced in Appendix 5 B.

Net turnover is defined as net of reductions in selling prices, value added taxes and other taxes calculated on turnover.

'Medium' companies, as described earlier, can, if a member state so wishes, show items 1 to 5 as a single figure called 'gross profit (or loss)'. 'Small private' companies, it will be remembered, can be exempted from publishing a profit and loss account.

Annual report

Section 43 of the proposed directive deals with the contents of *le rapport du gestion* (literally the management report, roughly equivalent to the British directors' report and referred to in the English version of the proposed directive as the annual report). The report is to contain a detailed review of the development of the company's business and the current position, and also give particulars of any important events that have occurred since the end of the accounting period; also the company's likely future development. The annual report is subject to audit (see below).

Audit

The proposed fourth directive makes only very sketchy references to audit. It is understood that this will be dealt with in detail in a later directive. Meanwhile, as a foretaste of what may be coming, it is worth looking also at the relevant articles in the draft statute for a European company.[10]

It is clear from Articles 44 and 49 of the proposed directive that the annual accounts of all three types of companies are to be audited, although member states, if they so wish, may exempt what I have called 'small private' companies The EEC Accountants Study Group feels that the quantitative criteria for 'small private' and 'medium' companies have been set too low and that small businesses will be subject to more stringent legal requirements than their economic importance justifies. They further suggest that the monetary levels of criteria should be tied to an index linked with changes in currency values in the EEC; that medium companies should be allowed, for a transitional period of 10 years, to have as auditors persons who would not be qualified to act as auditors of 'large' companies; and that audit of the annual report be limited to verifying that it is in conformity with the annual accounts.

Article 207 of the English text of the proposed statute for a European Company provides that 'If, on completion of his audit, the auditor has no objection to make in respect of the annual accounts, he shall *certify* them without qualification' (italics added). This is not a wording which will appeal to British auditors. The last clause reads as follows in the French version: '...il est tenu de délivrer un visa sans réserves'. Perhaps a more acceptable English translation could be found.

Although the auditor is to be appointed by the general meeting of shareholders he is to report, following German practice, to the supervisory board (*Aufsichtsrat*). Apart from ascertaining 'whether the accounting system and the annual accounts comply with (the draft European Company) statute and with the statutes of the company and with the principles of regular and proper accounting' he must also report 'any matters which he discovers in carrying out his duties and which might jeopardise the existence of the company or significantly affect its development, or which indicate serious infringements by the board of management otherwise than in preparation of the accounts, of any of the provisions of this statute or of the statutes of the company' (Article 208).

The liability of the auditors is expressly limited to three years after filing the annual return in a European Commercial Register but it is also expressly stated to extend to third parties.

Conclusion

If the Council of Ministers approves the fourth directive in anything like its proposed form the effect on British financial reporting will be substantial. Even if all the suggestions put forward by the study group are accepted, a fair part of our present legislation will need to be rewritten. How soon this will happen is difficult to foresee.

Appendix 5A

Example of prescribed form of Balance Sheet

(Translation by the author of French original of article 8 of the proposed fourth directive)

Assets

A. Unpaid capital (showing separately amount called up).

B. Preliminary expenses to the extent that national legislation authorises showing them as an asset.

C. Fixed assets:
  I Intangible assets:
    1. Research and development costs, to the extent that national legislation authorises showing them as an asset.
    2. Concessions, patents, licences, trade-marks, and similar rights which:
      (a) were acquired for consideration and do not have to be included under C-I-3,
      (b) were created by the company itself, to the extent that national legislation authorises showing them as assets.
    3. Goodwill acquired for consideration.
    4. Pre-payments (on account of intangible assets).
  II Tangible fixed assets:
    1. Land and buildings.
    2. Plant and machinery.
    3. Other plant, tools, furniture and fittings.
    4. Fixed assets under construction or being paid for by instalments.
  III Investments and other financial assets:
    1. Shares in associated undertakings.
    2. Claims on associated undertakings.
    3. Investments.
    4. Claims on undertakings in which the company has an investment.
    5. Securities representing financial assets.
    6. Other claims.
    7. Own shares (with an indication of their nominal value or book value) to the extent that national legislation authorises showing them in the balance sheet.

D. Current assets:
  I Stocks:

1. Raw materials and supplies.
2. Work in progress and scrap.
3. Finished goods for resale.
4. Pre-payments (on account of stocks).

II Debtors:

(The amount becoming due and payable within one year must be indicated separately in each case.)

1. Trade debtors.
2. Claims on associated undertakings.
3. Claims on companies in which the company has an investment.
4. Other claims.

III Securities forming part of current assets; liquid assets:

1. Shares in associated undertakings.
2. Bills of exchange.
3. Balances with banks and on post office current accounts, cheques and cash.
4. Own shares (with an indication of their nominal value or book value) to the extent that national legislation authorises showing them in the balance sheet.
5. Other securities (forming part of current assets).

E. Pre-payments.

F. Losses:

I Of the current period.

II Brought forward from previous periods.

Capital and Liabilities

A. Subscribed capital:

(The shares must be grouped by category with an indication of their nominal value or their book value).

B. Reserves:

1. Legal reserve.
2. Share premium.
3. Revaluation reserve.
4. Reserve for own shares.
5. Statutory reserves.
6. Free reserves.

C. Valuation adjustments to the extent that these do not appear on the assets side or in the notes:

1. On preliminary expenses.
2. On intangible assets.

3. On tangible fixed assets.
4. On investments and other financial assets.
5. On stocks.
6. On debtors.
7. On investments forming part of current assets and on liquid assets. (Items included under 2 to 7 should be broken down in the same way as the corresponding assets.)

D. Provisions for contingencies and charges:
1. Provisions for pensions and similar commitments.
2. Provisions for taxes (showing future taxation separately).
3. Other provisions.

E. Creditors: (Creditors due and payable within a period of less than one year or more than five years must be shown separately for each item, as must also fully secured creditors.)
1. Loans (convertible loans being shown separately).
2. Bank borrowings.
3. Instalments received on orders.
4. Trade creditors.
5. Amounts due on bills of exchange.
6. Amounts due to associated undertakings.
7. Amounts due to undertakings in which the company has an investment.
8. Other creditors.

F. Accruals.

G. Profits:
I Of the current period.
II Brought forward from previous periods.

Appendix 5B

Example of prescribed form of Profit and Loss Account

(Translation by the author of French original of Article 22 of the proposed fourth directive)

I Trading results (excluding income and expenditure, if any, included under II):
1. Net turnover.
2. Cost of goods sold (including valuation adjustments).

3. Gross profit.
4. Distribution costs (including valuation adjustments).
5. General administration expenses (including valuation adjustments).
6. Other trading income.
7. Trading profit or loss.

II Financial results:

8. Income from trade investments, income from associated undertakings being shown separately.
9. Income from other securities held and from claims forming part of the financial assets, income from associated undertakings being shown separately.
10. Other interest and similar income, that arising from associated undertakings being shown separately.
11. Valuation adjustments relating to trade investments and other financial assets and to securities forming part of current assets.
12. Interest and similar charges, those arising in respect of associated undertakings being shown separately.
13. Financial profit or loss.

III Exceptional income and expenditure:

14. Exceptional income
15. Exceptional expenditure.
16. Balance of exceptional items.
17. Sub-total.

IV Taxes:

18. Taxation of profits
    (a) current,
    (b) future.
19. Other taxes not included under I, II, or III above.

V Profit or loss for the year.

Notes

[1] First directive of the Council of 9 March 1968 with a view to coordinating, in order to render of equal value, the safeguards which member states require of companies and firms within the meaning of the second paragraph of Article 58 of the treaty, so as to protect the interests of both members and outsiders.

[2] Proposal for a directive to co-ordinate, with a view to making them equivalent, the guarantees demanded in the member states from companies within the meaning of Article 58, 2nd paragraph, of the Treaty of Rome for the purpose of protecting the interests both of the members of such companies

and of third parties. Annual financial reports (form and valuation); contents of the notes and the report of management; audit by an accountant and publication (Düsseldorf: Verlagsbuchhandlung des Instituts der Wirtschaftsprüfer GmbH., 1969). See also Elmendorff's article, 'Coordination of the Legal Accounting Requirements in the Various Countries of the European Economic Community', *Journal UEC*, October 1967.

[3] Commission of the European Communities, 'Proposal for a Fourth Directive on the Annual Accounts of Limited Liability Companies', *Supplement to Bulletin of the European Communities*, 1971, no. 12. The directive appears to have been translated from the French by persons who are neither native speakers of English nor accountants. It should therefore be used with care!

[4] Study Group of Accountants in the European Economic Community, *Observations on the Council's Proposal for a Fourth Directive Pursuant to Article 54(3)(g) for Coordination of Measures to be taken by Companies in the Member States to Safeguard the Interests both of their Members and of Third Parties as Regards the Presentation and Content of the Annual Accounts, Management Report, Methods of Valuation and Publication of these Documents* (10 July, 1972).

[5] This passage is so important that it is worth comparing the above translation (taken from the source quoted in note 3) with the original French:

> Ils doivent être établis avec clarté et donner, dans le cadre des dispositions en matière d'évaluationet de structure des comptes, une image aussi sûre que possible du patrimoine, de la cituation financière ainsi que des résultats de la société.

Compare also section 149 of the German Aktiengesetz (Companies Act) 1965:

> Der Jahresabschluss ... muss im Rahmen der Bewertungsvorschriften einen möglichst sicheren Einblick in die Vermögens- und Ertragslage der Gesellschaft geben.

[6] The French equivalent is said to be *fidélité*. The Dutch Act of 10 September 1970 on the Annual Accounʇs of Enterprises uses the phrase *getrouw en stelsmatig* (fairly and systematically).

[7] The Institute of Chartered Accountants in England and Wales and allied accountancy bodies, November 1971.

[8] E. Stamp and C. Marley, *Accounting Principles and the City Code: The Case for Reform,* London: Butterworths, 1970, p. 150.

[9] See the interesting discussion in H. C. Edey and Prot Panitpakdi, 'British Comijany Accounting and the Law 1844–1900', in A.C. Littleton and B.S. Yamey, *Studies in the History of Accounting*, London: Sweet and Maxwell, 1956.

[10] Commission of the European Communities, 'Proposal for a Council Regulation embodying a Statute for European Companies', Brussels, 24 June 1970 (*Supplement to Bulletin of the European Communities*, 1970, no. 8).

6 British Accounting and the EEC

by R. H. PARKER

One consequence of British entry into the European Community will be that continental European ways of thought and practice will have a much greater influence than formerly on British accounting. In the first section of this article I shall look at past, present, and future external influences. The second section examines the diversity of current accounting practices within the enlarged EEC; the third looks at the problem of uniformity in company financial reporting in its European context; and in the fourth there is a brief discussion of regulation of the accountancy profession.

External influences on British accounting: past, present, and future

British accounting is of European origin. A useful reminder of this is the extended title of the oldest surviving text in English on double entry, Jan Ympyn's *New Instruction*, published in 1547:

> A Notable and very excellente woorke, expressyng and declaryng the maner and forme how to kepe a boke of accomptes or reconynges ... Translated with greate Diligence out of the Italian toung into Dutche, and out of Dutche, into French, and now out of Frenche into Englishe.

Despite this historical background Britain's accounting and financial links with her colonies and former colonies (including the United States) have been much stronger than with Europe, especially during the last hundred years or so. Until fairly recently, it was fashionable to visualise Britain as at the fortunate intersection of three circles representing the Commonwealth, Anglo-America (U.S.A. and U.K.) and Europe, the latter rather vaguely defined, but taken here to mean the European Economic Community. At various periods in our history we have influenced, or been influenced by these three areas in varying degrees. Table 6.1 shows how trading relationships changed during the decade 1961/71. The growing importance of the EEC and the declining importance of the Commonwealth are clearly evident.

Accounting influences tend to follow trading and commercial ones, though often with a time lag. As might be expected, our accounting relationship with the countries of the Commonwealth has been, at least until recently, a rather

Table 6.1

Direction of UK imports (% of total)

	1961	*1971*
Commonwealth	35	22
EEC	15	21
USA	11	11

Direction of UK exports (% of total)

	1961	*1971*
Commonwealth	35	22
EEC	17	21
USA	8	12

Source: Overseas Trade Statistics of the United Kingdom

one-way affair. British accounting practices and company and tax legislation were exported and later modified to suit local circumstances. In some instances the child has grown up to be as active as mother, but mother has not on the whole paid much attention.

A much more important influence on British accounting has been that lusty step-child, the United States. Early American accounting owed much to the British example. When the Scots were celebrating in 1905 the fiftieth anniversary of the foundation of the Edinburgh Institute, Richard Brown could write:

> The history of the profession in the United States may be said to have commenced only about twenty years ago. Prior to that time there were comparatively few American accountants.[1]

Nevertheless American accounting, like the American economy, was soon to move to world leadership, particularly in cost and management accounting and accounting education. In these fields the American influence on Britain and the countries of western Europe continues to be greater than their influence on each other.

When one comes to consider cross-Channel flows of accounting thought and practice of the past, it is difficult to find anything beyond double entry book–keeping. Britain has not taken any more modern accountancy development from Europe. Consider a few examples. Few British accountants have even heard of, let alone adopted, the 'logismography' of Cerboni.[2] The early nineteenth century French development of cost accounting appears to have been independent of later developemnts in Britain.[3] Schmalenbach's *Dynamic Accounting*, first published in book form in Germany in 1919, had great influence on the continent but none in Britain: it was not even translated into English until 1959.[4] The accounting consequences of the German inflation of the 1920s inspired Sweeney's *Stabilized Accounting* (1936) which has influenced several professors but few practitioners. The national accounting plans of pre-war Germany and post-war France have likewise aroused little interest in Britain.[5] Dutch theory and practice concerning replacement value accounting have aroused academic interest but have not, so far as is known, been adopted in practice by any British-owned company. Equally, European accounting owes little to Britain.

Britain's entry into the EEC will inevitably mean a return of European influence, but not all aspects of accounting will be equally affected. There will be little effect on those areas of British accounting not regulated by law. The main external source of new ideas on management accounting, for example, will continue to be the United States: the Americans' technical supremacy in this field and a shared language will assure that.

Things are likely to be different in the fields of company financial reporting, taxation, auditing, and mergers. Not surprisingly, there has been a tendency within the EEC to harmonise towards the law in force in France and Germany, the most powerful founder members of the Community. Britain's failure to join the Community earlier has meant that the British viewpoint has not been considered. We have all the disadvantages of the member who joins the club after many of the rules have already been decided. Risking a very broad generalisation, one can say that the EEC is tending to adopt French ideas on taxation (see Chapter 11) and German ideas on financial reporting.

Accounting in the EEC: diversity and change

There is as yet no such thing as 'EEC accounting', and important differences of accounting theory and practice still exist among the member states. For instance, a footnote in the 1971 Dunlop Annual Report records that the loss of about £10 million reported by Industrie Pirelli SpA, the Italian half of the Dunlop Pirelli Union, was 'significantly greater' under the common accounting principles adopted by the Union because of 'the application of different criteria which result in accelerated provision for depreciation and severance indemnity'. Again, Professor G.G. Mueller in his book *International Accounting*[6] distinguishes four types of accounting (accounting within a macro-economic framework, the micro-economic approach, accounting as an independent discipline, uniform accounting), and is able to find within the enlarged EEC examples of the last three. The Dutch, he claims, have a micro-economic approach to accounting, the British regard it as an independent discipline, and the French and Germans practise varieties of uniform accounting.

When it is said, therefore, that European ways of thought and practice will have a greater influence in Britain, it does not mean that British accountants are confronted with a monolithic European approach to accounting. Moreover, there is, as we shall see, not only diversity but also change. Most of these changes seem, fortunately, to be towards British ideas, or rather Anglo-American ideas, than in the other direction.

Change is coming for a number of reasons, but the most important factor is undoubtedly the need of large European companies to raise money on the international *capital market*. The philosophy of disclosure which now characterises British company financial reporting has arisen not just because of governmental pressure but because of the need to attract investment from a wide range of shareholders. The capital markets of the six founder members of the EEC ,on the other hand, are relatively underdeveloped. It has been estimated that the number of quoted companies, the market capitalisation and the equity turnover in the U.K. are all greater than that of Germany, France, Italy, Holland and Belgium put together (see Table 6.2).
Compared with the U.K., the capital markets are, the Netherlands apart,

Table 6.2

	Number of quoted companies	Market capital-isation at 31.12.71 £'000 m.	Equity turnover year to 31.12.71 £'000 m.
Germany	550	13.3	1.7*
France	830	9.4	1.7
Italy	140	4.0	0.9*
Holland	400	5.3	1.3
Belgium	580	2.7	0.4
Totals	2,500	34.7	6.0
U.K.	3,300	50.2	6.9

* Year to 30.6.71
Source: Institute of Chartered Accountants in England and Wales, *The United Kingdom and Company Law in EEC*, 15 March 1972.

tightly controlled by government regulation or by the banks and as a consequence the need for disclosure has not been so great.

One obvious example of non-disclosure is the relative rarity of published consolidated accounts in continental Europe. In France, for example, there is still no legal requirement for any company, however large, to prepare group accounts. Pressure is, however, coming from at least two sources: within France the powerful Commission des Opérations de Bourse has insisted since 1 July 1971 that consolidated statements be included in *notes d'information* (prospectuses); outside France the need for a quotation on, for example' the London Stock Exchange has led to change.

An interesting recent example is Ciments Lafarge, a company with group sales in 1971 of nearly 3,000 million French francs, and subsidiaries and associated companies in Canada, Africa, Germany, Britain, the U.S.A., and elsewhere. It was not until the company successfully sought a quotation on the London Stock Exchange in 1972 that it published consolidated financial statements. The advertisement issued to comply with the regulations of the exchange announced the company's intention in future to publish annual consolidated accounts which will show a true and fair view (a concept as yet unknown to French law) of profits and financial position and which, while in the main retaining methods of presentation commonly used by French companies, will be prepared 'using bases of accounting consistent with those used for the purpose of the Accountants' Report included in this Advertisement'.

These bases differ in some respects from those used in the U.K. In particular, the consolidation follows principles defined in France by the Conseil National de la Comptabilité and approved by a decree of the Ministre de l'Economie et des Finances in 1968. The extent to which consolidation practices differ in the EEC can be judged from a case study appended to a paper presented in October 1970 to the 6th Congress of the European Federation of Financial Analysts Societies at Montreux.[7] From the same inputs, accountants in various countries produced the following varying outputs (all figures are Swiss francs):

	Consolidated Annual Surplus	*Consolidated Total Assets*
Germany	27,522	612,018
Belgium	25,217	609,372
France	24,971	603,257
Britain	25,219	609,372
Netherlands	25,086	624,659

In the German Federal Republic the present position is that only domestic subsidiaries *have* to be consolidated, the inclusion of foreign subsidiaries being optional. It is interesting to note, however, that Farbenfabriken Bayer AG, one of the few German companies quoted on the London Stock Exchange, publishes not only a set of normal German financial statements but also what it calls *Bayer World* accounts, 'prepared in accordance with recognised international accounting practices'.

An area in which change is more likely to affect British and Dutch accounting than French and German is *uniformity*. The French *Plan Comptable Général* is the most striking example. First published in 1947 and revised in 1957, its requirements are imposed by law on the nationalised industries (an important sector of the French economy) and on State-controlled or subsidised firms and organisations. Decrees of 28 December 1959 and 13 April 1962 prescribe the eventual extension of its field of application to all industrial and commercial enterprises. There is no equivalent national plan in Germany though uniform charts of accounts are widely used. Uniformity expresses itself rather in the model balance sheets and profit and loss accounts and detailed valuation provisions set out in the Companies Act, 1965. (Uniformity is considered at greater length below.)

In all nine members of the enlarged EEC *company and tax legislation* play an important though sometimes indirect role in financial reporting. There are significant differences of detail, however. It is only in German company law that one finds the kind of provisions set out above. The French law of 24 July 1966 contains only generalities; the British Companies Acts of 1948 and 1967, and the Dutch Act on Annual Accounts of Enterprises (1970)[8] concentrate on disclosure rather than prescription. The accounting philosophy of the former is expressed by the phrase 'true and fair view', and of the latter by the phrase 'fairly and systematically' (*getrouw en stelsmatig*).

The extent to which taxation laws affect reports to shareholders also varies. In Britain there is no compulsion to follow tax rules in published financial statements, but there is no doubt (to give but one example) that the main reason for the almost complete non-use of the last-in first-out method of stock valuation is that it is not available for tax purposes. In France, on the other hand, fiscal benefits cannot be obtained unless appropriate entries are made in the accounts intended for the shareholders.

While all members of the EEC have an organised accountancy profession its influence varies greatly, being much stronger in Britain, the Netherlands and Germany than in France and Italy (see Chapter 4). Only in Britain is there an Accounting Standards Steering Committee. It would be difficult in most other EEC countries for an independent professional body, not backed by any statutory authority, to attempt to determine financial accounting principles and practice in the way that the British accountancy bodies are currently doing.

Uniformity in company financial reporting

The authors of the proposed fourth directive on company law harmonisation seem to assume that a major purpose of company financial statements is to help shareholders make investment decisions (see Chapter 5). What are the implications of this?

If company financial statements are to be of help to shareholders deciding which company to invest in, it is important that they should be prepared and presented in such a form that: (a) meaningful comparisons of the statements of one company with those of others are possible, (b) a misleading impression is not given of a company's profitability and financial status.

The second point is as important as the first. It is clearly no good establishing rules which lead to perfect comparability of irrelevant and misleading information. It follows that it is essential that all companies:

1. Make adequate disclosure of relevant information.
2. Agree and act on the same concepts of income measurement and asset valuation.
3. Adhere to those concepts consistently with time.

Standards of disclosure are in general higher in Britain than in continental Europe. The requirements of the proposed fourth directive are, however, with the two exceptions mentioned in Chapter 5, reasonably in line with current British practice. It is now being recognised in Britain that agreement on concepts of income measurement and asset valuation is just as important as disclosure. A sometimes heated controversy has taken place around such words as 'comparability' and 'uniformity'. What do these words mean? Comparability, it is suggested, merely means consistency of accounting treatment of like items, not only for individual companies through time, but also for all companies at any one point in time. Comparability is not the same as uniformity, but it is difficult to see how it can be achieved without some degree of uniformity.

Mueller[9] has usefully distinguished three kinds of uniformity. At the book-keeping level there is the 'uniform chart of accounts'. This is 'a classification device. It assigns classes and subclasses to account categories and provides general guidelines on how appropriate account classification is to be achieved for each account appearing in a given system of accounts'. Such a chart can be extended to become a 'uniform plan of accounting' which includes rules for the reporting of accounting data to users of financial information. Both charts and plans can be national or sectional. Adding rules of asset valuation and income measurement which go beyond mere book-keeping procedures, one moves from a uniform plan to 'uniform accounting', of which the best example is the French national accounting plan. This prescribes, for instance, that cost in inventory valuation shall always be interpreted to mean 'weighted average cost' (a rule not always adhered to in practice).

Does this give comparability? Not really, since weighted average cost may not fit all situations. Instead, what is needed is *uniformity of principle*, i.e. like procedures for like circumstances. Paradoxically, this sort of uniformity can also be regarded as *diversity*: not diversity of principle, but *diversity of procedures*. We are thus led to uniformity of principle, combined with a *justifiable* diversity of procedures. This will give true comparability, i.e. comparability of information which is worth comparing. The contents of the proposed fourth directive imply mainly 'uniform accounting', but with no guarantee of 'uniformity of principle' and no means by which it could be obtained.

Harmonisation at the international level is to some extent an extension of uniformity at the national level. If, at the latter, one believes that every company should be free to choose and apply its own accounting principles in its own way, then international harmonisation obviously has few attractions. It comes easiest to countries such as France where uniformity—at least of the rather superficial kind described above—has already been partially achieved.

Regulation of the accountancy profession

The accountancy profession in most continental European countries is more subject to government regulation and less independent than the profession in the U.K. The British profession, despite a not entirely unmerited reputation for conservatism, has shown itself during its relatively short history capable of adapting fairly rapidly to new social and economic needs. The original work of the members of the accounting societies founded from 1854 onwards was bankruptcies, liquidations, and trusteeships. Towards the end of the nineteenth century there was an increased emphasis on auditing. During World War I, taxation replaced bankruptcy as the most important branch of work, after auditing, in most accountants' offices. Cost and management accounting grew rather more slowly: partly, perhaps, because the newly recognised professionals were anxious not to compromise their prized social status as gentlemen by descending to the factory floor and becoming employees. Times have changed, and management accounting and consultancy is now regarded as the glamorous side of the profession.

The continental European experience has been rather different (see Chapter 4), and there has been some discussion within the EEC concerning the restriction of accountants who act as auditors of companies from undertaking other accountancy services such as management consultancy and taxation work. The Institute of Chartered Accountants in England and Wales issued a statement in 1971 strongly arguing against such a restriction.[10] At the time of writing, the situation is still rather uncertain but the following paragraph translated from the French text of the explanatory notes appended to the proposed fifth directive on company law harmonisation is of interest:

> The laws of some member states regard it as incompatible with the demands of independence that persons not forming part of the personnel of the company but acting continuously for the company and being paid for so doing should be its auditors. On the other hand, in other member states it is permitted and current practice for a person to combine the positions of auditor and adviser of the same undertaking. This difference in law is not abolished by the directive.[11]

Conclusion

If the only criterion for Britain's entry into Europe was the short-run effect on the British accountancy profession one could be forgiven for having doubts about the wisdom of entry. The wider and longer-run view is more cheerful. An accountancy profession can only flourish within the framework of a healthy and expanding economy. If, as the writer believes, the only chance of achieving this for Britain is to join the EEC, then accountants will clearly benefit from entry. But it will not happen automatically. There is a lot of hard work ahead.

Notes

1 R. Brown (ed.), *A History of Accounting and Accountants*, Edinburgh: Jack, 1905, p. 271.
2 The curious should consult E. Peragallo, *Origin and Evolution of Double Entry Bookkeeping*, New York: American Institute Publishing Co., 1938, pp. 112–120; J. -H. Vlaemminck, *Histoire et Doctrines de la Comptabilité*, Brussels: Editions du Treurenberg, 1956, pp. 175–180; and, surprisingly, R. H. Inglis Palgrave, *Dictionary of Political Economy*, London: Macmillan, 1894, vol. 1, pp. 165–7.
3 D. Solomons, 'The Historical Development of Costing', in his *Studies in Cost Analysis*, London: Sweet and Maxwell. 1968,
4 E. Schmalenbach, *Dynamic Accounting*, London: Gee, 1959, twelfth edition translated from the German by G. W. Murphy and K. S. Most.
5 See P. Lauzel, *Le plan comptable français*, Paris: Presses Universitaires de France, 1967, 2nd edition, especially Chapter 20.

[6] G. G. Mueller, *International Accounting*, New York: Macmillan, 1967.
[7] The paper is reproduced as Chapter 7 of the present book.
[8] A bilingual Dutch and English version of the Act was published by the Nederlands Instituut van Registeraccountants in 1972.
[9] Mueller, op. cit., Chapter 4.
[10] Institute of Chartered Accountants in England and Wales, *Against the Restrictions of the Services Auditors May Carry Out*, July 1971. See also J. P. Grenside, 'Freedom of Practice in EEC', *Accountancy*, June 1972.
[11] *Proposition d'une cinquième directive tendant à coordonner les garanties qui sont exigées dans les Etats membres, des sociétés, au sens de l'article 58, paragraphe 2 du Traité, pour protéger les intérêts, tant des associés que des tiers en ce qui concerne des sociétés anonymes ainsi que les pouvoirs et obligations de leur organes.* Presented by the European Commission to the Council of Ministers on 27 September 1972.

7 Consolidation of Company Accounts in Europe

A paper[1] presented at the 6th Congress of the European Federation of Financial Analysts Societies, Montreux, October 1970.

Members of the international preparatory committee were:

C. Stalder, Zurich, chairman
P. Costis, Geneva
R. Henggeler, Winterthur
P. Hügle, Zürich
F. Stoll, Zürich
Dr. W. Wirth, Zürich
R. Debroux, Brussels
H. L. Gans, Luxembourg
E. Fernandez Pena, Madrid
D. B. Knox, London
E. A. M. R. Laane, Amsterdam
J. Løken, Bergen
E. Schwartzkopff, Cologne
F. Simmonet, Paris
N. Urbain, Brussels

Throughout this chapter 'consolidated accounts' means a comprehensive statement of the assets and earnings of a group of legally independent companies which form a business unit and which are controlled by a single management. Such consolidated accounts are made up by adding together the balance sheet and profit and loss account items of the individual companies, while eliminating inter-group operations. They are based on the individual accounts of the individual subsidiaries, and not on accounts especially drawn up according to a different set of accounting standards applicable only to the consolidated figures.

Our work on the problems which this raises is divided into three sections: *Basic theoretical questions.* This is a list of the chief problems encountered in consolidation; it attempts to summarise current opinions in Europe on the main problems without taking a particular view of them. *Questions and answers.* Here we have set out in the left-hand column a list of questions, and against them, answers from the members of working parties of investment analysts in eight countries. The last column gives their joint opinion of the practice at which companies should aim. From these answers it is possible to see what response the enunciation of the 'basic theoretical questions' has aroused, and how far the actual practice of consolidation has progressed in Europe so far. *Case study*. This comprises a practical problem of consolidating the accounts of a Swiss-controlled group, as it was put to the various national analysts' working parties; and the treatments of the figures which each of them proposed.

Basic theoretical questions

Principles of consolidation

Object of consolidation

Accounts showing the financial position and development of a number of companies which are separate legal entities, but which together form an economic unit under central management (i.e. a group). These accounts may refer to the past, the present and also to the future.

Purpose of consolidation

Better management of the group and its legally independent members with regard to finance, liquidity, profitability, etc. (i.e. internal purpose).
Fuller information for the proprietors, i.e. the shareholders of the group (i.e. external purpose)

Conditions for consolidation

(a) The same fiscal closing dates for the companies of the group under consideration. (b) A uniform system of valuation of assets within the group. (c) A uniform system of accounting within the group.

Scope of consolidation

Consolidation dependent on extent of ownership

With certain exceptions it is agreed that the inclusion of a group company in the consolidation depends in the first place on the extent of financial involvement between the parent company and the subsidiary company in question, and secondly, on the extent of the actual power of the parent company over this subsidiary company. Opinions differ, however, on the definition of the financial involvement and the power required. They can be classified under the following groups:

1. Consolidation of the accounts of subsidiary companies, in which the parent company owns at least:
   (a) 50% of the risk capital,
   (b) 51% of the risk capital,
   (c) 75% of the risk capital,
   (d) another percentage of the risk capital.
2. Consolidation of the accounts of subsidiary companies, in which the parent company owns at least:
   (a) 50% of the total share capital or registered share capital,
   (b) 51% of the total share capital or registered share capital,
   (c) 75% of the total share capital or registered share capital,
   (d) another percentage of the total share capital or registered share capital.
3. Consolidation of the accounts of subsidiary companies in which the parent company owns at least:
   (a) 50% of all votes,
   (b) 51% of all votes,
   (c) 75% of all votes,
   (d) another percentage of all votes.
4. Consolidation of the accounts of subsidiary companies whose operations are important for the group as a whole, e.g. those whose turnover or net profit forms a certain minimum percentage of that of the group or of the parent company.

Contrary to the difference in opinions regarding the criterion for deciding on inclusion in consolidation, there is full agreement that in case of consolidation, the exclusion of minority interests in the net assets and net profit of a subsidiary company is solely dependent on the extent of the ownership of the risk capital.

Consolidation dependent on geographical situation

As with regard to the extent of ownership required, there is also disagreement on the question of whether subsidiary companies abroad or in certain countries should be consolidated. The following opinions are presented:

In so far as the extent of ownership requires consolidation, all subsidiary companies are to be consolidated, irrespective of their geographical situation.

Only those subsidiary companies are to be included in the consolidation that are situated in countries with politically and economically stable conditions. In general, this limitation aims towards the exclusion of those subsidiary companies situated in less industrialised countries (the so-called under developed countries).

Only those subsidiary companies are to be included in the consolidation that are situated in countries from which assets and net profits can be transferred without hindrance.

Only those subsidiary companies are to be included in the consolidation that are situated within the same country as the parent company.

Consolidation dependent on activity

However desirable the consolidation of subsidiary companies operating in the same field of business may indisputably be, it is contested where, through consolidation, subsidiary companies with different activities would be combined. The following views have been expressed:

Only subsidiary companies with the same activities are to be consolidated. Consolidation of subsidiary companies with different activities is firmly rejected.

All subsidiary companies are to be consolidated whose functions are essential for the activity of the group as a whole, irrespective of what are considered to be their individual activities. All other subsidiary companies, on the other hand, which do not contribute to the essential activities of the group, and whose activities are different, are to be excluded from the consolidation.

As the over-all results achieved by the group and the total assets available in the group represent the most important data for the shareholder of the parent company, all subsidiary companies should always be consolidated, irrespective of their activities.

The extent of consolidation for subsidiary companies not 100% owned by the group

There are also varying points of view on the procedure in the case of subsidiary companies that are not 100% owned by the group. These can be grouped as below:

Independently of what percentage of a subsidiary company is owned, all the items on the balance sheet and the profit and loss account of this group are—in so far as consolidation is appropriate according to the criteria previously mentioned—to be *fully* consolidated. The interests of other owners of the subsidiary company, i.e. the so-called minority shareholders, are to be shown as separate items in the capital and net profit of the subsidiary company, and thus also in that of the group (full consolidation).

The items on the balance sheet and the profit and loss account of the subsidiary company are–in so far as consolidation is appropriate according to the criteria previously mentioned– to be consolidated only in proportion to the share of the subsidiary company's risk capital held by the parent company.

Elimination of minority interests in capital and net profit of the subsidiary company, and with it in that of the group, is superfluous (quota consolidation).

Implementing the consolidation

The purpose of the consolidation is to obtain as exact a reflection as possible of the assets, financing, and results of an economic unit composed of a number of legally independent companies under central management. This results in the requirement—so far undisputed—that for consolidation, only those items are to be brought together that can influence the external image of the group. All the items which affect only internal relations, which appear in the individual accounts of the parent and subsidiary companies, are therefore to be eradicated.

The consolidation of turnover (profit and loss account)

All sales between companies in the group, no matter in which direction they are made, are to be omitted in the consolidation, i.e. they are to be deleted under expenditure as well as under income. In order to avoid the accounting differences which can result from delivery expenses (transport, insurance, customs, etc.), it is an advantage to take the amount charged in his invoice by the supplier belonging to the group.
Those deliveries which are treated by one subsidiary company as sales, but by another not as expenditure or an increase in stocks *but as an addition to fixed assets* are to be excluded from turnover and to be shown separately *as the value of internal production of fixed assets.*

Consolidation of other items of income and expenditure, with the exception of investment income (profit and loss account)

As with internal deliveries, all other internal services—irrespective of the direction of their flow—are to be excluded from the consolidation. These will be mainly interest on loans outstanding between companies in the group, licence fees, administration expenses, shares in expenditure on research, etc. Their treatment leads to no differences of opinion, or to other difficulties.

Consolidation of investment income and profits (profit and loss account)

Income from subsidiary companies included in the consolidation is also to be excluded. Its treatment also, does not lead to differences of opinion or to difficulties. On account of the exclusion of investment income, which may represent a part or the whole profit of a subsidiary company, the profit itself is always to be fully included in the consolidation. This leads to no differences of opinion, or to difficulties in cases of 100% participation.

When dealing with subsidiaries which are less than 100% owned, i.e. the profit of subsidiary companies in which minorities still participate, opinions do differ, however, The following points are noted:

According to their position in relation to the group, the minority shareholders of the individual subsidiary companies differ from the shareholders of the parent company in that they have no influence over the group as a whole. Those responsible are only the shareholders of the parent company, while the minority shareholders of the individual subsidiary companies do not play a much more important role than creditors, as a result of their limited participation from the group's point of view. For the group and the shareholders of the parent company, their interest in the profits of the subsidiary company is equivalent to a debt to a third party. Thus minority interests are to be shown as creditors' claims (theory of interests).

According to their position in relation to the group, the minority shareholders of the individual subsidiary companies differ from the shareholders of the parent company only in the extent of their interest. Both are cases of capital that has been invested in the group for the purpose of realising a profit. Thus the interest of minority shareholders in the profit of a subsidiary company when it is consolidated is to be shown in the same way as that of the shareholders of the parent company. The former is merely to be separated from the latter, and listed as a special item (theory of uniformity).

Consolidation of debts (balance sheet)

In the consolidation, debts outstanding between group companies must be fully excluded, irrespective of their mode of origin, i.e. for one they are to be deleted as a credit (assets side), and for the other as a debit (liabilities side). Both the question of consolidation of debts as well as the procedure to be followed are undisputed.

Consolidation of stocks (balance sheet)

In so far as stocks have not been accumulated through deliveries from other group companies, no difficulties are involved in their consolidation, nor do they give rise to differing points of view. However, there are difficulties in accounting if the value of the goods supplied by a group company as shown in the consignee's stock includes not only the supplier's overheads, but also its profit. The latter, since it has not in effect been made in the external turnover of the group, must be removed from the net profit of the group. In the case of the stocks of 100% owned subsidiary companies, this gives no rise to difficulties, nor are there any varying opinions on the procedure.
Where, however, ownership is not 100% the following question leads to differing points of view: What proportion of the delivery included in the stocks of another group company can be regarded as external turnover, and to what extent this proportion affects minority shareholders. The following opinions should be distinguished:

The consolidation should exclude only that share of the profit made by a supplier belonging to the group on goods held in stock within the group which corresponds to the proportion of the subsidiary company owned by the group. The share corresponding to the interests of minority shareholders can be regarded as realised, and included in the value of stocks, since the corresponding part of the delivery is external turnover (theory of interests).

All profits made by a supplier within the group on goods held in stock within the group are to be excluded. As this exclusion results in a reduction of the net profit, and with it also of the company's net assets, this amount must be deducted proportionately from the share of the group as well as from that of the minority shareholders of the relevant subsidiary company (theory of uniformity, first case).

All profits made by a supplier within the group on goods held in stock within the group are to be excluded. However, the reduction in net profit and with it also in the company's net assets which result is to be charged fully only to the parent company's interest, and not to that of the minority shareholders (theory of uniformity, second case).

Consolidation of fixed assets (balance sheet)

With regard to fixed assets which have not been supplied by group companies, there are no difficulties. In the case of fixed assets received from within the group—as for deliveries of goods—those items must be excluded which represent a profit for the supplier belonging to the group. This correction is necessarily also applied to depreciation. Although the corresponding accounts could turn out to be complicated, no problems and differences of opinion arise where the group owns 100% of the subsidiary company owning the fixed assets. In other cases opinions differ. The following points of view have been put forward:

The minus correction to fixed assets and depreciation, resulting in reduced net assets and higher net profit, is to be effected for subsidiaries less than 100% owned only to that extent which corresponds to the proportion of the subsidiary company in question owned by one group. The minority shareholders' interests are not to be corrected, on the assumption that this represents external turnover (theory of interests).

The minus correction to fixed assets and depreciation, resulting in reduced net assets and higher net profit, is made in full. The minority shareholders' interests in the net assets and in the net profit of the relevant subsidiary company, as well as that of the group, are reduced or increased proportionately, as applicable (theory of uniformity, first case).

The minus correction to fixed assets and depreciation, resulting in reduced net assets and higher net profit, is made in *full*, and exclusively added to the group's share of the net assets and deducted from the group's share of the net profit. The minority shareholders' interests in the net assets and in the net profit of the relevant subsidiary company remain unchanged (theory of uniformity, second case).

Consolidation of shareholdings and net assets (balance sheet)

It has not been disputed that in the consolidation the value of shareholdings in subsidiary companies included in the consolidation is to be set off against their consolidated net assets, deducting minority shareholders' claims. This usually results in a difference. If this difference is positive, i.e. if the consolidated value of the net assets of the subsidiary is greater than the value shown for the holding in it, in the accounts of the parent company, it is shown as a special item in the net assets of the group. If the difference is negative, i.e. if the book value of the shareholding in the parent company's accounts is greater than the consolidated net assets of the subsidiary, it is shown as 'goodwill' on the assets side of the group's balance sheet under the item 'intangible assets'. The negative difference is rather rare, and is limited to the case of new acquisitions.

In general, attempts will be made to write off goodwill of this type within the shortest possible time. While there are no longer any great differences of opinion in essential questions about dealing with the differences resulting from consolidation, two schools of thought have formed on the question of how to identify the iterests of minority shareholders in the net assets of subsidiary companies. They necessarily correspond with remarks already made in connection with the consolidation of net profit:

The interests of minority shareholders in the net assets of subsidiary companies do not represent net assets of the group, but the group's debt to the minority. The interests of such minority shareholders are therefore to be shown among the group's debit items (theory of interests).

Besides the parent company's shareholders, the minority shareholders in subsidiary companies have also put capital into the group. Their interest is only distinguished from that of the parent company's shareholders by its limited extent. It is not therefore to be shown as a debit, but as an interest in the group's net assets attributable to the minority shareholders, and not the parent company's shareholders (theory of uniformity).

Consolidation when there are interlocking shareholdings

The presence of interlocking shareholdings within a group complicates the operation of consolidation, without on the whole changing it appreciably. For any subsidiary company must necessarily represent the parent company from which the consolidation must originate. In case of complicated conditions the procedure is the following: all inter-group relations are set out in an organisation chart which illustrates the system of shareholdings. Steps may be taken towards consolidation on this basis.

If the same procedure applies as in the case of groups without interlocking shareholdings, opinions differ in one special case. This is the instance of interlocking shareholdings between the parent company and one or more subsidiary companies. Views represented are the following:

In the case of interlocking shareholdings between the parent company and individual subsidiary companies, the same procedure is to be followed as previously, i.e. inter-group relations are set out in an organisation chart. The shares of the parent company held by the subsidiary company are regarded as being a small shareholding in a third company, and shown in the balance sheet of the group as a non-consolidated trade investment.

In the case of interlocking shareholdings between the parent company and individual subsidiary companies, that part of the parent company's capital which is held by subsidiary companies is to be regarded as being re-purchased by the parent company. In this way, consolidation is effected from the point of view of the parent company's shareholders outside the group, and the shares of the parent company held within the group are regarded as not being issued.

The choice of the rate of exchange and dealing with rate of exchange fluctuations when consolidating foreign investments

With regard to the choice of the rate of exchange there are the following possibilities, if for the time being rate of exchange fluctiuatons are disregarded:

1. Choice of a fixed book rate which is to be used for consolidation over a period of years. This may be the simplest course.
2. Choice of a current rate valid as at the date of consolidation, i.e. at the date on which accounts which are to be consolidated are closed.
3. Choice of an average rate, based either on the mean of several rates over the whole period, or on the mean of rates at the end of the consolidation period.

Whereas these possibilities for the choice of the rate of exchange are only of slight influence on the accounts of the group as a whole, there are great differences which result from rate of exchange fluctuations. To assess their effect exactly it is necessary for an interim balance sheet be made by the group companies affected on the date of the change. The resulting loss through devaluation, or the gain through revaluation, for the group may then be ascertained on the basis of this interim balance sheet. The profit and loss account, however, does not influence this result, as it refers not to the particular moment of the parity change, but to the period before this change. The exchange profit or loss will more readily be shown in the balance sheet. As far as the method of determining this is concerned, opinions differ, the following points of view being put forward:

All items in the balance sheet of the subsidiary company whose country has experienced a parity change are converted to the new rate, and the difference arising as compared with the previous net assets is regarded as a profit or a loss through the parity change. If the country in which the parent company is situated changes its rate of exchange, the loss or the gain is reflected by a special account which encompasses all the foreign subsidiary companies.

Out of the balance sheet items of a subsidiary company whose country has experienced a parity change, only those of *current assets* and *liabilities* are converted to the new rate of exchange, while the old rate of exchange is used for that of fixed assets. In this way a figure for net assets is obtained which differs from that before the parity change. The difference represents the loss or the gain of the group resulting from the parity change. If the parity change takes place in the country of the parent company, a corresponding account is to be opened which encompasses all the foreign subsidiary companies. This procedure of converting fixed assets at the old rate is based on the view that the fixed assets, as expressed in the rate of exchange of the parent company's country, still have the same value for the parent company, even after a parity change.

Questionnaire and answers

Questionnaire and answers

Basic Questions

	Germany	Belgium	Spain	France
1. Do the notes on the theory of consolidation meet with your approval as regards				
(a) Matter?	Yes, provided that the internal items are set off against each other.	Yes, apart from the difficulty of producing consolidated future estimates.	Yes.	Yes.
(b) Purpose?	Yes, but the main accent is put on the external aims: better information for shareholders and creditors—both present and possible future ones—, for the general public and the staff—.	*Internal aim:* To produce several consolidated balance sheets per annum. *External aim:* The main purpose is not only to inform shareholders but also the general public.	Yes.	Yes.
(c) Conditions?	The German legislation requires: (i) the company has to belong to the group, (ii) the leading company has to be a limited company or a company with private limited liability if one of the subsidiaries is legally constituted as a limited company, (iii) the conformity of the accounting period has to be guaranteed, if necessary through interim accounts. The legislation does not require an identical method within the group of valuing the assets. The validity of each set of accounts is	An identical closing date is not absolutely necesary since a consolidation could as well be based on interim accounts. An identical basis of valuation of assets within the group seems to be necessary. If foreign legislation (depending on the countries) imposes different means of valuation, the accounts of the subsidiaries have to be adjusted. A uniform method of accounting is desirable but not absolutely necessary since the difficulties resulting from it are solvable.	Yes.	Such a harmoni is desirable, bu no fundamenta condition.

.	Norway	Netherlands	Switzerland	Analysts' recommendations
	Yes.	Yes.	Yes.	Yes.
we emphasise rmation for e outside.	Yes.	Yes.	Yes.	Yes.
dard accounting s are not lutely necessary ur practice, are disregarded e interests of ker production ccounts). rwise the only ciple is to add ther like and	Yes.	Yes.	Yes.	Yes.

	Germany	Belgium	Spain	France
	accepted. To make consolidation possible, a consistent structure of balance sheets is necessary—without it, it would hardly be possible.			
2. What are the criteria for the consolidation: (a) Share of the risk capital? (b) Share of the registered capital? (c) Share of the voting rights? (d) Other criteria?	According to paragraph 329, section 2, of the German Companies Act: consolidation if more than 50% of the registered capital is held by the group. There will be no consolidation if the subsidiary is of little importance or if meaning fulness of the group's balance-sheet would be affected. Consolidation has to take place in the case of less than 50% controlling power when the subsidiary is located in the home country and when consolidation results in a different view of the group's assets and profits.	The characteristics such as risk capital, registered capital, and share of voting rights are all valid if any reach a minimum of 51%. If this share is below 51% consoidation should be imposed if the parent company has issued medium-or long-term loans which exceed a certain percentage of its own capital and reserve. The criteria of turnover and net profit are not in general used. However, the information of the public should be kept in mind. Therefore, consolidation should also take place in the case of less than 50% controlling power if it changes the group's results by 10% or more.	(b) more than 50%.	(b) and (c) if the parent company, is in legal conti of the subsidiarie (direct and indire as well as of the group's associate companies (50% a more), is fulfilling an important financi and economical r participations in companies of whi the group has mc than one-third of voting rights (33–50%), has an actual participation in c of closed compan (10–50%). d) Companies wh realise a turnover and which have capital and reserv of over FF 1 mill The same is effe for companies wh capital and reserv equal at least 5% the parent compa capital and reserv See also answer t question 5 of 'Ba questions'. A certain latitude should, however, left to the group order to consider special situations

K.	Norway	Netherlands	Switzerland	Analysts' recommendations
:ording to the : more than 50% :quity capital or lity to control ointments to the ard. In the U.K. re is a growing ctice of consol- ting major ociated companies which less than 50% eld. Some exam- s of voluntary solidation with than 50% con- lling power are: C and Rank.	The Companies Act requires that a minimum of $66\frac{2}{3}\%$ of the registered capital is retained by the group. A new suggestion recom- mends 50% of the registered capital or the voting rights.	50% of the reg- istered capital.	In general more than 50% of the registered capital. If the par- ticipation is below 50%, consolidation should only take place when the com- panies belong economically to the group and if their management is guaranteed by the parent company or another subsidiary.	Consolidation of subsidiaries in which 50% of the reg- istered capital is held with indication of minority interests in turnover, cash flow, and net profit.

	Germany	Belgium	Spain	France
3. Which companies are excluded from the consolidation for geographical reasons: (a) All foreign companies? (b) Foreign companies with high currency and political risks? (c) None?	The consolidation of a foreign subsidiary is not required by law; it is an entirely voluntary act by the parent company. In case of special monetary or political risks consolidation can take place, but these risks should be mentioned.	Only subsidiaries whose profits and/or the proceeds of a possible liquidation could not be repatriated. (Explanatory note is necessary.) If only the profits can be repatriated they should be included in the consolidated profits.	(c)	(c) except for extr ordinary facts (wa etc.). Weak currencies, the blocki of capital by a foreign governmer and inability to repatriate capital a not necessarily an obstacle to consolidation.
4. Which companies are excluded from the consolidation because of their activities: (a) All companies whose activities differ from those of the majority of the group? (b) As(a), with the exception of those companies fulfilling an important role within the group? (c) None? (d) Companies in liquidation?	Only companies which would affect the meaningfulness of the group's accounts are excluded from consolidation. Different activities are no obstacle to consolidation.	The area of activity should not be taken into consideration, only the controlling power exercised by the parent company. Exception: companies with purely complementary activities, when the parent company has invested only a very small proportion of its assets in them.	(a) (d)	(c) if the parent is financial holding company. (a) if the parent is listed as an industr or commercial holding company. (d) in principle no
5. In the event of a holding being less than 100%, is it (a) Completely consolidated, indicating the minority interests? (b) Consolidated *pro rata*?	(a)	*Majority interests:* (a) *Minority interests:* Consolidation proportional. Consolidation as (a) would be acceptable with a minimum share of 33% and if the remaining 67% is widely spread.	(a)	(a) for companies which legal contro between 50% and 100% is held. *mise en équivalence* (replacement of the net bookvalue of th holding by the shar of the parent company in the capital and reserve of the subsidiary) for participations between 33 and 50%, possib 10 to 50%.

.K.	Norway	Netherlands	Switzerland	Analysts' recommendations
basic U.K. rule hat accounts must published for *all* sidiaries, *either* consolidating n or by setting n out in detail arately. But direc- have a limited retion to omit sidiaries whose solidation would of no real value to reholders.	(c) if the other criteria are fulfilled.	(c) although a foot-note seems to be necessary if the risks are higher. %	(c)	(c) yet if special risks are involved a footnote is abso-lutely necessary.
3 above ne subsidiaries y be exempt from ishing accounts wn up on normal ciples, e.g. be- se they are banks; parate statement st be published them.	(c)	All companies whose activities derive from those of the group in general.	(c)	(c) but a breakdown should be given for turnover, cash flow, and net profit from the various main activities (e.g. in-dustrial, financial and commercial activities).
	(a)	(a)	(a) mainly.	(a)

	Germany	Belgium	Spain	France
				(b) for closed cor panies for which participations exc 10%.
Profit and Loss Account				
1. Is a consolidated profit and loss account: (a) Published on the basis of the external group turnover? (b) Published on the basis of the gross return or a similar unit? (c) As (b), indicating external turnover? (d) Not published, but consolidated figures are issued (which?)	Three forms are possible according to § 332 and § 333 of the Companies Act: (i) separate statements of external and internal turnover, (ii) only external turnover has to be published, internal figures can be set off against one another, or indicated by changes in stocks and similar times, (iii) the group profit and loss account in simplified form (§ 333) requires publication of external turnover figures. But this permits internal turnover to be offset by changes in stocks and so forth, as well as in other expenditures shown under (ii) an entry which does not have to be split up exactly.	The publication of the results (operating as well as profit and loss account) has to be as detailed as possible; it will be based on turnover, after eliminating all internal transactions. The company will have to publish: consolidated turnover (consolidated at 100%) according to the general regulations for consolidation, domestic turnover, and turnover attributed to the subsidiaries abroad.	(a) If the parent companies are American companies.	(a) is recommend
2. Which internal group transactions (e.g. deliveries of raw materials, manufactured goods and equipment, payments of interest, patents, overheads and others, such as dividends)	Costs and revenues resulting from group transactions are to be eliminated.	All group transactions are excluded.	Inter group transactions are eliminated at the time of consolidation.	All mutual transac tions which influe the net profit at ti of consolidation.

.	Norway	Netherlands	Switzerland	Analysts' recommendations
ıover figures are standard; some ps publish total , some sales to l parties, and e both. The nan type of unt which begins *Bruttoertrag* is ıown. A few panies publish kdowns of wages supplies costs, these are not al- s on the same s as the profit loss account. latter show de- iation, interest and received, t hire, investment me, directors' auditors' remu- tion, profit be- tax, tax, minority ·ests, dividends and proposed, other appro- tions (special 'isions, such as pension funds, also be shown).	According to the Companies Act it is not necessary to publish a consolidated profit and loss account (unfortunately, the new proposal does not include this either). Most of the companies quoted on the Stock Exchange do produce a consolidated profit and loss account, and the tendency is to publish it on the basis of external group turnover.	(c) is usual.	The profit and loss account (on a consolidated basis) is very rarely published; in general it is based on the turnover with third parties.	(a) with an indication of the added value, or a very detailed profit and loss account in order that the added value can easily be calculated.
traditional tice to exclude group trading its, except for proportion of n attributable to ority interests, there is a movet towards includ-	All internal group transactions are excluded.	All internal group transactions have to be excluded.	In general, internal group transactions are excluded.	Elimination of all internal transactions if this does not require excessive work in comparison with the result.

	Germany	Belgium	Spain	France
are excluded from the consolidation (or which are included?)				
3. How is the participation of minority shareholders in the net profit indicated? (a) As a part of the group's expenses? (b) As a part of the group's net profit? (c) In another way?	The participation of minority shareholders in the profit and loss has to be separately indicated before the item 'profit/loss'.	The participation of minority shareholders is indicated as follows: FB 100000000 group profit FB 20000000 minority participation FB 120000000 consolidated profit.	The share of the minority shareholder interests is deducted to determine the consolidated net profits.	The consolidated profit is divided into: share of the gr (majority interest share of minor shareholders.
4. Is the cash flow (net profit, depreciation, etc.) of the group easy to distinguish in the consolidated profit and loss account?	Yes.	Basically yes.	In most cases yes.	Yes, for the cash flow before dedu tion of minority i terests; it is more complicated for t cash flow of the group (majority i terest).

Balance sheet

	Germany	Belgium	Spain	France
1. Is a consolidated balance sheet drawn up on the basis of: (a) A standardised valuation of the assets of all the group companies? (b) A valuation of the assets of group companies, which is determined by the book value of these holdings? (c) The results of the group companies, according to their own valuations?	Standardised valuation methods for all the items of the balance sheet are not required by law. The figures in each individual balance sheet can be accepted.	(a)	Consolidated balance sheets are drawn up on the basis of the balances of the various companies belonging to the group if those are made out according to the book-keeping principles usually accepted.	(b) The Conseil tional de la Com tabilité recomme that adjustments made before consolidation in ord to harmonise as much as possible items which will consolidated. Los on assets must be ascertained for ev company in the group. It is diffic to take into consideration increas in the value of

	Norway	Netherlands	Switzerland	Analysts' recommendations
rofits on trans- ns at market , and adjust- s for minority ests are becom- ss common.				
	Various practices, the tendency is alternative (b).	Various practices, the tendency is alternative (b).	Various methods, with a slight preference for (b).	(b)
	Not always, but it has become better in recent years.	Yes.	Generally yes, except for insurance companies.	Special items should make it possible to calculate the cash flow on a *pro rata* basis, as opposed to the group's fully consolidated cash flow.
	(b)	(a)	Usually (a), sometimes (b) considering partial adjustments.	Figures are necessary which reflect economically and truly the assets and earning power of the group.

	Germany	Belgium	Spain	France
				assets, since a re- valuation can on take place with t agreement of the authorities.
2. In the valuation of stock, is the profit on internal deliveries among the various group companies excluded?	Yes, the cost of sale should be excluded too.	Yes.	Yes.	Yes, both in the consolidated bal. sheet and in the consolidated pro and loss account
3. In the valuation of holdings, is the profit on deliveries of capital goods among the various group companies excluded?	Only if it concerns an asset acquired out of the ordinary way of supplying or pro- ducing. Through this, the law seeks to prevent that the group's profits being increased artificially (e.g. through the sale of property at an excessive price).	No, the acquiring company should use the acquisition price in order to calculate depreciation.	Yes.	Yes.
4. In the event of there being minority shareholders, does the exclusion of profits, mentioned in question 2 and 3 above, result in a reduction of the participations in the net profit and reg- istered capital for: (a) Both the mi- nority shareholders as well as the group? (b) Only the group?	The exclusion of profits affects only the group's profits. These measures do not affect the minority share- holders' participation.	(a)	(a)	(b)
5. Are the differ- ences resulting from	(a) The relating items are called	(b)		(a) item: differen on consolidation.

	Norway	Netherlands	Switzerland	Analysts' recommendations
the answer to ion 2 under it and loss ac- t' is applicable	Yes.	Yes.	There are different opinions because the relationship be- tween the work required and the result is sometimes out of proportion.	Elimination is desir- able if this does not require excessive work in comparison with the result.
the answer on tion 2 under it and loss ac- t' is applicable	In theory yes, in practice uncertain.	Yes.	Basically no, this case very seldom occurs.	Elimination is desir- able if this does not require excessive work in comparison with the result.
	(a) and (b), depend- ing on the company.		(a)	(b)
for differences ng, for example,	(a) In most cases, using the nominal	(b) is usual in most cases.	(b) in most cases.	(a) or (b)

	Germany	Belgium	Spain	France
consolidation: (a) Indicated as a separate item (which?) (b) Set off against the shareholders' funds?	*Konsolidierungsausgleichsposten* or *Konsolidierungsrücklage.*			
6. How are the parcipations of minority shareholders indicated in the registered capital of the individual group companies: (a) As group debts? b) As a part of the registered capital of the group? c) In another way?	On the liabilities side as a compensatory item for the part belonging to the minority shareholders. Legally and in practice this item is part of the equity. But it does not belong to the shareholders of the main company.	e.g. Capital of the parent company Retained earnings of the group Capital and reserves of the group Minority interests Total capital and reserves.	This is listed as a special item before the capital and reserve. Some companies include it in the equity.	As share of the t capital and reser e.g. majority and minority interests together. The wo ing 'group' only means the majori interests.
7. In the case of bilateral holdings, are shares of the parent company which are in the hands of an affiliated company regarded as not outstanding, and therefore deducted from the indicated capital of the parent company?	These shares are considered as group assets and appear as a separate item in the current assets. Setting them off against the issued equity is not possible under German law.	According to Belgian law no company is entitled to hold its own shares. In the case of a group it seems to be more logical to hold the shares of the parent company in the group's portfolio than to cancel them.	Yes.	Yes; but the Act commercial companies (24.7.1965 prohibits a Frenc limited company from holding sha of a company if this latter holds in return more th 10% of the capita of the first one.

Conversion rates for the consolidation of foreign group companies

1. Which conversion rates are used: (a) Internal group book rates? (b) Rates corresponding to the currency parities? (c) Rates of the official foreign exchange market?	(c) at the buying date for fixed assets, longterm loans and advances. (c) for current assets and short term liabilities. (e) yearly average exchange rate for the calculation of	(c) for hard currencies the rate applied at the closing date for the accounts, with the possible exception for fixed assets, for which sometimes (a). In the case of weak currencies it is	(c) in principle.	In general the off conversion rate a the day of closing the accounts. The problem of chosir a conversion rate has not been solv

	Norway	Netherlands	Switzerland	Analysts' recommendations
different ac- ting dates; or differences ıg for example, een cost of isition of a diary and book : of net assets.	method: difference between book value and value of assets in subsidiaries.			
separate item, ıally placed een the capital reserves of the ıt company and group's long term s.	(c) in most cases, as a separate item between debt and equity.	e.g. Capital of the parent company Retained earnings of the group Capital and reserves of the group Minority interests Total capital and reserves.	(a) in most cases or (b) depending on the company.	(b)
but because of ictions placed ssues of shares ıbsidiaries this ıw almost un- wn in the U.K.	In some cases deducted from the capital, in other cases shown as asset.	Yes.	This case seldom occurs in Switzerland.	In general they should be deducted unless they are a temporary investment.
fixed assets, version rates at time of acquisi- are commonly l. at the end of accounting od for the other ıs of the balance t.	(b)	(b) and (c) are usual. In the case of weak currencies it is advisable to create provisions for depreciation. This should be done in any case.	(c) rate of the closing date (the majority of companies). A considerable minority of companies proceed according to (a).	(b) or in some specified cases different rates, provided that the reason for using another rate is mentioned (e.g. to insert the lowest possible value (d), if this rate of ex-

	Germany	Belgium	Spain	France
(d) Free market rates? (e) In the case of (c) and (d) rates from the end of the financial year, or average annual rates?	costs (except for depreciation) and revenues. In case of considerable discrepancies between the official exchange rate and the black market rate the latter should be applied.	advisable to create provisions for depreciation. This should be done in any case.		
2. Are the same conversion rates used for the conversion of the items on the profit and loss account and the balance sheet? If not, which rates, and why, for which items?	No, see above.	Yes, in case of hard currencies; adequate provisions should be made if this is not the case.	Yes, if no modification of the currency parity has taken place.	In general the sa conversion rates all items of the balance sheet. F subsidiaries locat in countries with weak currency it possible to use fo fixed assets the ra valid at the time of acquisition (w corresponding ac justments for depreciation), and the items in the profit and loss account the aver of all monthly figures converted the month-end ra or if impossible, a balanced avera rate.
3. Following a change in parity of the domestic and/or foreign currency (currencies), are the old or new rates used for converting: (a) Current assets? (b) Invested capital? (c) Debts? (d) Profit and loss account?	The use of internal exchange rates for fixed assets and long-term liabilities requires the same rate for the calculation of depreciation. Any changes in exchange rates are in this case evened out. For short term assets and liabilities, the latest exchange rates. Average rate is re-	New rates for (a), (c), and (d), duly considering the above restrictions. An exception could be made for (b) rates at the buying date.	(a) and (c) new rate Old rate for (b), on condition that exchange value in the currency of consolidation does not exceed the market or liquidation value of the assets. Old rate for (d), otherwise the rate at time of modification of the currency parity.	(a) new. (b) new (with exc tions, see answer to (a).) (c) new. (d) new (with de tions).

	Norway	Netherlands	Switzerland	Analysts' recommendations
ill used but end is to use the end of the nting period.				change is lower or higher than the lower or the highest official intervention point.
ce sheet items l year rates. and loss ac- s have, in the often been at ge rates for nting periods estion, but is a movement ds end-year for all items, t remittances en members of oup, which nverted at the actually used.	Yes.	The official rates of the foreign exchange market for remittances. Rates corresponding to the currency parities for items of the balance sheet and the profit and loss account.	Most of the companies use the same rates, yet for the profit and loss account there are various adjustments.	If there was no change in parity during the fiscal year in question, the same rate for all items of the balance sheet and the profit and loss account.
ew rates. ormally at the n force when sset was ac- d, although this s problems in rting subse- depreciation es, and for full stency between ce sheet and and loss ac- s the new rate pler.	(a), (b), (c), and (d) new rates.	(a), (c), and (d) new rates. (b) various practices.	(a), (b), (c), and (d) new rates with some exceptions for (b) old and internal rates. (d) average or adjusted rates.	(a), (b), (c), and (d) new rates, but the effect on fixed assets and net assets of a change in parity should be shown. (Increase of earnings and decrease of losses due to changes in parity should be added or charged direct to reserves and not shown as a special item in the

	Germany	Belgium	Spain	France
	commended for items in the profit and loss account.			
Questions on the information policy with regard to consolidation				
1. Are group companies, which are not included in the consolidation, indicated in the annual report?	All domestic companies of the group have to be listed in the annual report; those included in the consolidation require special mention.	Yes.	It is necessary to indicate exactly which companies are consolidated and which are not.	Sometimes.
2. Is a change in the number of companies consolidated indicated in the annual report?	Yes, provided that a comparison with earlier balance sheets is of importance.	Yes.	It is not necessary to mention any change in the number of consolidated companies. Yet it is customary to list them all in the annual report.	In general, yes.
3. Are details given in the annual report on: (a) The cost of fixed assets? (b) The replacement value? (c) Previous economically required depreciation? (d) Previous bookkeeping depreciation which does not correspond to that economically required?	Although this is required from an individual limited company this is not required from a group.	(a), (b), (c), and (d) yes.	(a) generally no. (b) generally no. (c) generally yes. (d) yes.	(a) yes. (b) no. (c) no. (d) no.
4. Does the annual report mention auditing of the consolidated accounts: by whom, how and how far?	Yes.	No.	No.	No.

K.	Norway	Netherlands	Switzerland	Analysts' recommendations
new rates. new rates.				profit and loss account.)
;, this is required law.	The reader of the annual report is in most cases left with bad information on this point.	Yes in most cases, but sometimes no.	The information of the shareholders is in this respect not always complete.	Indication of unconsolidated group companies is necessary.
ports must list significant osidiaries, with proportions of ir equities held.	Same as above.	Yes.	Not always.	Indication of any changes in the extent of consolidation is absolutely necessary.
yes, unless acred before 1948. no; the Comies Act, 1967 's that directors st publish the rent market value land and buildings t is substantially 'erent from that own in the counts. No. Yes.	In some cases as additional information to the balance-sheets.	Various practices.	(a), (b), (c), and (d) in general no. Some companies publish the insured value of their fixed assets.	All four figures are desirable.
s (a note will made when the counts of a foreign osidiary are not lited.)	No.	In general yes.	In general no.	Checking by independent chartered accountant desirable.

	Germany	Belgium	Spain	France
Questions about attitudes to consolidation				
1. What is the state of consolidation in your country? Has there been any legislation on: (a) The need for consolidation? (b) Individual questions concerning consolidation?	The Companies Act, 1965 declared consolidation obligatory for the 1967 accounts for the first time. It contains detailed instructions regarding the figures to be published. The consolidated balance-sheets published before this date often differed from these instructions.	There is no liability to publish consolidated results. A insignificant number of companies publish consolidated figures without using a standard method.	At an early stage. There are neither legislation nor any legal rules about consolidation.	An increasing num ber of companies publishes consolidated accounts (1967: 22, 1968: 4 1969: 64). No lega decree exists. In th long run the recommendations the Conseil Natio de la Comptabilit (1968) and the Patronat Français should favour the of a standard meth
2. Does tax legislation: (a) Favour consolidation? (b) Restrict consolidation? (c) Neither (a) nor (b)?	The tax authorities ignore consolidated accounts.	(b) due to the Belgian attitude towards the tax authorities. This attitude will continue to sustain an opposition to publishing consolidated figures.	(c)	The tax authoritie attitude towards r valuation of the assets has a retard influence because companies fear disadvantageous effect if the real figures were published. A special remission of taxes 1965 enables appr priate companies fix their taxable n profits on the bas of those of the ent group without sho ing the consolidat accounts.
3. Do the stock exchange authorities encourage consolidation by: (a) A positive attitude alone? (b) Certain regulations governing admission to the stock exchange? (c) Other measures?	(a)	Only the Bank Commission has officially requested consolidated accounts. The Stock Exchange Commission certainly shares the same point of view but has not yet taken action.	No compulsory stipulation exists from the Stock Exchange Committee.	As of 1.7.1971, th Security Exchange Commission plans request consolidat documents accord to the principles c the Conseil Natio de la Comptabilit from all companie coming to the cap market.

K.	Norway	Netherlands	Switzerland	Analysts' recommendations
advanced as any- ere in the world. e liability regard- consolidation es back to the mpanies Act, 1948 ich first made olication of sidiaries' ac- unts obligatory.	The Companies Act, 1957 requires that the parent companies publish the figures of the holdings of which they possess at $66\frac{2}{3}\%$ of the capital. The new proposal is 50% of the capital or the voting rights.	There are neither legal obligations nor instructions regarding consolidation. Many leading companies publish consolidated results yearly.	There is no legal obligation regarding consolidation. More and more, companies accept their duty to consolidate; the number of companies publishing consolidated accounts or statements increases little by little.	
	(c)	(c)	(c) except groups with an important part of their activities in a foreign country. These companies will not publish a consolidated tax charge, in order to prevent any fallacious interpretation.	
need for encour- ment beyond that vided by the law.	The Stock Exchange Commission has taken a neutral stand.	(a)	The Stock Exchange Commission has only recommended consolidated accounts.	Intervention by the national and European Analysts' associations with stock exchange authorities to ensure that all companies whose shares are traded on stock exchanges publish consolidated accounts.

	Germany	Belgium	Spain	France
4. Is the attitude of the trade unions to the publishing of consolidated accounts: (a) A help? (b) A hindrance? (c) Neutral?	Certainly, the trade unions are interested in the publishing of consolidated balance sheets although officially they did not recommend it.	To date the trade unions have not dealt with this question.	Neutral.	(b) in the short te but(a) in the long term. Due to the staff's involvemen in self-financing, t companies will be obliged do deal wi the trade unions o behalf of the entir group which agair proves the usefuln of consolidated accounts,
5. Have consolidated accounts made the development of share prices more logical?	In order to answer this question a lot of time for observation is required. The reply cannot be given right now.	To date this statement does not seem to be true. Once the general public is better informed on these questions the influence should be stronger.		Yes.

K.	Norway	Netherlands	Switzerland	Analysts' recommendations
	(c)	(c)	To date the trade unions have not taken an official stand.	
s.	In general, this is a question of information, terminology, and the company's desire to solve the problem. There is a clear tendency towards emphasising the consolidated figures.	Consolidated accounts have a positive impact on share prices and make them, generally, more logical.	At present an answer is impossible since Switzerland has only just started having consolidated accounts.	

Case study

Composition of the Swiss metal-working and machinery concern which is taken for the case-study.

	Holding (%)
Parent company Switzerland (CH)	
Finance company Switzerland (CH)	100
Subsidiary company Switzerland (CH)	100
Subsidiary company Belgium	100
Subsidiary company Germany	100
Subsidiary company Great Britain	100
Subsidiary company Spain	46.1

Rates of exchange used for the internal group transactions

100 FB	=FS	8.70
100 DM	=FS	108.--
1 £	=FS	12.10 before devaluation
		10.40 after devaluation
100 Ptas.	=FS	7.20 before devaluation
		6.20 after devaluation

Study plan

Consolidation of the whole group of companies on the basis of the indivi-ual annual statements of account of the group companies and using the consolidation sheets which have been included to reduce unnecessary work. A brief explanation should be given of the figures contained in the 'Adjustments' column, to simplify the evaluation of the results.

Balance Sheets 30.9.68

	Parent co. Switzerland Published	Parent co. Switzerland Internal	Finance co. Switzerland Published	Finance co. Switzerland Internal	Subs. co. Switzerland Published	Subs. co. Switzerland Internal
(in thousands)	FS	FS	FS	FS	FS	FS
Assets						
Cash and marketable securities	7243	7243	61788	61788	6490	6490
Accounts receivable	30150	30150	–	–	30507	30507
(Spanish subsidiary)	(–)	(–)	–	–	(482)	(482)
(other group cos.)	(–)	(–)			(6644)	(6644)
Miscellaneous current assets	3408	3408	1390	1390	8054	8054
Inventories	67582	67582	–	–	61274	61274
Total current assets	108383	108383	63178	63178	106325	106325
Land and buildings	51764	51764	–	–	51756	51756
Machinery and equipment	73725	73725	–	–	50440	50440
Investments	–	–	96815	96815	–	–
(in Spanish subsidiary)			(2679)	(2679)		
(in other group cos.)			(94136)	(94136)		
Holdings	9051	9051	12923	12923	403	403
(in Spanish subsidiary)	(–)	(–)	(550)	(550)	(–)	(–)
(in other group cos.)	(9051)	(9051)	(7457)	(7457)	(–)	(–)
Total fixed assets	134540	134540	109738	109738	102599	102599
Liabilities						
Current liabilities	23194	23194	769	769	54783	54783
(Spanish subsidiary)	(–)	(–)	(–)	(–)	(162)	(162)
(other group cos.)	(3744)	(3744)	(–)	(–)	(11480)	(11480)
Long-term debt, incl. pension funds	36032	36032	20644	20644	69392	69392
(to group companies)	(–)	(–)	(–)	(–)	(29942)	(29942)
Common stocks	52500	52500	10000	10000	24800	24800
Earnings retained and surplus	117917	117917	135607	135607	55772	55772
Stockholders equity (value of holdings)	170417	170417	145607	145607	80572	80572
Total assets	242923	242923	172916	172916	208924	208924
Profit and Loss Account						
Net sales	176659	176659	–	–	166395	166395
Inventory changes, own manufacture, etc.	+ 10523	+ 10523	–	–	+ 6951	+ 6951
Production	187182	187182	–	–	173346	173346
Supplies from group companies	– 21527	– 21527	–	–	– 38895	– 38895
Own production	165655	165655	–	–	134451	134451
Manufacturing costs (after deduction of group internal deliveries and depreciation)	– 88935	– 88935	–	–	– 76002	– 76002
Selling and administration costs, incl. taxes	– 40058	– 40058	+ 1272	+ 1272	– 35980	– 35980
Licence fees, patent and interest payment to/from group companies	+ 1553	+ 1553	+ 4179	+ 4179	– 1962	– 1962
Bonus (to staff)	– 6779	– 6779	–	–	– 4722	– 4722
Gross operating profit	31436	31436	5451	5451	15785	15785
Depreciation	– 18156	– 18156	–	–	– 11608	– 11608
Net operating profit	13280	13280	5451	5451	4177	4177
Sundry expenses and returns, incl. exchange differences	–	–	+ 445	+ 445	–	–
Annual surplus	13280	13280	5896	5896	4177	4177

ubsidiary co. Belgium		Subsidiary co. Germany		Subsidiary co. U.K.		Subsidiary co. Spain	
ublished	Internal	Published	Internal	Published	Internal	Published	Internal
FB	FB	DM	DM	£	£	Ptas	Ptas
6149	6149	938	938	0,7	0,7	21146	21146
11763	11763	13034	13034	562,0	562,0	32322	32322
(–)	(–)	(–)	(–)	(–)	(–)	(–)	(–)
(5839)	(5839)	(583)	(583)	(34,3)	(34,3)	(2616)	(2616)
1455	1455	2065	2065	4,1	4,1	5283	5283
3428	3428	22367	22335	932,6	932,6	42648	42648
22795	22795	38404	38372	1499,4	1499,4	101399	101399
7154	8575	15485	16645	569,2	523,5	40303	43750
499	644	7647	24340	426,3	615,6	55211	63000
–	–	–	–	–	–	–	–
–	–	–	–	–	–	–	–
–	–	–	190	–	–	–	–
			(–)				
			(–)				
7653	9219	23132	41175	995,5	1139,1	95514	106750
21551	21551	10484	10484	786,5	786,5	48910	48910
(–)	(–)	(–)	(–)	(–)	(–)	(–)	(–)
(17322)	(17322)	(457)	(457)	(46,5)	(46,5)	(7767)	(7767)
3600	3600	32622	32622	1942,2	1942,2	51015	51015
(–)	(–)	(31875)	(31875)	(1942,2)	(1942,2)	(43209)	(43209)
1000	1000	16000	16000	500,0	500,0	62522	62522
2469	3931	998	19139	– 725,4	– 579,9	25852	36408
3469	4931	16998	35139	– 225,4	– 79,9	88374	98930
30448	32014	61536	79547	2494,9	2638,5	196913	208149
17057	17057	89569	89569	2281,3	2281,3	161604	161604
+ 1556	+ 1556	– 1921	– 855	+ 106,2	+ 106,2	+ 5466	+ 5466
18613	18613	87648	88714	2387,5	2387,5	167070	167070
– 11877	– 11877	– 27417	– 27417	– 787,1	– 787,1	– 1959	– 1959
6736	6736	60231	61297	1600,4	1600,4	165111	165111
– 3479	– 3479	– 31052	– 31052	– 1044,7	– 1044,7	– 105873	– 105873
– 14023	– 14023	– 18400	– 18400	– 438,3	– 438,3	– 26222	– 26222
+ 13054	+ 13054	– 3856	– 3856	– 8,4	– 8,4	– 10562	– 10562
– 149	– 149	– 1714	– 1714	–	–	– 1608	– 1608
2139	2139	5209	6275	109,0	109,0	20846	20846
– 311	– 207	– 3777	– 4973	– 117,4	– 119,3	– 12232	– 11552
1828	1932	1432	1302	– 8,4	– 10,3	8614	9294
–	–	–	–	–	–	–	–
1828	1932	1432	1302	– 8,4	– 10,3	8614	9294

Solutions

Balance-sheets

Country	Germany	Belgium	France
Figures used	published	published	published
Method of consolidation in Spain: balance-sheet and profit and loss account	100%	100%	*mise en équivalence*
Conversion rates	new rates for short-term items and old rates for long-term items	new rates	new rates
Assets (in 1,000 fr'.s)			
Cash and marketable securities	78,387	78,387	77,076
Accounts receivable	74,823	74,823	73,464
Short-term investments	15,580	15,580	15,252
Inventories	165,654	165,653	163,009
Total current assets	334,444	334,443	328,801
Land and buildings	130,655	129,285	126,786
Machinery and equipment	141,600	140,325	136,900
Other fixed assets	–	–	2,679
Holdings	5,319	5,319	5,319
Mise en équivalence	–	–	2,772
Total fixed assets	277,574	274,929	274,456
Total assets	612,018	609,372	603,257
Liabilities in 1,000 fr.s			
Current liabilities	84,803	84,804	82,415
Long-term debt	97,808	97,730	97,246
Current liabilities and long-term debt	182,611	182,534	179,661
Minority interests	3,481	3,241	–
Issued capital	52,500	52,500	52,500
Earnings retained and surplus	117,917 227,987	345,880	117,917 228,208
Stockholders' equity	398,404	398,380	398,625
Annual surplus	27,522	25,217	24,971
Total assets	612,018	609,372	603,257

U.K.	Norway	Netherlands	Switzerland
published	internal	internal	internal
100%	100%	*Mise en équivalence*	*pro rata*
new rates	new rates	new rates	new rates; fixed assets at old rate
78,387	78,387	77,076	77,680
74,823	74,823	73,463	74,090
15,580	15,580	15,252	15,403
165,654	165,619	162,975	164,194
334,444	334,409	328,766	331,367
129,285	130,400	127,687	130,029
140,324	160,816	156,910	160,048
–	–	2,679	1,444
5,319	5,524	5,524	5,524
–	–	3,093	–
274,928	296,740	295,893	297,045
609,372	631,149	624,659	628,412
84,801	84,804	82,414	83,515
97,731	97,730	97,246	97,469
182,532	182,534	179,660	180,984
3,240	3,615	–	–
52,500	52,500	52,500	52,500
303,784	325,318		
		367,413	371,105
42,097	42,096		
398,381	419,914	419,913	423,605
25,219	25,086	25,086	23,823
609,372	631,149	624,659	628,412

Profit and Loss Account in 1,000 fr.s

Country	Germany	Belgium	France
Figures used	published	published	published
Method of consolidation in Spain	100%	100%	*mise en équivalence*
Conversion rates	average rates U.K. 10.70 Spain 6.40 (depreciation excluded)	new rates	new rates
Net sales	476,026	475,017	464,997
Inventory changes, etc.	17,020	16,977	16,639
Production	493,046	491,994	481,636
Supplies from group companies	− 99,612	− 99,373	− 99,251
Own production	393,434	392,621	382,385
Manufacturing costs (after deduction of group internal deliveries and depreciation)	−216,730	−216,204	−209,641
Selling and administration costs, incl. taxes, net of tax reclaims	−102,226	−102,042	−100,416
License fees, patent and interest payments to/from group companies	− 24	− 1	+ 655
Bonuses	− 13,468	− 13,464	− 13,365
Gross operating profit	60,986	60,910	59,618
Depreciation	− 36,172[1]	− 35,850	− 35,092
Net operating profit	24,814	25,060	24,526
Sundry expenses and returns, incl. exchange differences	+ 2,759[2]	+ 445	+ 445
Annual surplus	27,573	25,505	24,971
Minority interests	− 51	− 288	–
Annual surplus (consolidated)	27,522	25,217	24,971

Notes:

[1] Since in England and Spain fixed assets are converted at the old rate this rate is also applied for depreciation.

[2] Contains some differences in consolidation.

[3] Accounts are based on sales, not production, and thus neither sales nor costs include the increase in stocks of finished products. By deducting the

U.K.[3]	Norway	Netherlands	Switzerland
published	internal	internal	internal
100%	100%	*mise en équivalence*	*pro rata*
new rates	average rates UK: 10,6125 Sp: 6,325	new rates	new rates (depreciation excluded)
375,646[4]	376,162[4]	464,998	469,616
–	16,352[5]	17,790	17,947
–	392,514	482,788	487,563
–	–	– 99,251	– 99,307
375,646	392,514	383,537	388,256
–199,228*	–216,559	–209,641	–212,667
–102,042*	–102,168	–100,416	–101,165
	–	+ 654	+ 353
– 13,465	– 13,465	–13,365	– 13,411
60,911	60,322	60,769	61,366
– 35,849*	– 37,109	– 36,394	– 36,724[7]
25,062	23,213	24,375	24,642
+ 445	+ 2,183[2]	+ 711[6]	– 819
25,507	25,396	25,086	23,823
– 288	– 310	–	–
25,219	25,086	25,086	23,823

items marked with * an asterisk from the net proceeds a trading profit of FS 38,527,000 is established.

[4] Internal deliveries are deducted from net turnover.

[5] To allow for devaluation, stocks are adjusted in the U.K. and Spain.

[6] Of which 266, share of profits of unconsolidated Spanish company.

[7] Since in England and Spain fixed assets are valued in Swiss francs on the basis of a central investment index, depreciation is calculated in Swiss francs too.

The debate at Montreux

Members of the panel were:
C. Stalder, Swiss Credit Bank, chairman; J. Brunner, Aluminium Suisse SA, Zurich; R. Debroux, Société Générale de Banque, Brussels; P. Hügle, Swiss Reinsurance Company, Zürich; E. Kilgus, professor, Zürich University; D. B. Knox, Grieveson, Grant & Co., London; E. Schwartzkopff, Sal. Oppenheim Jr. & Co., Cologne; and F. Simonnet, Caisse des Dépôts et Consignations, Paris.

The debate was staged to discuss in slightly greater detail some of the differences of opinion which had emerged in the answers to the questionnaire and the treatment of the case study. It dealt with the following problems in particular: (1) Should consolidated accounts be based on individual companies' published figures or on so-called 'internal' ones? (2) What holding should the parent have in a subsidiary for it to have to be consolidated? (3) Should any subsidiaries be excluded because of their nationality, their activities, or the currency in which they operate? (4) Which exchange rates should be used when rates have changed during the accounting period?

In general, the panel's remarks on these points diverged little from the answers to the questionnaire. There were the same differences of opinion, some of them significant, but it none the less seemed reasonable to believe that they could be reconciled, and that this could be done on the basis of the 'analysts' recommendations' published in the questionnaire.

Professor Kilgus pointed out that methods of valuing assets could not but be to some extent subjective. Thus 'internal' figures could be as deceptive as published ones. What he thought really mattered was full information about the methods by which the figures had been produced; particularly when there had been any change in the basis of accounting from one year to the next, detailed notes were needed.

P. Hügle thought it would be unfortunate to pursue this argument to the point of accepting any basis of valuation whatever. The long-term objective must be to get figures which came as close as possible to economic reality. Subjective though they might be, there were prudent accounting rules already established in the industrial world. Of course, the accounts which were being published contained a lot of undervaluations, and if they were to give all the help which they should these ought to be eliminated.

F. Simonnet described the very comprehensive French legal rules for the inclusion of companies in consolidated accounts, and said that they were complicated and at times barely comprehensible. Simpler rules would be better and would encourage the production of consolidated accounts. J. Brunner agreed. He thought what should really decide whether a subsidiary was included was whether its absence would make the accounts notoriously unhelpful; and that the rules should not be so strict that they produced over-frequent changes in the composition of the group and thus affected comparisons of one year with another.

Questions from the audience

One questioner asked about the lack of information about the credit-worthiness of the parent company when only consolidated group accounts were available. Professor Kilgus again went into the problem of valuing assets and said that a borrower's standing really depended on his expectations of future cash flow and profits, and that these could best be estimated from statements of the source and disposition of funds. Mr. Knox pointed out that in Britain the law required the publication of a separate parent company balance sheet: this also applies in Germany.

Members of the panel from countries in which consolidation is required were asked if bank and insurance companies also had to produce consolidated accounts. D. B. Knox and E. Schwartzkopff said that in Britain and Germany they did. F. Simonnet said that in France they were not yet compelled to, but that it had been recommended that they should. P. Hügle added that analysts naturally wanted consolidated accounts as much from them as from anyone else.

Another questioner doubted the value of amalgamating the accounts of businesses whose accounts differ substantially in structure, such as industrial and utility companies. The panel thought the best answer was to publish separate accounts in full for different activities; at least separate turnover and profit figures should be given, as is required in Britain by the 1967 Companies Act.

Other questions were in general answered in the terms of the commission's published report.

How to encourage the publication of consolidated accounts

The speakers agreed that the publication of consolidated account should be encouraged. Their general feeling was that at this stage it would be better not to try to obtain new legislation but to seek the help of the stock exchange authorities. This seemed to offer the best way to the *international harmonisation of accounting methods so badly needed in Europe; only this for instance, would make it possible to compare the consolidated accounts of different European groups in the same industry.*

The European Financial Analysts therefore put forward four basic principles which they consider essential:

1. Consolidation should include all subsidiaries of importance, including those abroad.

2. The number of subsidiaries included should be changed as little as possible, and changes should be fully explained.
3. Valuation methods should be as consistent and as close to reality as possible, and should be fully explained in the notes.
4. There should be separate accounts, or at least separate figures for the most important items, for sections of the group with widely different activities.

Notes

[1] Reproduced by kind permission of the European Federation of Financial Analysts Societies.

PART III

Industrial and Financial Developments

8 Industrial Policy in the Community

by A. T. McLEAN

The enlargement of the European Economic Community to include the United Kingdom, Ireland, and Denmark provides some interesting comparative economic and political statistics. Estimates based on 1970 figures[1] yield the facts in Table 8.1.

	EEC-9	*U.S.A.*	*U.S.S.R.*	*Japan*
Population (millions)	253.3	205.4	244	103.5
Area (thousand square miles)	590	3,600	8,800	143
Gross National Product ($000 million at market prices	626.0	993.3	288	196.2
Energy production (million metric tons coal equivalent)	500.2	2,151.4	1,386.1	71.4
Crude steel output (million metric tons)	138.0	122.1	116.0	93.3
External trade:				
Imports ($ million)	57,966	39,963	11,739	18,881
Exports ($ million)	54,259	43,226	12,800	19,318
Development aid (net flow of capital—official and private. $ million)	6,142	5,971	204	1,824
Motor vehicle output (millions)*	10.8	8.3	1.0	4.9
Computers in use (thousands estimated)*	26	80	7	9
Merchant fleet (million tons gross)	57.97	18.46	14.83	27.0

Note:

* Approximate figures only.

In many respects the Community compares favourably with the three other leading economic powers, land mass and energy production being the only 'unfavourable' comparisons. If Norway had decided to join the Community a significant contribution would have been made to geographical area and the size of the merchant fleet. On the whole, the bald figures may tend to give the unwary the impression that the enlarged Community should be a thriving industrial society. A better picture, however, may be obtained by looking at the Common Market's achievements in its years of existence.

Trading between the original Six increased rapidly from 1958 onwards, and by 1968 all existing tariff barriers between member states had been abolished and a Community customs tariff was introduced for third countries. The free movement of workers is at an advanced stage despite the existence of some remaining administrative obstacles. The free movement of capital has been advanced somewhat and value added tax has been introduced by all of the founder members. Economic expansion and rising standards of living are evident and key sectors of the economy growing rapidly. Yet in areas of advanced technology, matters seen to be less than harmonious. One commentator[2] has observed that bilateral collaboration in the aircraft industry was limping forward, that the multilateral European space programme was a flop and that Euratom, the joint nuclear research community of the member states, had been dying a lingering death for years. Yet another commentator[3] has concluded that key sectors of the economy seemed to be proceeding at a much faster rate towards internationalism than their own national governments, for the simple reason that a number of EEC countries seemed to prefer a national policy to safeguard their own interests—this is evident in a wide variety of support measures. The attempts, therefore, of industry threatened to founder on an inadequate realisation of earlier thoughts with regard to European integration.

No doubt with these criticisms in mind the Commission published in 1970 a statement of intent as a basis for thorough discussion within the Community, not only with the Parliament, Council, Economic and Social Committee, Consultative Committee of the ECSC ,and the European Investment Bank, but also with all groups representing economic and social forces.

Memorandum from the commission to the council

In presenting a memorandum to the Council on Industrial Policy, the Commission noted that the policy they recommended was deliberately orientated towards future expansion and progress in the widest sense. Rapid growth in production and consumption was also related to a better deployment of workers and improved living and working conditions. It recognised that industrial policy has to take account of the requirements of regional policy which aims at distributing economic activities evenly through the territory of the Community, thus avoiding excessive industrial concentration in particular areas. In presenting their report to the Council, the Commission emphasised some interesting aspects which had been taken into consideration in the preparation of the report.

Firstly, it sought an improvement in the conditions and dignity of labour. The necessary increase in productivity should not be achieved by a worsening of working conditions and an increase in the rate of work, but rather by organisation of a nature which not only reduces worker fatigue, but also develops job interest. Secondly, it required more active participation by workers in policy creation and organisation. The Commission seems to be convinced that industrial expansion could be accelerated by combining on one hand the concept of private enterprise, competition and the right to make profits with, on the other hand the influencing of economic development by commonly defined objectives between management and workers. Participation, the Commission maintained, was not only a requirement for human progress, but a factor of industrial efficiency.

Thirdly, it viewed the absence of harmonisation in the educational sector as an impediment to the freedom of movement and of establishment of managerial staff, and thus an obstacle to economic and industrial union. A call was made for closer cooperation between all European universities, for the mutual recognition of diplomas and for the harmonisation of methods and programmes. The reconciliation of humanistic and economic aims was emphasised as one of Europe's foremost missions.

Fourthly, the natural environment required protection. By failing to deduct from the value added by industry, the value such activity is destroying in the environment, national accounts concealed the extent of what are known as 'external diseconomies'. Common standards were therefore required in connection with the development of collective facilities, research into new appliances and products, and town and country planning. Thus European industrial policy should not aim exclusively at increasing the volume of goods put at the disposal of consumers but should also set itself the taks of improving the citizens' living conditions.

Finally, the Commission advocated a more even distribution of wealth throughout the world. They emphasised that the industrial development of the third world should be encouraged, as the Community would benefit if the number of its solvent trading partners increased. Such was the Commission's justification of the special efforts in favour of the European and African Associated States.

With these principles in mind the Commission devised the following course of action:

Achievement of a single market

The establishment of a single internal Community market demanded elimination of technical obstacles to trade, free access to public contracts, and the abolition of the tax frontiers within the Community. Substantial variation remained in national regulations designed to ensure the protection of workers, consumers, or the natural environment; such differences preserved the obstacles to intra-Community trade. These technical obstacles remained in existence mainly due to the slowness of the experts in removing them. It was apparent that there was a need to avoid uncoordinated national initiatives which could lead to the emergence of new technical obstacles, that common methods of analysis and standardisation were required and that a concerted attitude on the part of the member states was advisable.

The Commission also noted the practice of reserving public or semi-public contracts for national industries within each member state. Even though such practices were illegal from 1 January 1960, this effectively deprived certain key industries in the Community of the advantages of a large internal market. The Commission felt compelled to emphasise to member states that public buyers should be given careful instructions as to their duty to comply with the provision of the treaty, and the part they can play in achieving a single market by seeking the best supplier irrespective of nationality. Clearly the goodwill of buyers is important to the effective implementation of directives designed to ensure free access to public contracts.

The existence of tax frontiers was identified as a factor which kept certain markets closed. Therefore, firms' investment, sales and buying strategies could not be worked out in terms of the Common Market. To eliminate controls and compensatory frontier taxes, indirect taxation harmonisation was essential.

Unification of the legal, fiscal, and financial framework

The Commission noted that legal, fiscal, and financial obstacles still remained to frustrate firms wishing to extend their activities throughout the Community. The legal obstacles effectively hampered cross-frontier collaboration which is seen to be essential to the spirit of the treaty and also essential for industrial growth and strength to meet foreign competition. To overcome these hindrances the Commission considered it necessary that the proposed statute for the European Company should be adopted as soon as possible, subject to all matters contained in its articles being agreed to, or amended where necessary (see Chapter 2); also that all member states introduce legislation on corporate groups such as currently exists only in Germany, and that domestic company law be harmonised (see Chapter 1).

Investigation into the possibility of facilitating cooperation between public corporations and the possibility of adoption by all member states, or at Community level, of a *groupement d'intérêt économique* (GIE) statute, such as exists at present only in France, was recommended by the Commission.

As far as tax harmonisation was concerned, it was deemed to be of the utmost urgency that the Council adopt the directives on fiscal law relating to mergers and the rules governing parent companies and subsidiary companies which were submitted on 15 January 1969. Noting the absence of a common capital market, together with the difficulties stemming from the structure of national financial markets, the Commission suggested that the banking and finance machinery in most member states required modernisation, that the taxation system applicable to stock financing could be improved, and that an increased volume of capital from euro-bonds could be made available to Community firms (see Chapter 12).

Reorganisation of industrial structures

In this case the competitive economic challenge from third firms, was recognised; also, that Community firms should be able to face such a challenge. There was no doubt in the minds of the members of the Commission that a higher degree of concentration was required to ensure optimum development, but the dangers of national concentration within member states could not be ignored. At the same time, powerful firms from third countries had established considerable control over member state firms. The conjunction of the two phenomena—national concentration and acquisition by third country firms—could, if care were not taken, reduce or even wipe out the possibility of a common European development policy in the advanced technology sectors.

The Commission, therefore, considered it necessary: (a) To eliminate obstacles which make the formation of transnational European firms difficult, (b) To use for this purpose public funds for industrial development in the advanced technology centres. In this respect, trans-national firms were defined as not only those which spread their activities over several countries, but those whose capital and management came from several countries and whose decision centre is in Europe. It is of interest to note that the Commission were not contemplating setting up a public body such as the late-lamented Industrial Reorganisation Corporation of the U.K. to achieve its aims but envisaged both itself (using funds it administers under the Treaty of Paris) and the European Investment Bank offering financial facilities for the grouping of firms in different member states.

Technical developments, reorganisation of industrial structure, cross-frontier economic interpretation and economic development both by European and third country firms present a major challenge to the Commission and, as is clear from further appraisal of its report, they are almost an obsession.

Adjustment to changes

The Community's requirements, argued the Commission, must always be borne in mind when the rate of change is speeded up in order to secure industrial progress which, in turn, governs economic and social progress. If jobs are abolished through the process of change then new jobs must be created in more dynamic sectors. The industrial exploitation of technological innovations and forecasting combined with the strengthening of regional policy should be encouraged as much as possible. This includes a necessary improvement in management methods and the training of future executives and managers of firms.

Extension of community cooperation in economic relations with third countries

As the foremost trading power in the world, the Community has considerable responsibilities with regard to the expansion of world trade. Economic relations with third countries now extend to fields that had been scarcely opened up at the time of drafting the treaties and it is clear, according to the Commission, that Community solidarity is not sufficiently organised. The interests of the Community will naturally be safeguarded by the Commission in its economic and political relationships with third countries but this in turn requires that each member state should attempt to achieve a concerted attitude and joint action with its Community partners in the new fields of external economic relations.

This over all strategy of the Commission may, at first sight, appear reasonable, sensible and even sound to those concerned with the Community as an economic being. British industrialists, trade unionists, accountants, lawyers, tax planners and workers may, however, regard some aspects of this plan of action with some reservations. Dialogue will ensue from doubt, and from dialogue we have delay. And this, in some respects, is the story of the Community. Debate among the representatives of the founder member states is not noted for speedy adoption of directives and regulations. The Commission complained to the Council in its 1970 memorandum that the work of the institutions was considerably behind schedule because of the slowness of experts. Only one directive was approved in 1969, whereas 44 were prescribed in the programme.

In 1970 the Commission advocated an acceleration of the decision-making process but at the time of admission of the new member states there was no evidence to suggest that the process of harmonisation was gaining momentum. For example, no further directives on company law approximation have been adopted since the publication of the memorandum in 1970. Indeed, two more years may well elapse before the second directive under Article 54(3)(g) of the Rome Treaty is accepted. The dialogue clearly continues.

I would even venture to suggest that the process of equivalence in the Community may even decelerate when the U.K. introduces further dissension into the chambers of the Commission, Council, Parliament, and their attendant expert committees. The Commission, for example, is convinced that an acceleration of industrial expansion could be achieved by more active participation by workers in policy creation and organisation. This in itself must be the subject of considerable debate. The disciples of Mayo must surely regard Europe as their El Dorado but they are not noted for rapid decisions. Worker participation has existed for some considerable time in several of the founder member states, hence the recognition of supervisory boards and works councils as part of a future Community company system (see Chapter 3). These organs, however, are totally foreign to British company structures and hence, while admitting and admiring the potential of such bodies, I would predict that the British delegations might well delay the processes of equivalence even further.

As an additional illustration of future controversy it is evident from an appraisal of the British accounting press in the latter half of 1972 that hostile reaction to continental European methods of financial reporting and auditing was growing. The aggressive attitude of those who represent interested parties in the U.K. may well be reflected in the debating chambers of Brussels.

The Commission's memorandum, which in itself, was partly designed to provoke discussion and secure debate was unavailable in English in the U.K. until the spring of 1972. As a publication of some large size it has considerable content, much of which can never be covered in an appraisal such as this. Some aspects of it are, however, well worth further consideration.

Cooperation and concentration

While recognising that the cult of bigness was not a valid reason for encouraging a higher degree of industrial concentration in the Community, the Commision had to acknowledge that the transition from a national economy to a continental economy demanded some measure of cooperation, reorganisation, and concentration at the European level, which had until now been postponed. Lesser undertakings with new opportunities should set up new establishments, and expand. Existing legal, fiscal, and political differences between member states, however, were not conducive to a healthy system of cooperation and concentration necessary for the economic growth of the Community. The Commission thus regarded as a major objective the requirement:

> ...to adapt or introduce, national or Community legal provisions relating to company law, so as to allow companies in the Community to cooperate, to enter into contracts, to set up establishments or to merge,

while respecting the rules of competition, anywhere in the territory of the Community, as simply and with as great a legal security as in their own country;

...to adapt existing legal provisions to ensure that there is no fiscal inequality in the relations between companies and establishments active in more than one Community country;

...to reach a stage where industrialists realise what new dimensions and opportunities the Community is opening up for them;

...to establish within the Community a political climate favourable to development of ties of all kinds between companies in different member states.

The achievement of the objective depended on member states and the Commission taking a number of steps to facilitate establishment of subsidiaries, cooperation and mergers across frontiers inside the Community. The Commission were of the opinion that the legal merger between companies was not the only method of achieving cooperation and concentration within the terms of the Treaty of Rome. Some methods of association appealed to the Commission as being particularly suitable under certain circumstances.

Cooperation agreements

Many variations of cooperation agreement exist, the best known being joint purchase or sales contracts, research and development agreements, and specialisation agreements. An inquiry by the German section of the European Committee for Economic and Social Programming covered nearly 1,500 cases of international cooperation and showed that, of 850 examples of association for a specific purpose (disregarding licence contracts), a majority related to cooperation in marketing, with somewhat less relating to research and development and production respectively.

Cooperation agreements do not constitute concentration as they neither create an irreversible situation nor in most cases, even an organic link. Opinion would have it, however, that this form of cooperation may lead in practice to a certain degree of unity since economic units eventually tend to overlap and become more or less permanently interdependent. Cooperation agreements are seen as an essential stage prior to a more integrated collaboration between two or more firms because they allow the status and independence of the partners to remain intact and, therefore, they do not arouse the same psychological inhibitions as a merger or a takeover. The benefits and difficulties of collaboration can be estimated during this cooperative phase, which may be regarded as an essential test-bench for more extensive economic integration at a later stage.

One of the difficulties facing cooperative ventures is that of finance—a problem which is not easily solvable due to the independent structuring of ventures. If external finance is required over and above the joint resources a more formal method of integration may be required. Other difficulties may be created with regard to the rules concerning competition laid down in the European treaties (see Chapter 10). Many would assert that the rules of competition are such as to hinder the necessary efforts towards cooperation between firms in the Community. The Commission, however, has indicated that it had not the slightest intention of hindering the efforts towards cooperation. In a 1968 communication the Commission gave notice of its intention to encourage and facilitate cooperation between small and medium-sized firms, and also of its conviction that cooperation between large firms was both permissable and desirable.

Note that the decisions of the Court of Justice and the Commission have specified that Article 85(1) shall apply only when competition is restricted to an appreciable extent. Article 85(1) of the Rome Treaty prohibits in general all agreements which have as their object or effect the restriction of competition within the Common Market. The Commission has confirmed that certain categories of agreement would not be prohibited. Cooperation may also be exempted from prohibition under Article 85(1), when it can be shown that constructive aspects of the agreement outweigh the appreciable restriction of competition.

Intermediate froms of cooperation and concentration

Legal procedures in the founder member states allow firms to exercise one or more of their functions jointly. The legal status and independence of the participating companies are not affected by this flexible form of almost purely contractual cooperation. Despite the recognition of a legal personality, these joint ventures are more akin to cooperation than concentration. In fiscal terms this is expressed as 'fiscal transparence' in the sense that profits shared among the parties are considered to have been earned by them directly and would not be taxed at association level, thus considerably reducing the risk of double taxation.

In most circumstances, with regard to the rules of competition, these methods of association would be regarded as cooperative ventures rather than as examples of concentration. Among the best known examples in most of the founder member states are the *holding partnership* and *temporary partnership* which are associations without legal status, and which have been formed with a clearly defined objective in view. This occurs frequently in the field of public works.

Under Italian law the *consorgio* is an agreement between firms whose activities are related or identical; this allows considerable latitude with regard to the definition of decision-making bodies and the rules for operation.

In Germany the *Interessengemeinschaft* is an agreement between independent undertakings jointly pursuing one or more objectives, and sharing the resultant income and expense in an agreed proportion.

By far the most important type of association in this area is the *groupement d'intérêt économique* (GIE) which achieved legal recognition in France in 1967, and is liable to be adopted by the Community as an official half-way house between association and merger. Originally in France it was conceived as a 'betrothal' for large firms wishing to experience an economic relationship with a partner prior to making it official by merger. In practice, however, the GIE has been the vehicle of association of small to medium-sized firms and the Commission recognises a potential Community organ.

The GIE has extreme flexibility, permitting two or more companies of whatever size or nationality to achieve made-to-measure agreements to combine certain of their activities, provided that they do not merge all the activities of the parties to the agreement. Most firms who create GIE's do so simply because they wish to retain their independence while rationalising certain of their activities. Budding cartels, however, receive short thrift from the courts. The GIE has a legal status and can be adopted by all types of undertaking, including individuals, and does not necessarily require capital to set it up. Apart from formalities of registration as a business enterprise, it requires no preliminary administrative authority. It can also issue bonds, and must have an economic purpose: either a profit objective for its members or in some way to improve the results of its members. As an association it is not taxable as a legal person.

A contract in writing determines its organisation, which is very much at the discretion of the members. Within the terms of the contract, members in general meeting may make decisions affecting the management of the GIE within the terms of its objects. In its dealings with third parties it will be bound by the acts of any of its officers which are within its objects. In the event of failure of the GIE its members will be fully responsible for its debts.

Perhaps the greatest significance of the GIE is its ability to cross national frontiers, for example the initial studies on the European airbus were made by a GIE whose members were SNIAS, Fokker, and Deutsche Airbus. Cooperation across fronters is much to the liking of the Commission, and should the adoption of the European company (see Chapter 2) be delayed further than expected, we may well find the Community readily accepting the GIE as a vehicle to promote greater and speedier cooperation among member states.

Methods of concentration

Concentration of industry can arise in a number of ways. Firstly, by financial participation, when one company invests in another by an acquisition of shares either to secure control of the firm or to guide its policy. This method of acquisition is used extensively by Community companies, though not nearly to the same extent as British and American companies which typically have greater financial resources. In the opinion of the Commission, acquisition of a company's shares on the open market does not generally lead to the concerted policy needed to derive the greatest advantage from concentration despite the inevitable restructuring of management boards. The phenomenon of industrial holding companies and financial holding companies, between both Community companies and third countries, is noted. Serious difficulties arise, however, on the taxation of subsidiary company profits and of the amount of capital available.

Industrial groups, as recognised only in the German Companies Act of 1965, have also been created in the Community, where companies associate themselves in economic groups but remain separate legal entities. Problems of the liability of officers of companies associated with groups—problems including doubts about the protection of minority interests and creditors—have provoked the Commission into suggesting a directive laying down common principles for a body of law governing such industrial groups.

The greatest, and presumably the most desirable method of concentration is by merger when by complete amalgamation, constituent companies either both lose their legal identity and assume together a new one, or one of them is absorbed into the other. Such operations are virtually impossible between companies of different member states, as respective national company laws present obstacles which are difficult to overcome. A merger, for example, between a German company and a company of another nationality is not allowed because merger operations in Germany are subject to judicial control which could not be imposed on a foreign company.

A further complication would arise if a French company decided to combine with a German company to form a single entity in Germany. The control aspect of German law would be satisfied but, by French law, the French company must have the unaminous consent of its shareholders before moving out of French territory. If shares are widely held then the chance of consent is remote. If consent was forthcoming, a further complication arises, as by French law, a national company cannot amalgamate with another one in one simple move. Liquidation in one country and reconstruction in another is an essential prerequisite of a merger across national frontiers. This process is naturally time consuming and expensive. Furthermore, capital gains taxes on the liquidation may be prohibitively expensive, and no concessions are granted by the authorities in the case of cross-frontier mergers, as they are with national mergers, Penal taxation in other forms is a final discouragement to most types of transnational merger.

Conclusion

This appraisal of industrial policy in the Community is difficult to conclude simply because it is a large and complex subject embracing a wealth of ideas, visions, and proposals. One outstanding aspect of the Commission's memorandum is that of cooperation and concentration, and some aspects of their proposals have been described. The Commission clearly envisages a more efficient European industry through concentration, hence their concern over the slowness of harmonising the conflicting and impeding company and fiscal laws of the member states, and their enthusiasm for such organs as the supranational European Company and transnational *groupement d'intérêt économique*. However, it remains to be seen whether the advantages of concentration in the form of economies of large-scale production, marketing and distribution, and greater capacity for research and development can be achieved in the manner suggested by the Commission.

The Commission clearly identifies concentration with 'efficiency' and the United States' industrial record is frequently used as comparison. There are dangers, however, in drawing too fine a comparison, and creating from this an economic policy. Little has been said about the need to harmonise the law of contract throughout the Community. The lack of such equivalence must create commercial difficulties between industrial groups which policy encourages, and between customers and creditors. The United States has the advantage of a federal law of contract, despite the absence of a federal companies law.

The Commission should also be mindful of a recent American observation.

> The current merger movement...has done more than merely increase the concentration of industrial assets in relatively few multimarket corporations. There is evidence of important and increasing connecting links between this growing centralization of industrial resources in a few hundred vast corporations and the performance of competition in particular markets.[4]

This is seen to pose a serious threat to America's democratic and social institutions by creating a degree of centralised private decision-making which is incompatible with a free enterprise system. It would appear that the Commission will be faced with a singular task in balancing concentration and competition in the interests of the Community.

Notes

[1] European Community: The Facts. European Communities Press and Information. London 1971.

[2] Rene Foch, 'The Great European Technological Mess', *Vision*, November 1970.

[3] Dr S. C. Bakkenist, 'Industrial Growth in the EEC. up to 1980' *European Intelligence*, 2 December 1971.
[4] *Economic Report on Corporate Mergers*, Staff Report to the Federal Trade Commission, 1969, p. 5.

Bibliography

Industrial Policy in the Community: Memorandum from the Commission to the Council, European Communities Press and Information Office. London 1970.
D. Swann, *The Economics of the Common Market*, Penguin. London 1972.
Small Firms and the Common Market, Confederation of British Industry. 1972.
Vision – The European Business Magazine, SEPEG, 9 Rue Charles-Humbert, Geneva.
European Community. European Community Press and Information London.
European Intelligence., European Intelligence Ltd., Agroup House, 16 Lonsdale Gardens, Tunbridge Wells, Kent.

9 Mergers in Europe

by J. R. SMALL

There can be little doubt that one of the most exciting areas in industrial Europe over the next ten years will be the potential concentration of industrial power through mergers and acquisitions. One of the main purposes of the EEC might be seen to be the creation of a climate favourable to such mergers. Its expressed intent to deal with the needs for a European company, the harmonisation of taxation, uniform accounting principles, and common standards for the disclosure of information would seem to be designed to overcome some of the factors which restrict the development of large industrial units, particularly those which cross national frontiers. Even the EEC's desire to ensure fair competition through Articles 85 and 86 do not conflict with this. As E.M.G.A. Sassen, a former member of the EEC Commission has said:

> ... a reduction in the number of independent firms can intensify competition. Such mergers are in harmony with the objectives of Community competition policy for, to use a quotation from the United States Supreme Court which aptly describes the Commission's policy 'it is competition not competitors which the Act protects'.[1]

The difference in meaning between merger and acquisition is not always clear. The word merger means different things to different people, and here it is used as a general term for the creation of a larger industrial group, either through acquiring an existing organisation (takeovers) or merging with one of a similar size. There are, however, other methods or industrial penetration—through subsidiary companies and trading agreements, for example—and the distinguishing characteristics between these and mergers is that they are either not of a significant size or do not involve the transfer of effective control to one centre.

In 1970 the EEC Commission published a memorandum on industrial policy in the Community. Included in this was a survey, which had been carried out on the Commission's behalf by Opera Mundi, analysing the trend in the EEC in respect of cooperation, acquisition of shares in other firms, and the creation of subsidiaries and mergers. The survey covered 1961 to the first half of 1969, and was restricted to important sectors of manufacturing industry. More than 15,000 operations were covered, as analysed in Table 9.1. From this analysis it can be seen that of the total number of penetrations subsidiary formation was most popular, accounting for 45% of the total, cooperation was next, accounting for 34% and mergers were least

Table 9.1

	1961–69: All sectors, unilateral establishment of subsidiaries in other countries			Cooperation: minority holdings reciprocal holdings Common subsidiaries Common parent companies			Mergers–takeovers (or controlling minority)				
Year	From Member Country to Member Country	From Third Country to Member Country	From Member Country to Third Country	between firms in the same Country	between Common Market firms	between Member Country and third Country firms	Same Member Country	Different Member Countries	By a Member Country in a third Country	By a Third Country in a Member Country	Totals
1961	241	351	71	100	104	362	131	19	26	102	1507
1962	232	348	76	141	114	343	162	11	21	85	1533
1963	195	379	63	55	61	228	157	28	9	82	1257
1964	273	476	139	132	123	335	172	34	18	110	1812
1965	247	409	142	177	140	364	228	17	20	70	1814
1966	320	467	154	205	112	289	221	31	20	93	1912
1967	320	496	196	166	104	292	253	32	36	115	2018
1968	304	381	191	231	160	387	272	35	29	106	2096
1969[1]	160	239	126	145	83	197	265	50	36	57	1358
Totals	2300	3546	1158	1352	1001	2797	1861	257	215	820	15307

[1] First six months
Source: Opera Mundi.

prevalent, accounting for 21%. However, when we exclude cooperation and mergers within the same country, then the role of mergers becomes even less significant, and there is little evidence that there has been a significant swing away from the predominance of the subsidiary as the principal means of penetration. For example, the relevant figures show:

	No.	%
Subsidiaries	7,004	58
Cooperation	3,798	31
Mergers	1,292	11

	%			
	1961	1965	1967	1968
Subsidiaries	52	56	63	55
Cooperation	37	37	25	34
Mergers	11	7	12	11

The importance of activity cannot be measured by numbers alone. One merger measured in terms of value may be much more significant than a number of cooperation agreements or the establishment of many subsidiaries, nevertheless it is one measure of activity which helps fill in one of the parameters of industrial concentration in Europe.

Activity between member countries within the EEC shows a similar position:

	No.	%
Subsidiaries	2,300	65
Cooperation	1,001	28
Mergers	257	7

However, in this case, growth rates have been in the other direction, namely 25% for subsidiaries, 54% for cooperation and 84% for mergers, indicating that perhaps the climate is becoming more favourable for integration via mergers within the Community. Not surprisingly, however, merger activity within single member countries is growing; 272 compared to 131, and has grown, 108% compared to 84%, faster than mergers between member countries. What is more surprising is that companies outside the Community have been more active under all three classifications with countries within the Community (see Table 9.1) as compared with activity between the member countries:

	Third country and member country	Member country and member country
Subsidiaries	3,546	2,300
Cooperation	2,797	1,001
Mergers	820	257

It has been estimated that between Community countries in the years 1965/68 total direct investment was approximately $1,700 million whereas investment in the Community from third countries was approximately $5,000 million. The reason for this was perhaps the desire of third countries to establish themselves inside the EEC tariff wall. This would seem to be borne out by the fact that within all classifications third country operations are only increasing slightly from year to year while member country operations on the other hand are developing rapidly. Again this indicates that the climate for inter-EEC activities is becoming more favourable – this is substantiated by a second report[2] by the EEC Commission on trends in industrial concentration.

Table 9.2

Year	Purchase of holding (minority or majority) inter-EEC No.	Creation of joint subsidiary inter-EEC No.	Creation of wholly owned subsidiary in EEC or third country No.
1966	254	315	781
1967	228	299	830
1968	241	292	890
1969	265	324	989
1970	327	345	1,199

Although the report does not isolate mergers as such, as it includes these along with purchases of minority holdings, it does indicate an apparent increase in the trend in this area. Further analysis, the report states, shows that there were twice as many EEC companies buying into other countries in the Community as there were third countries buying into the EEC. This would appear to indicate a swing away from the position as disclosed by the Opera Mundi survey, indicating perhaps that, within the EEC, conditions are becoming more favourable for, and EEC countries more aggressive in, cross-frontier activities.

The relatively low, though growing level of merger activity in the EEC, with the greater part being generated by non-EEC countries contrasts with the position in the U.K. Newbould's study,[3] for example, showed that in 1967 and 1968 1,068 and 1,433 mergers took place in the U.K. His work was based on an analysis of the U.K. press, and his figures were considerably in excess of official Board of Trade statistics which showed 661 and 598 mergers in 1967 and 1968 respectively.

Table 9.3

Numbers of companies acquired (Board of Trade data)

Year	No.	Year	No.
1954	275	1962	636
1955	294	1963	885
1956	246	1964	939
1957	301	1965	995
1958	341	1966	805
1959	559	1967	661
1960	736	1968	598
1961	632		

Even on the basis of Board of Trade information, Europe—particularly the EEC—would seem to have lagged behind the U.K. in terms of merger activity. Nevertheless the potential for all forms of industrial penetration, especially mergers, in Europe is bright, particularly where continental Europe is concerned.

Attitude of European management

How are mergers viewed by European management? Publications such as *Vision*, *Multi-National Business*, *Fortune*, *Management Today*, are filled with comments of individual managers, mostly viewing the prospect of an enlarged market as an exciting one offering great opportunities, provided that the behaviour of government and unions is realistic (and, of course, that of competitors, though this is rarely mentioned). However, little systematic work has been done in this area. A study on industrial concentration in Europe was commissioned by the European Federation of Financial Analysts Societies for presentation at their 6th Congress, and the following comments are based on this.[4] A study group consisting of financial analysts from Switzerland, Germany, Holland, France, Norway, Spain, Belgium, and the U.K. considered the following mergers:

Belgium	Gevaert/Agfa
	Grand Bazar d'Anvers/Supermarche
France	Gervais/Danone
	Thomson-Brandt/CSF
Germany	BASF/Wintershall
	Glanzstoff/AKU
Holland	AKU/KZO
	Heineken/Amstel
Norway	AS Norcem
Spain	Construccion Naval/Astilleros
Switzerland	Sandoz/Wander
	Ciba/Geigy
U.K.	GEC/English Electric
	Cadbury/Schweppes

A variety of reasons is always put forward to justify a merger and it is not always easy to isolate either the principal aim or the dividing line between the various aims. On some occasions the real reason is never disclosed to the public. While it was not possible to rank the importance of such aims in any quantifiable fashion in the cases considered, a subjective assessment indicated the following order of importance:

Improvement of market position.
Increased research capacity.
Increased marketing potential.
Broadening of production range.
Increased production capacity.
Improved potential financial position.
Acquisition of executives.

The acquisition of executives was the only aim on which explicit public comment was not made. All the others were to a greater or less extent put forward as reasons for the creation of a larger industrial unit. Rarely was any specific information provided to justify these, other than a general statement that benefits would be obtained in these areas. In this respect, continental management is even more paternalistic than U.K. management, particularly when a merger is 'friendly', i.e. agreeable to both boards of directors, and this in their eyes would seem to be all that they need say.

Relevant to the detailed analyses of past performance and future plans on capital investment, profitability, dividend policy, etc., a significant contrast can be drawn between mergers which are unfriendly, when one board of directors is seeking to fend off an approach made by another company—which stimulates the acquiring company, also, to produce detailed information—and mergers which are friendly. If it is possible to do this in one situation, there is no reason why it should not be so in all cases. Management's philosophy is usually that as little information should be disclosed as will enable them to achieve their objective. From their standpoint, this may well be a rational decision rule but if the EEC is serious in its desire to promote cross-frontier investment then it, not management, will have to determine what information is disclosed.

Marketing was undoubtedly the most important aspect in these mergers. Improvement of market position or increased market potential are among the most difficult factors to evaluate, and therefore perhaps the easiest justification to give in a merger, in order to get away with the 'minimum information disclosed' rule. However, even allowing for this, marketing was the dominant theme for management. The most common statement made was the need to create a company large enough to compete at an international level through a contrast of the proposed group with equivalent U.S. or EEC, or other non-EEC competitors. Not only was 'ability to compete' put forward as the reason for increased size but also 'ability to survive'; in other words, to become large enough in size or national importance to make the enlarged organisation economically or politically an undesirable take-over candidate. The cry of 'national interests' to justify a merger on one occasion, is one to which I shall return later because emphasis on this strategy by management is one of the factors which could work against a cross-frontier merger on another occasion.

The second most important reason for merging was increased research capacity and, by implication, improved research. Although this was a benefit which management said would result, little information was given to justify the belief that somehow there is an absolute limit to expenditure on research and development so that, if size increases, expenditure does not increase proportionately and a cost saving can be made; or that the benefits to be derived from research and development will be at least as good in one organisation as they will be in two or more; or finally, that large organisations are more responsive to technological change and innovation than small. Here again, continual reference was made to the U.S.A. where such benefits had resulted in better profit margins through lower costs on equivalent products, or price premiums on technologically superior products. Linked with the improvement brought about by better research and development were the improved productive benefits to be brought about through broadening the production range or by increasing productive capacity.

Although improved financial position was not particularly emphasized this was often deliberate on the part of management who were concerned not to do so lest, if the merger did not go through, this might undermine the confidence in any one of the participating companies. Management were particularly sensitive about this because of their appreciation that suspicion of financial difficulties can have a much more immediate impact on a company's rating than suspicion of any other factor.

Little prominence was given to the role of the acquisition of executives in these mergers, yet discussions revealed that this was a factor which received considerable attention. The reason for the lack of publicity was the possible effect on existing personnel. From the European viewpoint if the concept of management by ethnic centre becomes a practical reality, this factor will become more and more important. The lack of apparent success in the few true cross-frontier mergers which had taken place was often attributed to this problem of merging management from different cultures. This was seen as sufficiently important to have outweighed what might otherwise have been a worth-while 'European' acquisition. The point was regularly made that, until more experience had been gained in this area through the creation of small subsidiary companies and cooperative agreements, ventures would not be made into the more significant area of mergers. This would seem to be borne out by the statistics quoted earlier.

The study showed European management to have a profound belief that bigness meant survival through more certain profits and less likelihood of takeover.[5] The economies of scale brought about through the physical, human, and financial resources which the large organisation can command made it the only viable unit in an internationally competitive economy. In particular, where research and development is important and innovation requires expensive market penetration, small units, in international terms, were at a competitive disadvantage. Shipbuilding, photography, computers, electronic calculators, were just a few of the illustrations given of the European unit ineffective at the international level. Economies of scale have interested economists for many years but there is not unanimity for the view that bigness is best, One of the main proponents of this view is Galbraith[6] but there are others who do not accept it, for example, Jewkes *et al.*[7] are only one group whose studies have pointed out the lack of evidence that, in terms of the productivity of research and development, bigness necessarily means better. Indeed, what little evidence there is would seem to point in the opposite direction.

Table 9.4

Top 20: U.S.A. and European companies

	U.S.A.			Europe		
Ranking	Sales $ billion	Net Income % Sales	Net Income % Shareholders' Equity	Sales $ billion	Net Income % Sales	Net Income % Shareholders' Equity
1	28.3	6.8	17.9	12.7	7.1	9.1
2	18.7	7.8	12.6	7.5	3.3	11.3
3	16.4	4.0	11.8	5.2	7.0	9.3
4	9.4	5.0	16.8	5.2	1.9	4.7
5	8.3	13.0	16.2	5.0	0.8	3.6
6	8.2	6.6	11.2	3.8	1.7	6.1
7	8.0	1.0	3.7	3.7	5.6	8.7
8	7.5	12.0	13.4	3.5	3.7	8.6
9	7.3	4.6	10.5	3.5	2.4	6.9
10	6.0	4.3	9.3	3.5	3.3	22.2
11	5.9	9.5	10.2	3.3	—	—
12	5.1	9.9	10.4	3.2	—	—
13	4.9	3.1	4.4	3.2	2.6	8.0

Table 9.4 (continued)

14	4.6	3.8	9.9	2.9	0.8	4.2
15	4.0	8.4	9.6	2.9	0.5	2.7
16	3.9	6.3	8.7	2.8	1.4	6.6
17	3.8	9.3	11.5	2.7	—	—
18	3.7	—	—	2.7	0.7	4.4
19	3.6	4.7	11.7	2.6	2.9	7.7
20	3.4	—	—	2.5	2.3	5.0
				U.S.A.	Europe	Superiority Factor
Average sales $ billion				8.1	4.1	2.0
Average net income as % sales				6.0	2.4	2.5
Average net income as % shareholders' equity				10.0	6.5	1.5

With apparent average sales twice as high, net profit margins 2.5 times as high, and return on shareholders' capital 1.5 times as high, the answer to the European manger seems obvious; bigness is seen as the cause of profitability not the result of it.

Source: *Fortune*, May and August 1972.

The U.K. Monopolies Commission has recently rejected proposals for two mergers in the pharmaceutical industry on the explicit grounds that large companies are less efficient in research and development, and therefore it would not be in the national interest to allow them. In reaching this decision the Monopolies Commission came to the conclusion that there was little connection between size and research success, and that the largest firms have been responsible for proportionately fewer major innovations.

However, these latter studies have been concerned with invention and innovation, not with production and marketing (other than the marketing of innovation), and it is production and marketing which to the businessman are what matters when he considers economies of scale. He is less likely to study academic writing and more likely to look at publications such as *Fortune*, where the facts of Table 9.4 originated.

Although there is little evidence to support the view that, apart from stock exchange ratings, growth by merger is not, in terms of profitability, as successful as internally generated growth,[8] to the European manager this is the only way that growth can come about quickly enough. The scene would seem to be set for a substantial increase in the number of mergers in Europe, and the potential for this will be greater on continental Europe than in the U.K. From the U.K.'s viewpoint this is seen by some[9] as a position which the U.K.'s membership of the EEC should enable it to exploit to its advantage. Compared to the continental markets, the size of the U.K. stock market, for example, and the role of London as the capital centre—certainly of Western Europe, if not the world—have led many people to conclude that the City will undoubtedly benefit from U.K. membership of the EEC. Industrial concentration is only one of the areas where these benefits can be expected. However, because the U.K. has a greater capital market and in some respects more sophisticated financial institutions geared to this it does not mean that it will have it all its own way.

European financial institutions have a much better experience of direct industrial investment than their U.K. counterparts (see Chapter 12). This may have been a cause or a consequence of the relatively small open capital market in Europe; however, as Villiers points out,[10] such participation has given the European financial institutions a much greater appreciation and knowledge of both industrial investment and of industry; and concomitant with this a willingness to take more positive action than merely disinvestment—the traditional approach of the U.K. institutional investor—when things are not going well in the company in which it has investments. The recent action of the Bank of England in permitting commercial banks to acquire interest in merchant banks is indicative of the realisation that in this area we are at a disadvantage compared to other Europeans. While U.K. financial institutions may benefit, it must be remembered that only a small

Table 9.5

Country	Stock Market Capitalisation (at 30.9.71) £'000m	Equity Turnover Year to June 1971 £'000m	Turnover as % of market capitalisation	Stock Market Capitalisation as % of 1970 GNP
Germany	13.3	1.7	12.8	17.2
France	9.3	1.7	18.3	15.2
Italy	4.0	0.9	22.5	10.3
Netherlands	4.4	1.2	27.3	33.6
Belgium	2.7	0.3	11.1	25.2
U.K.	41.0	4.8[1]	11.7	93.7

[1] The London figure has been halved to make an approximate comparison with the turnover as recorded in broker/broker markets in the EEC.

part (12%) of the overseas financial services which they provide, and not a very profitable one, is concerned with Europe. It is therefore unrealistic to assume that major resources will be moved away from what is a substantial majority involvement in terms of size and profitability to a minority profitless involvement. What is more likely to happen is an increase in mergers and trading agreements between U.K. and continental financial institutions.

Cross-frontier mergers

While a growth in the rate of industrial concentration in Europe would seem likely, this growth through mergers will be at a national rather than international level. Cross-frontier penetration is more likely to come about through the establishment of joint subsidiaries and trading agreements. The reasons for this are mainly legal and technical (see Chapter 8). Different accounting standards and requirements for disclosure can lead to ex-ante caution and ex-post disillusionment. These still present grave problems at the national level,[11] and at the international level the position is even worse. Businessmen are going to be hesitant about accepting financial statements which have been prepared in accordance with the rule applicable and acceptable to the country in question: they would be foolish to do otherwise.

When the Dunlop/Pirelli merger was under consideration it was found necessary to get an independent firm of accountants to re-calculate the Pirelli profits according to what they would have been had U.K. practice been applied. When these figures were produced they differed substantially from those which had been reported by Pirelli. It will be interesting to find out in due course the extent to which the lack of success, according to the press, of this merger was due to things not being quite what they seemed to be. The accounting problem is only one aspect of the wider issue of the need for a European company subject to European company law. Till the Societas Europea becomes a reality there will, in a legal sense, be no trouble-free trading, so that European companies have the same advantages in the EEC as, for example, an American company has in the U.S.A.

Linked to the above is the taxation problem. The study of European mergers referred to earlier[12] disclosed that rarely was taxation the reason for a merger. However, once a merger had been agreed, taxation became an important factor in determining the method of implementation. Until the problems of dividend withholding taxes and gains taxes have been resolved at a European level, taxation—if not a stumbling block to a merger—could lead to less than optimum organisational form.

The U.K.'s lack of membership of the EEC has, according to some authorities,[13] restricted its ability to engage in cross-frontier mergers because of the various controls regulating and restricting the flow of capital funds. These have been introduced because of the balance of payment crises confronting successive governments. While such measures may well have helped cope with the balance of payments problem, in the short run it has created a situation in which U.K. firms wishing to invest abroad have been at a severe disadvantage compared with their EEC competitors except where they have been big enough to make use of the euro-bond market (see Chapter 12). The entry of the U.K. into the EEC should see a reduction in these restrictions, not only to comply with the EEC regulation, but also to ensure that U.K. companies are to compete on an equal footing with their fellow members.

In anticipation of complete liberalisation by the end of 1974, the Bank of England has already begun this process by raising the direct official exchange allowance to £1,000,000 in respect of EEC countries, i.e. provided approval is given, £1,000,000 in official exchange currency per annum per project may be used for direct investment. However, although the U.K. will conform to the EEC regulations by the end of 1974 and will have a policy in common with that of its partners, it cannot be assumed that this will mean that the European markets will then be identical in all respects to national markets. This is not what happens at present in the EEC and, despite the desire to implement the principles of free movement of funds, it is not likely to be the case for some time to come. As Manser has pointed out,[14] the liberalisation of capital movements is a nominal, rather than a real event and there are sufficient escape clauses in the Treaty of Rome to allow a country should she wish—as France did in 1968—to go against the spirit of the treaty and impose controls on the movement of capital funds. It is likely that the U.K., because of her particular sensitivity to inflows and outflows of capital as an international banker, will require to continue to have available much the same sort of regulations that exist at present. In any event it is questionable even if exchange controls were abolished that this by itself would result in a free flow of capital. There are many other factors which, again as Manser has shown, can impede such movements, e.g. legal, fiscal, administrative, and practical matters, and within the EEC there are no two countries who have an identical position at present. Neither is there any evidence that the freedom of capital movement which has existed within the EEC has stimulated a vast amount of cross-frontier activity. The figures quoted earlier do not disclose that this is so, and the Segré Report[15] pointed out that the relaxing of exchange control barriers in the EEC had not apparently had a significant effect on investment between member countries. The freeing of capital movement will certainly help the trend towards industrial concentration in Europe, provided that other barriers can be overcome and there are worth-while investment opportunities to be had, but it would be wrong to assume that overnight investment in the European market will be as easy as investment in the home market.

The multinational company

The final factor which is likely to inhibit the development of cross-frontier mergers is not technical, but emotional: fear of the multinational company. At one end of the spectrum there are those who see the multinational as the epitome of the modern new technological world—large, efficient, completely lacking in prejudice or discrimination, in that for the aspiring executive all that is required is an ability to satisfy the organisation's objectives. At the other end, it is seen as a form of imperialistic power with an army of mercenaries whose allegiance lies solely to its paymaster, and who are prepared to put his interest above that of their own nation's and any other's interest.[16] In recent years it is those at this end of the spectrum who have attracted most attention. The call for the control of the multinational comes from all quarters, political, management and unions. In a recent article[17] the criticisms of the multinational company were summarised as follows:

1. *General*

The multinational enterprise is a threat to national economic sovereignty as it operates under a global strategy which can be contrary to the perceived interests of nation states.

The ultimate source of decision making in the subsidiaries of multinationals is outside the host country, and therefore not under its control or jurisdiction.

Some multinational enterprises act irresponsibly on matters involving ecology and pollution.

2. *Financial*

Investment plans, both as regards location and method of financing may conflict with host nations' policies.

Multinationals sometimes engage in transfer pricing to minimise local tax requirements.

Multinationals move their substantial liquid financial resources across the exchanges, often aggravating speculative pressures on a currency.

3. *Employment*

Some multinationals do not respect the host country's tradition of trade union recognition, joint consultation or local industrial relations practice.

There is implicit limitation by some multinationals on the authority of indigenous management and their opportunity of reaching parent board level.

Multinationals 'export jobs' as well as capital by setting up factories in countries where labour and other costs are cheapest.

Some multinationals may switch production from one country to another so as to limit the effects of strike action.

4. *Procurement*

Multinationals often dictate the source of purchases, i.e. from parent company, irrespective of costs and local availability.

5. *Marketing*

Multinationals sometimes prevent overseas subsidiaries from exporting to the country where the parent company has its headquarters or sphere of influence, even when their products are cheaper or of higher quality.

6. *Research and development*

Some multinationals centre their research and development work in the parent country to the alleged detriment of the host nation's ability to build up its own independent technologies.

Multinationals export technology, thus undermining the parent country's competitive advantages.

Although there is little factual evidence to justify these conclusions there is equally little evidence to prove that they are invalid. Considerable work to obtain this information is currently under way in most countries, but it is doubtful even when it is available that it will present a clear-cut picture. In any event, when national interest is at stake, it is not actual abuse but potential abuse which causes most concern and because of this, governments are going to come under increasing pressure to enforce regulations restricting the activities of the multinational. For example, the U.K. Trades Union Council in 1971 resolved that the government take action by requiring greater disclosure of information, and obtain guarantees of behaviour from companies resident in the U.K., to cover industrial relations practice, manpower plans, intracompany trading and financial practice, research policy, and remittance and development policy, and to impose sanctions if these guarantees are broken. In the U.S.A. similar suggestions have also been made,[18] and considerable political pressure is being exerted to curb the multinational car manufacturers from using their overseas factories to supply the domestic market.[19]

The EEC has recognised the problem that under such pressure, national governments may take action which is contrary to the spirit of the Treaty of Rome and thus hinder the development of industrial concentration.

> At present there are few mergers between firms from different member countries. ... the Commission is working hard to eliminate the obstacles—especially in the area of tax and company law—to cross-frontier mergers. Unfortunately, some recent cases show that governments of some member countries prefer to restructure industries in a national framework and therefore use pressure to prevent multinational arrangements.[20]

An example is the French sugar industry where the market, with the positive assistance of the French Government, is totally controlled by French refiners. Tate and Lyle, the U.K. company wanting to extend into Europe, had taken steps to acquire Beghin one of the large refiners in France but this move was blocked by the French Government which forced a national merger to take place.

There is no shortage of advice on how, on the one hand, the EEC should deal with the problem on an international basis and how national governments, on the other, should deal with it on a national basis. Even though many feel that multinational control can only be made effective through multinational policies and action which, theoretically at least, a structure like EEC should be able to provide for its members, the proponents of unilateral action on the part of national governments are likely to be the more successful in the short run, and such action is bound to hinder the cross-frontier merger, though it could lead to more national mergers.

Those who have tried to obtain concentration significantly and quickly by mergers such as Agfa/Gevaert and Dunlop/Pirelli have apparently had experiences which are scarcely designed to fill other businessmen with enthusiasm for this method of industrial concentration. Mergers of such a size cannot be expected to prove themselves successful overnight and it would be wrong to assess long-term decisions on the basis of short-term performance. Nevertheless, in the absence of long-term performance and unless success is obvious, other less dramatic methods such as trading agreements, the creation of joint subsidiaries, or small wholly owned subsidiaries, etc., are likely to be more attractive.

Conclusion

It is likely that over the next few years much will be written, much will be suggested, but little will be done in the field of cross-frontier mergers. The merger movement in Europe is, in the main, going to be confined within national frontiers. Industrial concentration will take place but largely through the media of subsidiary companies and trading agreements. Nevertheless the barriers will be broken down, albeit slowly, and experience will be gained; the company which ignores these developments may find that it may be serving in hell without even having had the opportunity of reigning in heaven!

Notes

[1] E. M. G. A. Sassen, Ensuring Fair Competition in the European Community, Community Topics 35. European Communities Press and Information, London 1970

[2] *Premier Rapport sur la Politique de Concurrence* (joint au 'Cinquième Rapport Général sur L'Activités des Communautés'),
Communauté Économique Européenne, 1972, Brussels.

[3] G. Newbould, *Management and Merger Activity*, Guthstead London 1970.

[4] See proceedings of the 6th Congress of the European Federation of Financial Analyst Societies, *Financial Analysis and Industrial Concentration in Europe*. In particular, see a report on the study group (of which the writer was a member) on concentration of European enterprises 1970.

[5] In this latter case, survival probably referred to management rather than the firm or its shareholders.

[6] J. K. Galbraith, *American Capitalism*, New York: Houghton Mifflin.

[7] Jewkes, Sawyers, Stillman, *The Sources of Innovation*, London Macmillan, 1961.

[8] Newbould, op cit.

[9] Mainly the advocates for the U.K. joining EEC.

[10] C. H. Villiers, *The Merchant Banks and Cross-Frontier Mergers in an Enlarged EEC*. Paper presented at a *Financial Times* conference on 8 December 1971.

[11] In 1968 the problem of profit reporting caused Sir Frank Kearton, chair-

man of Courtaulds Ltd, to write to the president of the Institute of Chartered Accountants in England and Wales, expressing concern over the difficulties in reconciling pre- and post-acquisition profits because of the wide variety of acceptable rules for reporting financial results. Since then attempts have been made through the Accounting Standards Steering Committee to improve the situation. However, in the specific area under consideration—accounting for acquisitions—it has not been possible to find an acceptable way of dealing with the problem.

[12] See *Proceedings of the 6th Congress of the European Federation of Financial Analyst Societies*, op cit.

[13] Villiers, op cit.

[14] W. A. P. Manser, *UK and the EEC: The Prospects for Finance.* National Westminster BankQuarterly Review, London, February 1972.

[15] *Development of a European Capital Market*, EEC Commission. Brussels 1971.

[16] This is not so far-fetched as it might sound. On 4 December 1972 the President of Chile in an unprecedented statement to the United Nations accused a large U.S.A. multinational— ITT— of aggression and interference and said: 'Before the conscience of the World, I accuse the ITT of attempting to bring about civil war in my country'.

[17] 'Controlling the Multi-Nationals—is it Necessary', *Multi-National Business*, 1972, No. 1.

[18] *A Trade Policy for America*, AFL/CIO Programme, May 1971.

[19] 'National Politics v International Economics—Pressure to keep the US Motor Industry American', *Multi-National Business*, 1972, No. 3.

[20] E. M. G. A. Sassen op cit.

10 Competition Policy in Britain and the Common Market

by R. SHIRLEY

British monopolists, actual or aspiring, are faced with a substantial change in official attitudes on entry into the Common Market. Instead of the gentlemanly disapproval they are used to, they will be likely to undergo the ungentle condemnation of the Commission of the European Community, accompanied possibly by painful fines.

This is not to say that the competition policy of the EEC is dissimilar in principle to that of the U.K.; it is, however, much more severe in practice. Both policies seek to ensure that the prices of goods and services are held at the lowest level compatible with the proper development of business; this would be achieved by the prohibition of restrictive practices and the discouragement of monopoly. On the other hand, each permits exceptions when it can be shown that such practices or situations are beneficial to the public interest.

Yet, the application of these principles has been very different. In the U.K. the worst punishment meted out to the cartelists or monopolists has been an injunction to desist. In the Common Market, fines of the equivalent of up to £40,000 have been imposed (the quinine cartel case, 1969), and the Commission's impressive power to fine is accompanied with a thorough-going power of investigation. In the United States, to round out the comparison, policy is much simpler. This is due to the proposition on which U.S. legislation is founded, that competition is of itself good, and anything that restricts it, even if only in potential, is of itself bad. Indeed U.S. policy appears now to be developing towards a further proposition that mere bigness is bad, even though the bigness does not involve dominance in particular industries. The International Telephone and Telegraph Corporation was recently directed by the U.S. Department of Justice to divest itself of subsidiaries valued at one billion dollars in order to be allowed to keep the one billion dollar Hartford Fire Insurance Company.

The subsidiaries of which ITT had to divest itself were engaged in food retailing, fire protection, life insurance, car rental (Avis), and house building. The Justice Department claimed that these subsidiaries were related to the business of Hartford Fire. The connection, however, is rather indirect, and the neat balance in asset value between the retained and the relinquished, strongly indicates that mere size, and not actual dominance, was the basic objection to ITT. Bigness intimidates potential competitors, so it must be restrained.

As will be seen, the European Community may be moving towards this extreme, though possibly necessary and logical position.

Monopoly and restrictive practices: a synopsis

A brief review of monopoly and restrictive practices in general will set the stage for a detailed account of the situation in the European Community and the U.K.

There is a natural tendency in business and industry to maximise profit and power. This may be done by means of rabid competition designed to destroy one's competitors and so create a situation of dominance or monopoly. Or, where firms are too evenly matched to destroy or absorb each other, an *effective* monopoly might be created by an agreement to act in concert. This may be expressed by the proposition that a monopoly is a one-firm cartel, or a cartel is a multi-firm monopoly.

Between these two possibilities there is the oligopoly, where the number of firms is so few that they might act as a cartel without actually engaging in explicit agreements; their prices and other relevant data are easily ascertained so that they might follow each other without making any kind of contact. A similar relationship is exhibited by the situation of dominance, where one firm occupying a large section of the market can assert price leadership, and be followed by numerous small firms, ostensibly competitors, but in reality members of an effective cartel, content to abide by and support, the price policy of the leader.

A fifth and frequent possibility is seen in the firm which, although it has many competitors in its general line of business, enjoys nevertheless a monopolistic position by virtue of, for example, its location, or of a trade-mark or brand name which distinguishes its product from otherwise indistinguishable ones. Competition here is effected by advertising or to put it another way, *price* competition is stifled by advertising. This condition might be conveniently called idiopoly. An idiopolistic situation, then, would be one in which a single firm enjoys a monopoly, not because of lack of competition, but by virtue of some particularity of its product, often its mere name and reputation. Even high price itself could give a firm an idiopolistic character, since many consumers prefer highly priced articles on the assumption that they must be better.

A final consideration in our review of polistic structures is that of the incipient monopoly, by which I mean a proposed merger. The difficulty experienced in controlling established monopoly has directed attention towards the policy of stopping it developing in the first place. Both in Europe and Britain, as well as the United States, great emphasis is being placed on the scrutiny of proposed mergers, and their prohibition, if it is concluded that they might lead to an undesirable monopolistic situation.

The practices by which polistic structures seek to exercise themselves are numerous. They include: (a) horizontal and vertical price fixing, (b) allocations of production, territories, bids, etc., (c) joint production, sale, or purchase, (d) limitation of character, variety or quality of production, (e) share of patent and trade-mark rights, or of technical information. Some of these restrictive practices are fairly rare, and others may have a socially beneficial purpose, e.g. the sharing of technical information. The most prevalent, and undoubtedly the most objectionable of the restrictive practices are horizontal and vertical price fixing, and I shall confine attention to these.

Horizontal price fixing implies collusion of some kind between several suppliers of the same product to sell it at the same price; this price, of course, would be higher than the marginal price. In fixing a common selling price, notice must be taken of terms and discounts, since the provision of favourable terms would be a means of expanding one's sales at the agreed price, to the detriment of the other members of the cartel; in other words, there would be hidden competition. Indeed, sometimes a cartel concentrates on fixing terms and discounts, rather than prices, in the hope that in regulating the secret elements of competition, the open or public element will tend to equalise spontaneously.

Vertical price fixing, or resale price maintenance (RPM), is a means of ensuring similar prices amongst distributors; it gets its vertical aspect from the fact that it is usually enforced by the supplier. In other words, although it has a horizontal effect in that it establishes uniform prices to all consumers, it derives in the first instance from some agency lower down the tree of distribution. There may be several levels, or interfaces of RPM, to the extent that the whole range of exchange is covered, i.e. manufacturer/distributor/wholesaler/retailer/customer.

Originally, RPM was established at the instance of retailers who wished to bring about a cartel situation and found it easier to work through their supplier, in getting him to determine a common price and to enforce it. To this extent the system was one simply of horizontal price fixing, with a rather novel enforcement mechanism. Latterly, as suppliers realised that benefit could accrue to them, they came to the fore in originating RPM agreements, which then took on a truly vertical character.

Attitudes both in the U.K. and among the original Six have evolved, or rather, revolved, since the war. Until the establishment of the European Community in 1958 there was a distinct tendency among the founder partners to favour restrictive practices, which mirrors the historical British attitude. And this approval of polistic situations was not restricted to businessmen and rightist governments, but also was evident among trade unionists. This is shown in Professor G. C. Allen's[1] comment on Ernest Bevin, Foreign Minister in the 1945 Labour Government, that he preferred dealing with monopolistic firms, since they were more amenable to trade union claims, i.e. they were more able to pass wage increases on to the customer. A similar view was prevalent among continental socialists, who saw in competition a source of low wages, inferior conditions, and instability.

Development of British policy

Monopolies and restrictive practices act, 1948

The 1944 White Paper on employment set the scene in the U.K. for an attack on restrictive practices. The maintenance of full employment became explicit policy of the Government, but full employment, which would increase competition for workers, necessitated competition for customers, or else prices would rise. The result was the 1948 Monopolies and Restrictive Practices Act. In this Act, monopoly was defined as a situation wherein one-third or more of home or export goods were supplied by or to a single firm or combine; excluded were services, trade unions, nationalised industries, public marketing boards, and professions.

The Act set up an investigative panel, the Monopolies Commission, which was limited by the Board of Trade at each end, i.e. it could undertake investigation only on referral by the Board of Trade, and if it found cause for objection, could not exercise control but could only make recommendations to the Board of Trade, who then decided whether to act. In fact, inactivity typified the Government's attitude. Until 1956 (when the Act was superseded), in only one case was an attempt at enforcement made. In the other cases the inclination of the Government was to obtain voluntary agreement, which besides being long drawn-out, usually resulted in compromise even though the Commission's recommendations had been formally accepted.

This is not to say that the work of the Commission was futile. The reports themselves were widely published, and this undoubtedly had an effect on businessmen in general, serving to alert them to possible investigation and criticism. In Professor Allen's words, 'the former complacency was disturbed'.

Restrictive trade practices act, 1956

The next stage in the evolution of British policy was the Restrictive Trade Practices Act, 1956. The main difference—and a crucial one—between this and the former Act was in procedure. It was now incumbent on parties to restrictive practices to register and describe them (though strangely, there was no penalty for failure to do so). The Registrar of Restrictive Practices was responsible for initiating proceedings, which he would bring before a specially constituted court, the Restrictive Practices Court, composed of High Court judges and competent laymen. Thus the Government was relieved of the political onus of discovering and terminating restrictive practices.

There were two other important provisions of this Act. One was the prohibition of *collective* resale price maintenance. RPM by *individual* companies was permitted, however, and indeed, their power to enforce such agreements by recourse to the courts was increased. A third feature of the Act was that the restrictive practices it envisaged were described, and a presumption established that they were illegal. The onus of proving otherwise lay on the practitioners. Again, no penalty attached to the making of an 'illegal' agreement prior to its being registered and prohibited.

However, 'gateways' were provided: if it could be proved that benefit accrued to the public from the practice complained of, and if the benefits outweighed the harm—a nice judgment—then it could be permitted. A public benefit of this nature would be, for example, a favourable effect on employment, or the improvement of exports.

Most of the agreements brought by the Registrar before the Court were disallowed. Those that were accepted were upheld on apparently obvious grounds of public benefit. An agreement between the manufacturers of water-tube boilers was held to aid exports, and so was allowed. The Cement Makers' Federation claimed that their agreement allowed them to charge lower prices to remote customers, and further, that their industry was efficient, and their rate of return reasonable; this agreement was also allowed. A claim on the part of the black nuts and bolts trade that their price fixing relieved the customer from 'shopping around' was allowed. This impregnable defence could be used by any cartel that existed, and its acceptance by the Court in this case is taken to be a vagary and not a precedent.

The negative effect of the Act on restrictive practice agreements is undoubted. Apart from the preponderance of cases disallowed by the Court, hundreds of agreements were abandoned voluntarily. Until June 1963, of 2,430 registered agreements, 1,610 were abandoned.

This, however, still leaves the unanswerable questions: How many agreements were never registered? And how many abandoned agreements were continued, however imperfectly, on a tacit and informal basis? Even those agreements found to be in the public interest on the grounds that the industries represented were efficient, and their return not unreasonable, are suspect, since one wonders how a legal entity can fairly judge the efficiency of an industry, and whether, in the absence of competition, productivity and innovations are likely to be pursued.

The Monopolies Commission was not entirely supplanted by the Registrar and the Restrictive Practices Court. It was reconstituted and charged, principally, with the investigation of dominant firms, which included monopolies and oligoplies. This also led to its assuming the function of vetting proposed mergers, as will be discussed later.

The 1956 Act had little effect on RPM. True, it abolished *collective* enforcement of this practice, but this made no difference to the large firms who were able to enforce minimum prices themselves. The smaller firms, who depended on collective action to enforce compliance, were now debarred from doing so, but even here the effect was modified by their being empowered, albeit individually, to penalise price cutting by retailers, even if the retailers had been supplied through an intermediary and had no direct contact with the manufacturers. The purpose of this concession was to allow the small firm an advantage in law, which the large firm enjoyed by virtue of its size and power. It could be argued that the framers of the collective enforcement prohibition, realising that large firms could nullify its purpose, decided that in fairness, provision must be made for small firms also to nullify its purpose.

It is estimated that between the Act of 1956 and the Resale Prices Act, 1964, some 200 injunctions were obtained by manufacturers to prevent price-cutting,[2] and this undoubtedly led to a much larger incidence of 'voluntary' price maintenance by retailers who feared a court action. The sanctioning of individual RPM by the 1956 Act, therefore, had the effect only of making it more of a nuisance to maintain prices; prices nevertheless were maintained. It became clear that competition among retailers could be achieved only by virtually prohibiting enforced RPM in all cases. This was the object of the Resale Prices Act.

Resale Prices Act, 1964

The tenor of this Act of 1964 was similar to that of the Restrictive Trade Practices Act, 1956. First, as to principle, the Act contained a presumption that RPM was against the public interest: it was up to the firm that wished to uphold the practice to prove otherwise. Second, as to procedure, it lay with the claimant firms to register their claim, and with the Registrar to bring the case before the Court.

Exemptions could be claimed by means of several gateways which allowed the firm to cite the public interest in seeking leave to uphold the practice. These were, that prohibition would result in:

1. Quality or variety being substantially reduced.
2. The number of shops being substantially reduced.
3. The price of goods being increased in general and in the long run.
4. Health being endangered.
5. Pre- or post-sales services being substantially reduced.

However, it was the *net* public interest that was to be considered, and the detriment in prohibiting RPM should, in the judgment of the Court, outweigh the detriment in permitting it.

The first resale prices case decided by the Court was in 1967 concerning the supply of chocolate and confectionery. The manufacturers claimed that the number of retail establishments would be substantially reduced if price maintenance could not be enforced. This defence was recognised as a valid matter in the public interest in the Act, but the Court found that the chocolate manufacturers had not proved that the number of retailers would in fact be substantially reduced, and did not therefore grant exemption.

This case is of particular interest, since, though the enforcement of resale prices was prohibited by the Court, resale prices of chocolate and sugar confectionery have in fact remained uniform; these appear to be goods in which retailers see no advantage in departure from the recommended price. One reason for this may be that since chocolate bars are usually bought singly by relatively affluent children and parents, the absolute saving would be too small to induce them to go to a less convenient outlet. Another reason may be that the absolute price is so low, and the smallest unit of currency, the new halfpenny, so relatively valuable, that the retailer would have to cut prices by as much as 10% (from 5p to 4½p) or even 17% (from 3p to 2½p) in order to get a price advantage.

Whatever the reason, this case illustrates that, however much the law opposes organised restrictive practices, there are situations in which they can develop spontaneously and tacitly in a manner that cannot be dealt with by legislation.

Monopolies Commission

At the outset of its career the Monopolies Commission, though charged with the general function of investigating restrictions of the market, concerned itself mainly with cartels. This particular function was taken from it in 1956 and charged to the Registrar and the Restrictive Practices Court. The Monopolies Commission was then able to turn its attention to dominant firms.

Monopoly of scale is the most difficult of the polistic situations to handle. Restrictive practices that involve collusion, agreement, and enforcement can be halted or at least modified by simply ordering them to cease. But how does one foster competition when the market is supplied by only one firm? Should the Government cause one or more competing firms to be established? In most cases this is practically and politically impossible; when governments involve themselves in the ownership of industry it is generally to *eliminate* competition, albeit in the public interest.

For this reason the Monopolies Commission was forced to concern itself less with fundamental organisation of a market than with actual practices. Two reports, though, did try to bring about a change in organisation. These were the reports on rubber footwear and colour film. The Commission's recommendation here was that import duties should be removed, i.e., competing firms *from abroad* should be allowed into the market. The Board of Trade, however, did not accept this solution.

Most of the Commission's reports dealt, not with the fact of monopoly or dominance, but with the effect, and were concerned principally with unjustifiably high prices. In the case of industrial gases, wallpapers, spark plugs, potash fertilisers, and automobile electrical equipment, the high prices resulted in high profit margins. In one case, Imperial Tobacco, they were due at least in part to the retention of inefficient plants. An interesting situation was presented by detergent manufacturers where it appeared that *competition* was the cause of high prices, i.e. instead of competing on the price scale, the two dominant firms competed on the advertising scale, and thus increased costs and prices inordinately. Each tried to establish itself as an idiopoly.

The recommendations made by the Commission to deal with these situations were various, and even included nationalisation (on the part of some members). However, all tended to be treated with the same indifference by the Government.

Monopolies and Mergers Act, 1965

It became apparent that a stronger policy had to be developed, and in 1964 a White Paper named Monopolies, Mergers and Restrictive Practices was issued by the Conservative Government. The following year this was translated into the Monopolies and Mergers Act by their Labour successors. By virtue of this Act the Board of Trade had power to dissolve existing monopolies, prohibit proposed mergers, require the publication of prices, and regulate prices; these powers were to be applied to services as well as goods. Of these, only the power to prohibit mergers has been used with effect.

The procedure in regard to mergers was that the Board of Trade could refer to the Commission any merger that involved the takeover of more than £5,000,000 of assets, or where the merged companies would supply or buy more than one-third of the goods or services in question in the U.K., or 'any substantial portion thereof'. The Commission would then investigate, as always with the 'public interest' as the criterion, and report back to the Board of Trade with recommendations as appropriate.

To the end of 1969 twelve proposed mergers had been investigated by the Commission, and three disallowed. The most recent case to be scrutinised is that of the Glaxo Group Ltd, the pharmaceuticals firm, which was the object of takeover by both the Beecham Group Ltd, and the Boots Co Ltd. The history of this attempted takeover is curious. The first bid was made by

Beecham. It was not objected to by the Department of Trade and Industry (which had absorbed the old Board of Trade, and assumed its watchdog function), and was therefore not referred to the Commission. This was despite the fact that the Glaxo board did not favour the bid, and tried to induce the DTI to have it reviewed. Then Boots entered the picture with a rival bid, which had the concurrence of the Glaxo board. The DTI now reversed its decision in regard to Beecham, and referred both bids to the Commission. The Commission's decision after five months of scrutiny was that neither merger should be allowed. The fundamental objection was that the British pharmaceutical industry research programme would be impaired if Glaxo were united with either Beecham or Boots; it is better to have two relatively small independent programmes, than one large one. 'Duplication of research ... stimulates competition in innovation, and it doubles your chance ... of the lucky strike.'

The argument has merit though it is far from overwhelming. It would have applied particularly to the initial Beechams/Glaxo merger, each of whose components lead British R & D expenditure in pharmaceuticals with £7 million apiece; yet this merger was to be allowed. It applied only minimally to the Boots/Glaxo merger, as Boots spends only £750,000 on research, yet this is the merger that led to both being prohibited. It is easy to believe that a strong factor in the DTI's reversal of its Beecham decision, and of the Commission's disapproval of both bids, has been the desire to avoid invidious decisions. This is a human inclination but not a judicial one.

The Fair Trading Bill presented to Parliament in December 1972 envisages certain important changes in polistic legislation. A new office, that of Director General of Fair Trading is proposed. The Director General will be appointed by the Secretary of State for Trade & Industry for a term of five years. Besides other duties concerned with the protection of the consumer he will take over the function of the Registrar in initiating actions in the Restrictive Practices Court. He will also have the new power of referring monopolies to the Commission, which will now be called the Monopolies and Mergers Commission. Referral of mergers, however, will still lie with the Department of Trade & Industry, though the Director General will have the facility of proposing the scrutiny of mergers to the Department.

The qualifying share of the market that will bring a monopoly or merger within the ambit of the legislation is lowered from one-third to one-quarter. This, however, is not a significant change in the case of mergers; the alternative criterion which establishes a maximum asset value of 5 million pounds remains the same and is the more exacting condition, under which most mergers have been referred in the past.

More important, the scope of the legislation will be extended to include nationalised industries, the supply of services (though not professional services), local monopolies, and restrictive labour practices. Referral of a nationalised industry will be on the iniative of the DTI and not of the Director General. Finally, and most significantly, the penalties for violation will remain as ineffective as in former legislation. Extensive as these changes might be in some respects they will not of themselves substantially alter the situation in the UK, because by the time they are enacted they will be largely overridden by the more stringent rules of the Common Market.

Development of common market policy

Prior to the establishment of the European Community the attitude of its founding members towards monopoly and cartels was one of toleration, if not positive encouragement. The current policy of the Community is one of strong opposition. This opposition is innate. The very name Common Market suggests an organisation wherein market forces are given full play, and indeed, Article 3 of the Treaty of Rome states that one of the objects of the treaty is to establish 'a system to ensure that competition is not distorted'. The Commission's first general report speaks of 'a system of fair and healthy competition....'

The primacy of competition is seen both in the public and the private law of the Community. The principle of free competition between the member states themselves is expressed in numerous articles of the treaty aiming: (a) to abolish tariffs, (b) to establish free movement of workers, freedom of establishment, freedom to perform services, and free investment of capital, (c) to suppress or modify state aids or taxes that distort competition, (d) to approximate national laws that distort competition. In Italy tobacco retailing is subject to a state monopoly. The Italian Government sought to prevent tobacco companies of other member states from entering the Italian market. The Commission ruled against this governmental monopoly as contrary to the treaty.

Regional policy of individual member states, too, is subject to Commission scrutiny. The general principle is that state aids to improve the underlying structure of a region's industry will be permitted, but continuing aid (like regional employment premiums) will not. Once-for-all subventions that will bring a region up to competition standards are available, long-term production subsidies are not.

Policy in regard to private competition is contained in Articles 85 and 86, the first prohibiting restrictive agreements, the second forbidding the abuse of dominant positions. Article 85 permits certain exemptions to the general prohibition, but these exemptions envisage the promotion of technical and economic progress, and further, require that consumers enjoy a 'fair share of the resulting profit'. Thus this section of Article 85 is similar to the Restrictive

Trade Practices Act, 1956 and the Resale Prices Act, 1964, both of which permitted exemptions only if a net public benefit could be proved.

Article 85 applies only to intermember trade, and has no reference to practices confined to individual states. But Article 86 speaks of improper exploitation of a dominant position within the Common Market 'or a substantial part of it'. One might then wonder if one country, say Germany, or the U.K. for that matter, might not be regarded as a 'substantial part' of the Common Market in this regard. More recent developments support this interpretation.

The Treaty of Rome merely states policy in regard to competition. It does not, nor could it, lay down procedures and penalties; this task was left to the Commission, which attempts to implement the Treaty by means of regulations and directives. The key regulation in this respect is Regulation 17 promulgated in February 1962. The salient provisions of this are:

1. That all agreements are to be registered except:
   (a) agreements whose sole object is the development of common standards, or the conduct of joint research, and this only if the results of the research are freely available to all parties,
   (b) bilateral agreements where only RPM or industrial property rights, such as patents, are involved.
2. That all agreements other than the above exceptions are prohibited unless exemptions are granted under Section 3 of Article 85. This provides for exemption if an improvement in production or distribution is achieved, or technical or economic progress is promoted, and that consumers get a fair share of the benefit.
3. That the Commission is empowered to require information from undertakings, and can call on the appropriate member state to assist in this. The Commission also has the power to examine books, and make copies of them, and to enter premises and vehicles.
4. That undertakings intentionally or negligently infringing Articles 85 and 86 are subject to a fine of one million units of account (now slightly over one million U.S. dollars) or 10% of turnover for the previous business year. A periodic penalty of up to 10,000 U/A's a day could be exacted for continuance of a prohibited practice.

All decisions made pursuant to Articles 85 and 86, and to secondary legislation, are subject to review by the Court of Justice.

Another regulation, no. 67, was promulgated in March 1967, clarifying the position of exclusive dealerships. Article 85 did not apply to bilateral exclusive dealing. This was subject to certain restrictions among which were that:

1. The dealer should not be obliged to refrain from manufacturing or supplying other non-competing goods.
2. Manufacturers of competing goods could not enter into an exclusive dealership.
3. There should be no obstacle placed in the way of other dealers or consumers obtaining the goods from other parts of the Common Market.
4. There must be competition from goods considered by the consumer to be similar.
5. Prices should not be 'excessive'.

It has already been mentioned that Article 86 speaks vaguely of 'a substantial part' of the Common Market. I have suggested that one of the larger member states, such as Germany, could, in logic, be regarded as a substantial part. This interpretation appears now to have been given some validity by draft regulation no. 2 of 1970, which is intended to amend Regulation 17. The phrase 'substantial part of the Common Market' is here defined as Holland, Belgium, and Luxembourg together, or any one of the remaining member states.

The definition, it is true, is used in the context of a minor exception to the requirement to notify agreements, but it nevertheless reinforces an already plausible contention. Finally, the GEMA copyright case (see below), involving a dominant position in Germany only, was decided by the Commission who ruled that, for purposes of Article 86, Germany formed a substantial part of the Common Market. Thus, the treaty has now been clarified, and one might even say extended, by means of secondary legislation by the Council, and of case law by the Commission.

The GEMA case

Legislation is meaningless without enforcement, and enforcement inevitably implies judicial decisions. It will be instructive therefore to summarise a few cases decided by the Commission.

The GEMA case, a very complex one, was considered in June 1971 and resulted in a series of interesting decisions. GEMA is the fortunate acronym for Gesellschaft für Musikalische Aufführungs- und mechanische Vervielfältigungsrechte. This is a German authors' rights society, which occupies a dominant, indeed exclusive position as to the performing rights of musical works of German nationals. The purpose of this society is the protection of the rights of authors, the word 'author' being taken in its broadest sense to include composers, music publishers, cinematographic producers, and so on. GEMA also manages authors' artistic works, and indeed, this has become its main function to the extent that the ordinary member is required, as a condition of membership, to assign all his rights in present and future works, not only for Germany, but for the whole world.

This extravagant condition was one of the main objections of the Commission. It was held that this stipulation constituted an attempt to limit other authors' rights societies within the Community, and that GEMA was thus trying to convert a dominant position into one of monopoly, which constituted abusive exploitation of that dominant position. Another important decision derived from GEMA's restricting ordinary membership to German nationals, and to others with fiscal residence in the Federal Republic. This was regarded as discrimination against nationals of other member states, and so an abuse.

As pointed out earlier, being a purely German organisation did not save GEMA from the Commission's jurisdiction, for it was ruled that the Federal Republic was 'a substantial part' of the Common Market, as designated in Article 86.

The Commission found that GEMA improperly discriminated against importers of records. Records manufactured and distributed in Germany were charged a licence fee of 8% of their ultimate sales price. This same fee was also levied on imports, even though a fee had already been levied by the authors' rights society of the country of origin; worse, that anterior fee was levied by GEMA itself in the case of re-imports.

GEMA was also found to have unfairly discriminated against imports of optical and sound recorders. Under German copyright law the manufacturers of recording devices were obliged to pay a proportion of their sales price to authors whose works might be recorded privately, and whose copyright would thus be infringed; these fees were payable to a duly constituted authors' rights society, inevitably GEMA, who would distribute them. GEMA exacted less than 3% from German manufacturers but the maximum of 5% from importers.

Another abuse of dominance has found to lie in the practice of requiring the full licence fee of 8% per record, even though some of the pieces on the record might not be protected. In effect this meant that GEMA claimed the copyright fee for works on whose copyright it had no claim, and indeed works that might well be in the public domain. These and several alleged abuses, have made the GEMA process virtually a body of anti-trust case law in itself. Unfortunately the import of this case has been lessened by its being concerned with the entertainment industry, which one tends to regard as peripheral to the real world of industry and finance.

The Supexie case

Four French companies manufacturing chemical fertilisers set up a limited company, Supexie, for the purpose of joint marketing in other

Common Market countries, and abroad. Although the companies could each decide the amount of product they allocated to Supexie, and how much they would market individually, in fact, they charged the joint firm with all their exports out of France.

Supexie's payments system was such that all four participants received the same price ex-factory or ex-port, no matter where their product was sold, whether to other Common Market countries, or abroad. So instead of the separate firms making 'cocktail-party' agreements on prices and terms, they set up a separate limited company to do so. And not only was a uniform price to the consumer thus established, but also a uniform factory price to the producers, so eliminating differentials in distribution costs. The effect of this system, then, was cartel-like on three counts, first, that it eliminated price competition; second, that it established market quotas, and third, that it pooled distribution costs (and so would prevent purchasers gaining the advantage of the most efficient distribution).

The Commission ruled that a joint sales agency such as Supexie, with its own powers for exporting to other member states, has the effect of restricting and distorting competition in contravention of Article 85. Exports outwith the Common Market, on the other hand, would not come under their prohibition.

Before the case was decided Supexie amended the agreement so that it applied only to exports beyond the Community. For this reason no intervention on the part of the Commission was necessary.

The ceramic tiles case

An association, Interessengemeinschaft der Deutschen Keramischen Wand- und Bodenfliesenwerke, was formed by the German ceramic tile producers, whose purpose, according to its Articles of Association was 'to take decisions regarding cartel agreements within the limits of the German law, against restraint of competition, and to defend them before the appropriate authorities'. Evidently the association was able to defend the interests of the tile producers successfully before the German authorities, but it failed to do so before the Commission.

The twelve German producers comprising the association represented 99% of German tile production, and approximately 60% of sales. The balance of 40% of sales comprised imports from other member states (mainly Italy), and from Japan. The main function of the association was the regulation of discounts on the purchase of tiles, which were granted not according to the amount brought from individual producers, but indiscriminately according to the total amount bought from all participating producers, even if this meant only a relatively modest amount from each. The discounts at the upper levels were substantial as the following table shows:

minimum purchase (D.M.)	*discount rate*
6,500	10%
26,000	14%
65,000	17%
145,000	17% & 2% bonus
520,000	17% & 3% bonus

Notice the crucial condition that the discount applied to the total purchases, and not merely to the excess. If someone had bought say, D.M. 25,000 of tiles, and needed D.M. 2,000 more, buying the additional supply from any one of the association's firms would not only entitle him to 14% off the new tiles but also to a rebate of 4% off all tiles he had already bought that year. So at this level, tiles worth D.M. 2,000 at list price, were actually got for D.M. 2,000 less 14%, less a further 4% of D.M. 25,000, i.e. a total cost of D.M. 720, which represents an over-all discount on this purchase of 64%. This system represented a very cogent argument for restricting one's purchases to the group, especially at the point at which one was about to graduate to a higher discount rate. Another strong incentive was that the buyers started each year at a discount rate related to that reached in the previous year (one grade lower in fact). Thus they were encouraged to make purchases at least to the level that would justify this rate so as not to be obliged to reimburse the producers.

The Commission ruled that this system contravened Article 85 on the grounds that 'the non-German producers ... have to surmount ... an artificial obstacle introduced collectively'. In support of this decision they rejected the association's argument that non-German imports could not have been affected, as these have grown from well under 10% of the German market in 1960 to over 35% in 1969. The Commission asserted that but for the agreement, imports might have increased even more. They bolstered their contention by pointing out that in the discount range of 17% plus 2% bonus approximately 30% of the total turnover was represented by purchases within 20% of the qualifying minimum of D.M. 195,000. This, however, is precisely what one might expect, discount system or no; in any article for which there is an elastic demand, purchases would tend to be concentrated at lower rather than higher levels. Nevertheless, though the Commission's statistics are not convincing, there remains the strong presumption that the discount did in fact induce the German consumers to deal exclusively with German producers.

The association put forward several arguments to prove that their system benefited the consumers, and so exemption should be provided under Clause 3, Article 85. The Commission's reply was that these benefits might well be provided without the joint discount agreement, or alternatively, if the agreement were extended to all EEC producers and purchasers, that the benefit would be even greater. At no time, however, was it asserted that the system was detrimental to consumers. The detriment was that suffered by the producers of the five other member states.

The aniline dyestuffs case

An important case is that of the aniline dyestuffs cartel considered by the Commission in 1969. Seventeen companies were charged with concerted practice in fixing common prices for their products. The companies denied concerted behaviour, and claimed that it was merely parallel behaviour in that they simply followed prices set up by the price leader. The Commission's case rested on the following allegations:

1. The price increases were identical—15%.
2. Nevertheless, these increases applied only to resale prices; the prices to subsidiaries and agents did not always rise in the same proportion.
3. The range of products to which the new price applied was identical.
4. The announcements or application of price increases took place within a few days of each other.
5. Telex messages to subsidiaries instructing them to raise prices were in some cases worded identically.

However, the first four of these items of evidence are hardly convincing since they are perfectly consistent with a price leadership situation. Only item 5, concerning the telex wording, suggests collusion. If the companies had gone to the trouble of editing their telexes their case might have been decidedly stronger.

The difference between concerted action and normal oligopolistic behavior may be rather subtle. The effect, which is what counts, is identical; only the means differ. But this difference was enough to induce the Commission to find against the companies. Penalties of up to 50,000 U/A's were imposed.

A point of note is that four of the largest companies did not even belong to the Common Market: three were Swiss—Geigy (the supposed price leader), Sandoz, and Ciba, and one was British—ICI. In finding as it did, the Commission therefore asserted its jurisdiction over non-EEC firms that operate in the Common Market. ICI appealed the decision, principally on the grounds that the company, being headquartered in the U.K. was not under the jurisdiction of the Commission. The Court of Justice, however, upheld the ruling and the fine.

The German record case

Another case of some importance is concerned with exclusive dealing. Deutsche Grammophon GmbH, a joint subsidiary of Philips and Siemens, practises RPM for its records (Polydor) in Germany, which is permitted by national law. A Hamburg supermarket, Metro-SB-Grossmarkte, imported Polydor records from France, having legally bought them from a French subsidiary of Deutsche Grammophon, and undercut DG's fixed price. A German court found this to be illegal under national law. The case was then taken by the supermarket to the Commission who decided that inter-member trade was involved, even when it was a question of re-imports, and it was contrary to Article 85 to prohibit their resale or fix their price. This is of all the greater interest when we consider that bilateral RPM is allowable under both German and Community law.

The Europemballage case

I shall now consider a remarkable case involving market dominance, the subject of Article 86. A holding company, Europemballage, was set up by the Continental Can Corporation of the United States. In 1970 Europemballage, which already had a dominant position in metal cans in northern Europe, bought a Dutch firm, Thomassen en Drijver Verblifa NV. This position secured for the enterprise the entire Dutch and Belgian markets in metal cans for meat and fish products, and upwards of 75% of the German market. There was no evidence that the enterprise had abused its dominance in any of the obvious ways such as price inflation, but the Commission ruled that the very purchase of a competitor by an already dominant firm was an abuse of that dominance. In other words, the Commission had taken on itself the power to regulate large mergers, which is not directly invested in it by the treaty, or Regulation 17. It had put itself in a position to investigate and rule on not only the abuse of dominance, but the degree of dominance, even when there is no abuse. From this it could be argued that a dominant firm seeking to expand further by internal growth would be subject to control.

The ruling that the mere extension of dominance is an abuse in itself had already been given in the GEMA case. Here, though, in the matter of Europemballage, it stands out starkly, and definitively, unobscured by competing rulings.

Europemballage, appealed the decision and won the support of the Advocate General who argued that strengthening a dominant position was not necessarily an abuse; that actual abuse in the normal sense must be proved before Article 86 could be invoked. The opinion of the Advocate General is normally accepted by the Court and becomes substantially its final judgment, but even so the case illustrates forcibly the thinking of the Commission and indicates its determination to block mergers that will create or extend a dominant position. If this cannot be done by means of Article 86 a revision of the Treaty will be sought.

The sugar cartel

The stringency of the Commission's punitive powers is shown by fines totalling 7,900,000 U/A's imposed on twenty-two firms in December 1972. The largest of the fines, 1,500,000 U/A's ,was exacted from the Belgian firm Raffinerie Tirlemontoise SA. The Commissionaire for Competition Policy, A. Borschette, called the violations 'blatant and deliberate', though he was at pains to point out that the fines were rather lenient since they represented a maximum of only 0.9 per cent of the company's turnover, whereas up to 10 per cent could have been imposed.

The essence of the case was that there was concerted action to keep up prices in the various member states by means of a system whereby the Belgian and French firms, which produced surpluses, would sell only to the producers of the other member states, thus depriving merchants from buying in the cheapest market.

The firms have indicated their intention of appealing, a prospect which M. Borschette states he regards with equanimity because of the convincing proof of his case. Officials of the Commission have stated that while the British Company, Tate and Lyle, was not directly involved, they were concerned with its dominant position in the UK market and will be investigating whether this position is being abused.[3]

Future course of policy

It seems that the Commission is intent on pursuing its active anti-trust course. It is now engaged in what might be a major case against synthetic fibre producers. This follows the decision of the German Cartel Office, Kartelamt, which imposed a fine equivalent to £ 6,000,000 on nine German producers. This considerable sum was intended to represent three times the alleged illegal profits made by the producers in consequence of the cartel agreement. Glanzstoff, a subsidiary of the Dutch group AKZO, was the most heavily penalised, being fined the equivalent of £ 2,600,000.

The Commission are presently (November 1972) investigating whether this cartel crosses into other member states, and therefore contravenes Article 85.

In regard to dominance, the Commission is now proposing that contemplated mergers and takeovers be notified, so that they might be ruled on at a preliminary stage at which they can be conveniently nullified.

Competition policy may well be further refined, or possibly distorted, in the light of a recent statement by Albert Borschette, the commissioner for competition policy. This is to the effect that the Commission is about to work for the establishment of uniform wages, working hours, and labour conditions, 'so that differences under this heading between member countries shall cease to be a factor in determining where investment is located'.

There is no doubt that one company's low wage costs is a severe impediment to another company's sales; eliminating this differential would allow the high-cost company a better chance to compete. But it arbitrarily lessens the low-cost company's chance to compete, which surely, it is the object of the Commission to foster. It also arbitrarily inteferes with competition between regional groups of workers to sell their labour. At present a worker in Palermo can choose between a high paid job in Hamburg and a low-paid job in his home town. Under a uniform wage policy, the choice might well be between a high-paid job in Hamburg, and no job in his home town. On the other hand, the Commission's action may simply be the forestalling of pay-parity claims on the part of the unions in the enlarged market.

One also wonders how an expanding, highly productive company might attract new workers in a tight labour market. If it cannot offer more pay or better conditions, how can it increase production and offer consumers the advantages of its greater competitiveness?

Competition in Britain as a member of the community

Common Market rules permit the enforcement of bilateral RPM, and therefore— thought it is of limited practical importance— are less stringent in that respect than the U.K's outright prohibition. With this one exception, Common Market rules and practice for the control of monopoly and quasi-monopoly are perceptibly more exacting. The European Commission can initiate an investigation, enter premises, issue decisions, and punish the culpable and negligent. In Britain the Restrictive Practices Court has only a fraction of this power, and the Monopolies Commission even less.

Apart from its inherent powers, the European Commission has shown initiative almost to the point of aggression in pursuing and deciding cases. Possibly this avidity can be traced to the Commission's independence of government and business establishment. In Britain the Monopolies Commission is appointed by, directed by, and reports to the Government. The Restrictive Practices Court and the Registrar are more independent, but still have face-to-face contact with Ministers, civil servants, and businessmen. By contrast, in the Community, the Commission is insulated from the various national governments by the Council of Ministers, which itself, by reasons of its very internationality, has great independence of any one member state. In brief, under the British system personal and political influence has much more scope for its exercise.

To what extent will U.K. industry, following British entry, be affected by

Common Market rules on polistic situations? The picture is clear in regard to dominance. Following Regulation 67 and the GEMA case, Britain itself would be regarded as a 'substantial part' of the whole, and any company that enjoys a monopoly within Britain in any distinctive product might well come under the jurisdiction of the Commission. Note that the Commission has regard to particular products, and not to industries, in considering monopolistic situations. One company may well be in competition with another in a general field, say fibres, yet have a monopoly in a particular kind of fibre, say rayon: this would then fall within the purview of the Commission.

The Commission's jurisdiction becomes even more certain if we consider that a monopoly in Britain is likely to extend to Ireland, which even though a small market, will be a full member state; so the condition of inter-member trade will then be irrefutably established.

To prophesy which British companies might draw the attention of the Commission is at present impossible, for whatever monopoly might exist now might well be upset by the incursion of other member companies; this, after all, is a prime purpose of the EEC. Indeed, if membership in the Common Market brings its intended benefit, existing monopolies in Britain will inevitably be assailed by continental competitors.

So far as restrictive practices go, there will be no new circumstances, since British industry operating in the Common Market is already subject to the Commission; this was shown by the aniline dyes case, as it involved ICI. Restrictive practices confined to the U.K. will not come under the Commission's jurisdiction. However, there is some reason to believe that the Community might be advancing to the position where even purely national restrictive practices will be brought within its purview. The 'substantial part' condition of Article 86 could well be applied to Article 85 by means of judicial decision. It would seem a natural extension that, if monoply within national boundaries is subject to Community regulation, then a cartel, which is just a multi-firm monopoly, should also be subject. Besides this, national cartels are bound to affect intermember trade in some degree, however small. This would be reason enough for an intently anti-trust Commission to initiate an investigation.

Five months before Britain was due to enter the Community, the effects of competition policy were foreshadowed in a decision of the boards of Imperial Tobacco Group Ltd and British American Tobacco Co Ltd. For 70 years these two companies had a market-sharing agreement under which Imperial had the exclusive right to market all BAT brand names in the U.K, and BAT a reciprocal right to all Imperial brands elsewhere. The two companies foresaw that the Community Commision would not accept such an arrangement. A merger was contemplated, but this would give the merged company

29% of the Community market, with a much higher proportion in certain parts of it such as Germany, and notably, the U.K. The 'substantial part' condition of Article 86, as crystallised in the Europemballage case, would then probably govern, and the merger be disallowed. Because of this, the two companies agreed to abandon the market-sharing agreement, though they still intend to continue a joint buying, and a joint packaging agreement. The companies do not intend to enter into cut-throat competition on the market side. In the words of the British-American chairman, Richard Dobson, 'We both intend by all legal means so to arrange our affairs that we do not compete with each other with identical goods in the same market.' It is more than probable that the Commission will afford no 'legal means' to achieve this purpose.

Another effect already evident is the change in the British Steel Corporation's pricing policy. Formerly, steel prices were quoted uniformly throughout the U.K., and included transport charges. Places distant from the point of production enjoyed the same price as nearby areas. This will be changed under the EEC basing-points system, where prices are quoted net of transport charges, so that the further a consumer is from the point of production the more he pays. This contrasts strongly with the Cement Makers' Federation which, like BSC, charge uniform prices in all areas, of which policy the Monopolies Commission approved on the grounds of public interest.

In the end we have to consider whether legislation can really foster competition. It is one thing to prohibit explicit agreements and to break up dominant firms. It is quite another to ensure that the isolated firms work at peak efficiency for a minimum of profit; and this is what competition implies. If we accept that it is a natural tendency among producers to maximise profits or to minimise the effort of achieving them, then a means fundamentally different from normal competition policy would be required. Such a policy, involving price control and efficiency norms, is seldom resorted to, and in any case, would not necessarily work. For this would involve government much more intimately in the affairs of industry than most governments, businessmen, and unions would relish. Legislation can merely remove barriers to competition. We must depend on other forces, be they self-interest, public spirit, consumers' militance, or differential taxation, to ensure a fair distribution of wealth and effort throughout society.

Notes

1 G. C. Allen, *Monopoly and Restrictive Practices*, George Allen and Unwin Ltd, p. 62, 1968.

2 J. F. Pickering, in *Public Law*, Autumn 1965.

3 Reginald Dale, Financial Times 19 December 1972.

Bibliography

Common Market Law Reports, London.

G. C. Allen, *Monopoly and Restrictive Practices,* George Allen and Unwin Ltd., 1967.

Reports of the Monopolies Commission, H.M.S.O., London.

European Community, European Community Press and Information Office, London.

D. Swann, *The Economics of the Common Market*, Penguin, 2nd edition, 1972.

Swann and McLachlan, *Concentration or Competition: A European Dilemma?* Chatham House; P.E.P., 1967.

11 Trends in European Taxation

by T. D. LYNCH

A paper[1] presented on 16 September 1972 at the 20th Summer School, at St Andrews University, of The Institute of Chartered Accountants of Scotland, to review the general tax situation, particularly some of the more recent developments, in this country and in other countries of Western Europe to find out, if it is possible to do so, if there are significant trends in taxation as a whole, or in any specific taxes.[2]

Definitions

'Trends' in this context will be fairly strictly construed. That is, I shall be looking for symptoms of movements which are reasonably continuous and definite in direction. We shall also be watching for the converse, i.e. the absence of trends. 'European' means western European, very largely the present European Economic Community countries and those which are about to join the Community. 'Taxation' means the major indirect and direct taxes. There simply is not space here to deal with smaller taxes, temporary taxes, special levies, local taxes, etc.— we have to restrict ourselves to the principal taxes which produce, or are expected to produce, the bulk of the national revenue. Reference will be made to some of the lesser taxes, but only for the sake of completeness, or occasionally as a matter of interest.

The task

It is well to define our terms and to describe what we have in mind to do, but we must also be clear why we are doing it. There are, in fact, several reasons. Firstly, it behoves us as good accountants to look at the broader aspects of the subjects we deal with in our everyday practice. By so doing we hope to achieve a greater insight into, and therefore a better understanding of the subject; our practical application thereby becomes more interesting and efficient and more satisfying intellectually. Secondly, it is the duty of all professional men and women to be aware of new developments in their own professions, though such developments may affect some individual members more than others. This paper has a lot to do with new developments, both current and future. There are other reasons for looking at this subject, which may well vary from individual to individual, e.g. a special interest in EEC affairs: the political duty of accountant M.P.s or budding

M.P.s; a reassurance that we are still 'the greatest', and so on. But there is one final and most important reason which does affect everyone. Unless we are prepared to lift our minds from everyday matters and become aware of developments we shall miss the opportunity to make our contribution to these developments, which would be a loss not only to ourselves but to the common good. In other words, the work we aim to do here should help to equip us to influence the trends we may discern in European taxation and to ensure, as far as possible, that nothing disastrous happens, whether by evil design or, as is more likely, by accident. This is our doomwatch.

Principal topics

The following are the main areas of taxation we shall look at, and these will provide the subjects of main section headings for this paper: indirect taxes, personal tax (especially on capital), business profits, corporate taxes, and double taxation relief. Before dealing with these specific areas, however, it is worth reminding ourselves what taxes generally are all about: the need for cooperation between countries in tax matters, and the particular requirements of harmonisation and avoidance of trade distortions in the enlarged EEC.

Some general aspects

The Nature of Taxation

No form of civilisation is possible without taxation. That is how important taxation is. But what is it? In its most rudimentary form it is the process by means of which revenue is raised to pay collective expenses. In simpler times the producers gave part of what they produced to those who could not produce anything because they were engaged in the non-productive, but essential task of organising the producers as a whole, or looking after their collective welfare. Public revenue (taxation) was, and still is, required to meet public expenditure. Things have changed, however, and it is not quite so easy to say what is meant by 'public expenditure'. Nowadays this expenditure can take many forms. Apart from ordinary administrative expenses, which can include a large variety of services, such as defence etc; it is taken to include capital expenditure; equalisation payments by way of special incentives; investment grants, etc.; and by way of general incentives, e.g. removal of poverty and redistribution of income and wealth. Governments may raise loans, as well as taxation, to meet revenue expenditure or capital expenditures. Governments may also go into business, e.g. nationalised industries, or they may transact business on behalf of the community as a whole, e.g. licensing the exploitation of offshore oil.

These are but a few examples to indicate the underlying complexity of what appears to be on the surface a perfectly simple statement: that 'taxation is the process by which public revenue is raised to meet public expenditure'. One must, therefore, concern oneself with the design of the process (the tax system) and also decide what should be included in (or excluded from) the term, public expenditure. This is why reforms of taxation are basically difficult to agree. There are differences of opinion not only as to methods and machinery but also as to what constitutes the whole of, but no more than, the public expenditure for which the public revenue, taxation, is required.

The fundamental problems of taxation are therefore (1) What revenue is needed, i.e. why it is required, (2) How it should be raised.

Taxation Reform

There has been a great deal of talk about tax reform, and a great many reforms have been introduced. So much so that tax reforms and reforming Chancellors have become national bores as a result. The Chancellor hero coming to rescue us all from the mess we are in—which we of course made against his advice— should beware of going too far, of rescuing us too often from the same dire situation.

It is, however, necessary to remind ourselves of the principal reforms that have recently taken place, or which are proposed, in the U.K.:

Indirect Taxation

The introduction of value added tax (VAT) in April 1973, to replace purchase tax and selective employment tax (SET).

Personal Tax

A unified tax has already been enacted to replace income-tax and surtax, and there is a Green Paper on the possible reform of estate duty.

Business Profits

Replacement of grants with accelareted depreciation. This was followed by the reintroduction of grants and even greater acceleration of depreciation.

Company Tax

This was reformed in 1965 on a modified double-rate (classical) system. It is to be reformed again in April 1973 by the introduction of an imputation system.

International Income

There has been a steady reduction in relief for double taxation.

We have to ask ourselves how far these changes reflect European, or even world trends, or if they are merely reactionary, arising from self-interest—whether of country or of individual prejudice—or from doctrinaire views. It is hard to say, but we will take a rather closer look at them under various heads, in conjunction with changes elsewhere, and perhaps draw some conclusions.

Harmonisation

No paper on taxation trends would be complete without some reference to harmonisation in the context of the EEC. If the EEC is to be what it purports to be, an economic (comm)unity, i.e. one common market, it will be necessary to eliminate anything which distorts trade, or interferes with the free flow of investment by people, of their money or their business capital. Clearly this must be the most significant single factor in determining taxation trends in Europe, since taxation can so easily distort trade and prevent the free movement of capital etc., e.g. in the relief given or withheld for double taxation of international income.

One must avoid embarking here on a major essay on tax harmonisation, but it is a factor which is specifically required by the Treaty of Rome in respect of indirect taxation, and is implied, though not explicitly provided for, in relation to direct taxation. It is essential therefore to note what it means. Harmonisation in relation to taxation is not well defined, though its general nature is widely, if imprecisely understood. It will probably the sufficient for present purposes if we use the writer's own definition:[3]

> ...harmonisation of taxes... [is] any arrangement which has as its object the removal of barriers and causes of friction arising between States or their nationals by reason of divergences in their respective systems and rates of tariffs and taxes.

Harmonisation is therefore a process, not a state of things. It is essentially a process of alignment, of tax systems and of rates and reliefs. It may be present to a greater or to a lesser degree. The process must, of course, be capable of completion, and at that point harmonisation ceases and is replaced by a state of standardisation or uniformity. It is highly unlikely that this state of things will be reached before the turn of the century, and most probably not for a long time after that. We can therefore assume that the harmonisation process is to be with us for the foreseeable future, and consequently, that it will continue to influence taxation trends.

Indirect taxation

The Nature of Indirect Taxation

'Indirect' in the tax sense has always been equated with 'hidden'. The payer, the final consumer, pays but he is either unaware that he is paying, or aware only in a general way. This does not reflect its true nature, which it is important to appreciate: indirect taxation is taxation which is levied without *direct reference* to the taxpayer's capacity to pay, i.e. as compared with other taxpayers. It is often said to be regressive, while direct taxation is said to be progressive. These terms are not satisfactory, however, and require fresh consideration. First of all, 'regressive'. and 'progressive' are to some extent synonymous in people's minds with 'bad' and 'good' respectively. Indirect taxation is neither bad nor good. Like most things and most people has bad things and good things in its make-up and it may be *used badly*. The rates of indirect taxation and the total revenue raised thereby could be good or bad. If indirect taxation is geared properly to social security benefits and is increased for luxury goods it can be more progressive than a direct tax which is steeply graduated to deal with incomes which are, very largely, not there. The element of choice which seemed to be inherent in indirect taxes was welcomed by most taxpayers, but this was another myth which has been exploded with the introduction of VAT on almost all goods and services.

To summarise, indirect taxes are not regressive in nature; neither are direct taxes progressive. Both may be *used* regressively or progressively. The regressiveness or progressiveness of taxes must therefore be judged by reference to the system of taxation applied within a country as a whole.

Having put the pundits firmly in their places, it is probably time to get on more specifically with the job in hand and look at what has been recently happening in the indirect tax field all over western Europe.

Value added tax

Very largely, what has been happening is VAT. The existing Common Market countries have either adopted it or are on the point of doing so. The new EEC applicants will introduce VAT just before or just after joining.

Why VAT? Why not purchase tax or SET, turnover taxes, cascade systems, etc? Where were they found wanting?

First, it is important to appreciate what VAT is. It is a multi-stage tax levied on all goods and services. Because of the wide base, many people are involved in the administration, both within and without the Civil Service. By the same token, the rate of tax on most goods and services can be relatively low. Ideally there should be only one rate but, just as certain goods and services have had to be excluded from the tax, so also a number of rates have been introduced. The U.K. system boasts of only one rate, but in reality it has three: (a) zero, (b) 10%, and (c) reduced rate (to be announced). It may even be said that there are four rates, i.e. an effective rate of 16/17% on cars, by the introduction of a separate car tax to supplement the 10% VAT on new cars.

Thus the U.K. and all western European countries have introduced, or will shortly introduce, modified VAT systems at various rates. There seems little doubt that there is a strong trend towards VAT as the principal indirect tax. When properly applied it appears to be so vastly superior to other expenditure taxes that it is unlikely to be displaced for many years to come. The principal advantages claimed for it are that it is neutral in operation, self-policing, has a large and flexible yield, a low rate ,and allows full rebating on exports. It has disadvantages, notably the heavy cost in financial and human resources, due to the massive administration required, but even this quite major disadvantage is more than compensated for by the advantages. It is also liable to produce spin-off advantages, e.g. in better discipline in smaller businesses (including better accounting) and in the provision of more reliable trade statistics for industry and commerce, particularly for the retail trade.

VAT modifications

Vat is, then, the indirect tax of the next few decades in western Europe and it will probably be adopted by most of the developed countries of the world before the end of this century. Even Japan, with virtually no history of indirect taxation, is considering VAT. But, while VAT has replaced a lot of indirect tax, it has by no means replaced all indirect taxes. For example, in the U.K. we still retain our customs and excise duties on oil, on tobacco and on the very water of life itself. Where VAT has been introduced it has been introduced in modified form. These modifications will have to be amended and eventually harmonised throughout the enlarged EEC so that no one member can claim that another member is being unfair. Finally there is no point in having a single common market with a number of customs barriers zigzagging through it. The EEC must operate as a single entity if it is to mean anything at all. This means that eventually there will be no internal barriers, but before that can happen, the rates as well as the system will have to be harmonised.

VAT harmonisation

Thus VAT is in itself a trend, if not *the* trend, but it also points to further trends, towards harmonisation in fact. It seems certain that VAT will be harmonised, firstly as to the systems (i.e. all modifications will either be removed or, where they remain, they will be accepted throughout the EEC), and secondly, as to an eventual uniform rate or rates. This will in turn lead to a very significant thing. It will mean that, within the EEC, the VAT finally paid on goods and services will be collected by the revenue department of the country wherein the goods or services (or the relevant part of them) *originated*, whereas, at present, the VAT is collected by the country of destination, i.e. where the goods or services are finally *consumed.* Between the EEC countries, when the custom barriers go down, there will be no imports or exports. There will, on international, but intra-EEC, trade, merely be value added and final sales, as there is at present between, say, Scotland and England, where a common market has existed for a very long time. Thus, the VAT revenues will go to the countries with the most industrious and hard-working citizens and not to those with the largest appetities for consumption. What a wonderful chance for energy and enterprise, which should benefit too by the fact that EEC countries will now welcome the presence of a good business from another EEC country, instead of trying to keep such business out on nationalistic grounds.

National budgets

One other significant thing will happen. No Chancellor will be able to vary his VAT rate without the agreement of his counterparts in all other EEC countries, once the customs barriers are down and VAT is fully harmonised. This could well mean a gradual loss of flexibility, in operating indirect taxation, and in the longer term it would mean that an EEC budget would replace at least that part of the individual member states' budgets which are concerned with VAT and eventually with all other indirect taxes. This is, of course, such a material part of every budget that it will mean, in effect, the end of the truly independent national budget. There will be an independent EEC budget *vis-à-vis the rest of the world,* but within the EEC each member state will be required to limit action to fit into the EEC framework. The U.K. Government is at present examining the possibility of a change in its financial/fiscal years to the calendar year, which would bring this country into line with the EEC countries.

Summary

To summarise on indirect taxation, the following seems to be ascertainable trend:

1. The introduction of VAT to all countries in the EEC and to many, if not most, developed countries elsewhere.
2. Harmonisation of VAT, as national modifications are eliminated or aligned, first as to system and then as to rates.
3. Less volatile indirect taxes and therefore possibly more volatile direct taxes. (The opportunity may, however, be taken to find new sources of revenue because of the relative difficulty in 'moving' VAT; one fairly obvious target is that any factory or plant which in any way causes pollution will be taxed to pay for environmental protection and improvement.)
4. The rise of E.E.C. budgets and the gradual decline of national budgets.

Direct taxation: individuals

Framework for taxes on individuals

Direct taxes on individuals fall into three categories: (a) on income, (b) on capital gains, and (c) on capital (or wealth). It is not so very long ago that income was the sole (or only material) yardstick for computing the direct contribution of individuals to the national revenue. It is, however, now widely accepted that the distinction between income and capital gains is often not significant and that there is no difference in substance between capital gains, i.e. realised gains, and a growth in total wealth which has not been realised. All three factors are now generally taken into account. But no one is very clear as to how they are to be taken into account, and no one seems to have given any thought as to what public expenditure is to be financed from them. Is tax on income to be used for public capital works? Is tax on capital gains and on wealth to be used to meet public annual expenditure? What about redistribution of wealth? Is this quite literally to mean spreading capital around, in the way that income is spread around; or does it mean simply the destruction of capital by spreading it around in the form of income; or does it mean the reduction of capital in private hands and the building up of social or public capital? There is apparently no settled policy anywhere on these questions, except possibly in Russia. It is high time there was such a policy: a constructive policy which would encourage capital in private hands,—as many different pairs of hands as possible.

Income taxation

So far as taxes on income are concerned, there seems little point in going into much detail. Taxes on income are subject to a great variety of sophistication as to personal allowances and reliefs, the unit of assessment, i.e. the family as a whole or each member on his own, and the tie-in with social security contributions and benefits. Under the tax credit system which has been proposed for the U.K., and which seems to be a most sensible idea, the tax and the financial aspects of social security systems will be integrated. Income as a basis for taxation has been accepted by most countries for a long time, and it is not possible, therefore, to say that there is a trend towards income taxation, but it may be said that there is a trend towards better machinery for the assessment and collection of income-tax, and a more direct link between this and social security.

Capital gains tax

Tax on capital gains is well behind income-tax as regards acceptance, but the trend towards a capital gains tax throughout Europe is pretty obvious and requires no elaboration here. There are great differences in the computational rules, rates, etc., and in some cases unrealised gains are assessed annually, but the principle that capital gains should be taxed is well established, and it is likely that every European country will have a capital gains tax within the fairly near future. No doubt the harmonisation process will then commence so that, in the longer term, capital gains tax will be uniform in system and rates.

Taxes on capital: the present position

In March 1972 H.M. Government published a Green Paper entitled '*Taxation of Capital on Death: A possible Inheritance Tax in place of Estate Duty*' (Cmnd. 4930) in which they set down the general scheme of the British estate duty and the manner in which certain other countries tax capital on death, and in which they finally outlined an inheritance tax. The Green Paper is intended for discussion, and unlike earlier Green Papers on the subject of taxation reform, does not contain a specific proposal which has official blessing. The U.K. does not have a separate gifts tax, though there is an element of a gifts tax in the seven year restriction for estate duty purposes in respect of *inter višos* gifts.

The general situation is that the present EEC countries have an inheritance tax plus a gifts tax. Italy seems to be blessed with estate duty as well, but as no one takes Italian direct taxes very seriously, least of all the Italians, it may be as well to ignore this special case. One or two EEC countries have a wealth tax too, but as this tax is to all intents and purposes, because of its low rate, merely a tax on income under another name, as is all discrimination in income taxation with regard to income from capital, it is proposed to say no more about wealth taxes here. In any case the cry for a wealth tax would not arise if taxes on capital worked properly, i.e. effectively and fairly.

Taxes on capital: the need for a sound philosophy

Despite the wealth of information in the Green Paper, most of which is both interesting and instructive, it contains no fundamental philosophy for taxing capital. There is no sign that anyone has given the matter the slightest consideration. In part III of the Green Paper the opening paragraphs 43 and 44 are subtitled 'Basic principles'. Paragraph 43 states the essential differences between computing estate duty and inheritance tax ...whereas an estate duty is charged by reference to the value of the property left by the deceased, an inheritance tax is concerned (*sic*) with what the beneficaries get. Paragraph 44 is not concerned with principles at all but with procedure: it sets out in summary what appears in greater detail in the succeeding paragraphs of the Green Paper.

We are not concerned with the Green Paper itself, nor even with the technical differences between one kind of death duty and another. What we are concerned with are our two main principles:

1. The underlying reasons for charging tax on capital, i.e. the public purpose for which it is required.
2. Having established the above reasons, the best means of raising the revenue.

If we can answer the questions arising we may then be able to say whether recent changes represent a trend or not.

There is no official answer. The questions do not appear to have even been put down for discussion in official circles. It would appear that taxes on capital have simply been a convenient 'topping up' of the general national revenue. 'If we can get a few hundred million from this source [e.g. U.K. estate duty] this would probably be useful' seems to be as far as most governments (in or out of the U.K.) have thought about it, if they have thought about it all. If anyone doubts this he should look at the table on page 11 of the Green Paper (for convenience this table is reproduced and attached hereto as Appendix 11.A), from which it is clear just how little is at present derived from capital taxation, though present duties can fall very heavily on individual estates. Capital, and the taxation of capital, are sadly in need of urgent and prolonged consideration. Our whole way of life depends on this being done. There is a tension within each country as inherited capital becomes less and less accepted. There is a tension, too, between countries and especially between the developed and the undeveloped countries. The latter are no longer content with the annual hand-outs (i.e. the taxes voluntarily imposed by the developed countries upon themselves for redistribution to the less fortunate countries) which they have received in the past, or even with employment opportunities (subsidised or otherwise). They are hungry for food and clothing but they are even hungrier for capital. Except in times of utter disaster they will often prefer to do without extra food and clothing (just like the man who sets up in business with no capital), if it means the creation of capital.

But we are in danger of straying into a much larger field, and we must resist the temptation, and return to our main point. There must be a policy about capital, just as there has to be a policy about income. It is suggested that we should examine personal capital and ask ourselves what we want to do with it. Spend and destroy it? Protect and encourage it? Redistribute it to individuals or turn it over to the state? Having decided what we want to do with it, the tax system should be used to do it, a tax system which could be properly designed because it was clear what the system had to achieve.

Estate duty inheritance tax

Before I leave this part of the subject, perhaps a few comments on the estate duty/inheritance tax question and the possible short-term trends in practice would not be out of place. In other words, making the broad assumption that taxes on capital are desirable and that they will be fairly substantial—both reasonable assumptions—what is the likely vehicle for raising the revenue? There is not in fact a great deal of difference between an estate duty and an inheritance tax. They are both charged on death, or more correctly, the juxtaposition of the death of an individual and his ownership of property. The essential points of difference between the two systems are: (a) the quantum of the liability, (b) the incidence of that liability amongst the inheritors.

The total revenue raised must be assumed to be the same under either tax system so that there is simply a change in the incidence of the tax as between one taxpayer and another, which is given effect to by differing sets of rules. Some inheritance taxes are said to include a gifts tax, while others are said to be complementary to a gifts tax. But both taxes could be, and should be, part of a comprehensive system of capital taxation, where the chargeable base is capital *when it is transferred to a new owner for less than full consideration*. It will be seen that in this system, death is simply one of the occasions when this happens. The U.K. system, estate duty, is thus a partial gifts tax, which in turn is only part of a system of capital taxation.

A capital transfer tax

The question is, then, not so much as between an estate duty and an inheritance tax—these are mere names—but whether there will be a trend towards a full system of capital taxation or a partial system. As already noted, the incidence of the tax will be satisfactorily settled only when it has become clear why the capital is being taxed. Undoubtedly there is a vaguely expressed, but widely held view that some measure of redistribution of capital should be encouraged, and that in taxing capital, consanguinity should be acknowledged. The trend appears to be firmly set on a gifts tax/inheritance tax system, but this could be a short-term trend which in reality is the first part of the longer-term trend towards a complete system of capital taxation. Nomenclature is always difficult to foresee, but capital transfer tax (CTT) might be an appropriate name for such a system, especially as it may have to be paid on assets transferred out of a particular country (unless within the EEC), so that the *country of origin* gets back part of the wealth created there. CTT might also bring within its scope the present capital gains tax system and any stamp duties on capital. The whole thing could work as follows:

	Gift (or Inheritance)	*Sale at Full Value*	*Asset transferred on emigration*
Value (gross)	£10,000	£10,000	£10,000
Stamp Duty 1%	100	100	–
	£9,900	£9,900	£10,000
Original Cost	5,000	5,000	5,000
Gain	£4,900	£4,900	£5,000
Capital Gains Tax 20% on Gain	£980	£980	£1,000
Gifts Tax: Transfer Tax Value of Gift (gross): Transfer	£10,000		£10,000
Less: Stamp Duty and CGT	1,080	N/A	1,000
Gift: Transfer	£8,920		£9,000
CTT @ 20%	£1,784	NIL	£1,800

This is the kind of system which could easily develop over the next 20 years in respect of tax on personal wealth. *Something* will have to be done to alter the present system, which favours or destroys estates at random. This tax could, for example, finance a national building society which would encourage property ownership by those in lower income groups.

Taxation of business profits

Although short, this section is introduced to allow for a few words about business profits in general, outside the framework of the next two parts of this paper, which deal fairly extensively with company taxes and double taxation relief.

There are two points which require special consideration: (1) The right of a nation to tax (or to exempt) business profits arising within its boundaries. (2) Tax havens.

Taxing business profits

Generally, business conducted *within* a country is distinguished from business conducted *with* a country. Profits from the latter are not charged to tax by that country. Where a trade is carried on within a country by a non-resident, the latter usually does so through a 'permanent establishment', which is the taxable entity. These rules are fairly widely and well understood. The essential matter which we wish to note is that tax on business profits is regarded as the prerogative, or primarily so, of the *country of origin* of the profits, 'origin' meaning not the origin of the income from sales, but the locus of the business organisation which produced the profits.

It may be necessary to extend this general rule to the EEC itself, so that business profits originating within the Community will be taxed primarily by the EEC where the profits accrue to a business organisation which is not national but European, e.g. the proposed European registered company. If this were done in relation to other taxes too, e.g. the suggested capital transfer tax on capital permanently exported outside the EEC, the budget for running the Common Market could be financed directly by taxation instead of by way of annual subscription. This is, of course, very long term, but the multinational or international business is already with us, and we are looking for trends which may only have begun as well as those which are well under way. Possibly, however, this is an area where the trend has not yet begun, and perhaps all that can be said is that it is likely that European companies will emerge which owe their legal existence and their allegiance to the EEC as a whole rather than to any member state and that their duty to pay taxes will be primarily to the EEC.

Tax havens

Tax havens have always been a thorn in the flesh of national revenue departments and presumably will continue to be so for many years to come. Our immediate concern is those tax havens which exist within EEC countries or prospective EEC countries. There seems little point in standardising, rationalising, or harmonising taxes within the EEC when certain areas within member states or geographically closely allied thereto do not conform. I have in mind such territories as the Channel Islands and the Isle of Man and also the free ports such as Shannon. Certain member states, particularly Luxembourg, may be tax havens as respects certain classes of income falling to residents of other member states. All these factors cause distortion of trade and, while they may continue for the use of non-EEC members, one can well imagine that, within the EEC, something may have to be done as regards tax havens and the free ports. This is also a longer-term problem, but there is already a trend to tighten anti-avoidance legislation in relation to tax havens, and the gradual integration of business in the EEC will give this movement a fresh impetus. Since free ports bring additional trade to the EEC, there may be little desire to change these, but even here there could well be either a dismantling of existing free ports or a free port area in each member state—or the free ports may become EEC, rather than national institutions.

The EEC will continue to allow for regional development, including pioneer relief, but again there will be an increasing tendency to regard regional reliefs as an EEC matter rather than the concern primarily of the country in which the region happens to be situated. The actual reliefs may even be regarded as a matter to be debited to the EEC budget rather than to national budgets. If, in fact, a completely integrated system of income and capital taxation, as suggested above, could be developed, complete with exchange control and tax on permanent external transfers, there would be a natural decline in tax havens which would cause them to wither away in due course. It is perhaps possible to say, as regards this problem, that a trend has already begun which is aimed at the harassment of tax haven arrangements and their eventual elimination.

Company taxation

The U.K. has just reformed its company tax system by changing it from the double rate (or classical) system to an imputation system. While it has been doing so, the present EEC countries have been studying the van den Tempel Report, which recommends the general use of the classical system. Confusion! But fortunately, there is the clarity of confusion. The paradox of confusion is that, when it arises, it becomes clear that there is a problem and where it lies.

The confusion seems to be due entirely to a lack of appreciation of what a company really is, and much more research must be done on the subject of company taxation. The difficulty is said to lie in the legal status of companies, which varies from country to country, but it is here submitted that until the real nature, as distinct from the conventional or legal nature, of a company is recognised, confusion will continue to exist and will get worse.

Companies: the taxable entity

A company is in essence the collective entity of all its shareholders at any point of time. Those shareholders are engaged, albeit passively, in the company's business. They have limited liability, and this calls for special legal regulations. Companies are managed on behalf of the shareholders by non-shareholders or shareholders acting in a different capacity. This calls for further special rules, mainly in accountability, involving disclosure, etc. But nevertheless a company is nothing more than a group of shareholders who are, ultimately, individuals. Only individuals pay tax. Ideally, therefore, the profits of a company should be allocated to the shareholders according to their respective interests in the equity of the company, and tax should be charged on them accordingly. But this is not possible except in the smallest companies, where it is in fact done in some cases. It is done in the U.K. in the case of private investment companies. The principle is therefore admitted. Indeed it has a name—'fiscal transparence'—and has been advocated in continental Europe. This is probably idealistic and incapable of achievement, except in smaller companies which could be allowed an option to be taxed as a partnership. Many small companies can achieve a partnership position in practice by paying out annual income in full each year to their shareholder/directors and borrowing it back, but it is dangerous for a small company to disburse all its earnings in case it fails to get them back, since fresh capital is usually much more difficult to obtain in these cases. The fixed assets of small companies cannot be dealt with in the same way as earnings, and there is, accordingly, a disincentive in the form of a potential double charge to capital gains tax.

However, the small company is not really in the mainstream of this paper, and I shall return to the main propositions which have emerged for the assessment of company profits. These are that:

1. The company and its shareholders are one single entity.
2. The company and its shareholders are two entirely separate entities.

The single entity concept

This embraces the ideal of ignoring the company altogether and apportioning the income for assessment purposes to individual shareholders. Its usual expression is to be found, however, in the franking or partial franking of dividends paid to shareholders. In its simplest form, a company pays tax at the rate normally applied to individuals, i.e. the standard rate or basic rate in U.K. terms, and, in so far as it pays dividends, no further tax is due from the company, and the dividend is received by the shareholder tax paid. The company shareholder does not pay any more tax, but may use the taxed dividend to recover tax on losses, management expenses, etc. The individual shareholder may recover tax if he is exempt or liable at a lower rate than that paid by the company, and he is required to pay additional tax, e.g. surtax, on the gross dividend, if he is liable at a higher rate.

The main problem here lies in profit retentions. In so far as profits are not distributed, the converse of the effect on the shareholders, as just described, applies, i.e. no relief to loss-making company shareholders or to exempt or low-rate individual shareholders; and no additional tax from high-rate individual shareholders. The former are usually ignored as being of lesser importance numerically, and to extract something from the latter, on account of the high rate foregone, a basic additional charge can be made on the company (which cannot be franked on to the shareholders), usually in the form of a separate company tax, e.g. the former U.K. profits tax; or by restricted franking on, e.g. the proposed imputation system for the U.K., and the two-rate system which was originally proposed in the Green Paper on the reform of corporation tax. The mechanics of these systems differ, but they all give expression to the same basic principle, i.e. a company and its shareholders are a single entity for tax purposes.

The dual entity concept

This proceeds on the basis that a company must be treated for tax purposes as something quite separate and distinct from its shareholders. It finds expression in two principal forms: the nil-rate and double-rate (or classical) systems. In the nil-rate system a dividend to shareholders is allowed as a charge against profits, and to the extent of the distribution the company pays a nil rate. The dividend is not franked. It has paid no tax and enters into assessment for the first time as original income of the shareholder. Under the classical system the company pays tax on all its profits before distributions to the shareholder and, in so far as it pays dividends or other distributions, a separate and additional tax is borne by the shareholder.

Rates of tax

So much for the theory, but in taxation matters it is the practical aspects which matter, and here the rates of tax are crucial. After all, the total burden of tax on companies *as a whole* and on shareholders *as a whole* can be the same under the single as under the dual concept and similarly with any variation thereof. The differences arise from company to company and from shareholder to shareholder. For example, under the classical system the government may wish to assess companies as a whole at, say 50%, but this implies a rate of company tax lower than 50% and a withholding tax rate which, when added to the company's rate, is greater than 50%, simply because all companies do not distribute all their profits. Thus, we may have a company rate of 40% and a withholding rate of 25%, or a combined rate of 65%. But some companies do distribute all their profits, and others do not distribute anything (or they may not be liable to withholding tax, e.g. because of a double taxation agreement), so that some company profits will be assessed at 40% and others at 65%, while the majority of companies will pay tax at intermediate rates. This immediately raises the general point about fairness as between taxpayers. Other examples of inequality, such as foreign-owned companies (covered by DTR agreements) or branches achieving a preferential tax rate compared with home-based companies, will spring to mind. The economic arguments about encouraging or discouraging company distributions are complete red herrings. They certainly have nothing to do with tax. The rates of tax on companies should not vary from company to company (except in special cases, such as building societies etc.) and the tax should be neutral so far as distributions are concerned. The writer's preference is for the pre-1965 U.K. system, with the proposed imputation system as second best. But this paper is not about preferences, my own or others. It is about trends. It is therefore necessary to look at the present position in regard to company tax in western Europe and also at what is going on behind the scenes there. If these are viewed alongside the U.K. situation, then, bearing in mind the basic concepts already discussed, it may be possible to discern something, even if it is that there is no trend at all.

Company tax in western Europe

It is not proposed to give a detailed exposition of the company tax systems which operate in Europe. This would take far too long and would merely divert us from our real purpose. In any event, changes are going on all the time, mainly in the rates of tax, but also in the systems, which are the business of regular journals to record. Terminology is difficult too, and there is some confusion between local (municipal) taxes and national taxes, which makes true comparisons difficult. Suffice to say that, in general, the effective rate of company tax in the EEC, as about to be enlarged, is more than 40%, rising to more than 50% in some cases, but probably averaging out at around 50%. Nevertheless, bearing in mind that rates of tax are interesting, a brief narrative description of the various company tax systems with an indication of the individual national rates is attached to this paper as Appendix 11B.

The single entity concept predominates, and in most cases it is the imputation system which applies, although there are elements of the classical system in several cases, especially as regards non-resident shareholders. The German split-rate system is a single entity system. It appears to be classical, at least as regards the distributed profits, but it is in fact similar to the two-rate system proposed for, but not adopted by, the U.K. which, as everyone now agrees, is virtually the same as the imputation system.

The van den Tempel report

No review of the tax situation of companies in western Europe would be complete without a reference to this report, which was instructed by the European Commission and prepared by Professor van den Tempel, on the subject of corporation tax and individual income-tax.[4] The report was published in Brussels in 1970, and it must be understood that the views expressed in the report are Professor van den Tempel's personal views, and that these have by no means yet been accepted by the Commission. It is not possible to comment on, or even to summarise this excellent report here. The important point for the purpose of the present discussion is that the report recommends the classical, double-rate system which the U.K. is about to abandon and which both France and Germany abandoned some years ago. The report recognises six systems of company tax:

(A) Classical.
(B) Split rate, e.g. the German system.
(C) Imputation or other credit system.
(D) Nil rate, i.e. dividends allowed as a charge.
(E) Fiscal transparence (see above).
(F) Modified nil rate, i.e. dividends allowed to a certain extent.

These are classified, following the approach adopted by the present paper, i.e. two basic concepts with a number of forms or mechanisms, as follows:

Single entity systems	*Dual entity systems*
B	A
C	D
E	F

Double taxation relief

Double taxation

By double taxation we mean taxation of income more than once. 'Double' suggests twice only, but this is a relic of a simpler age when international trade usually involved only two countries at a time, usually Britain and one other. Income can, of course, be taxed, or be liable to be taxed, more than twice, and it is probably more correct to refer to multiple taxation rather than to double taxation. There are occasions when income is taxed more than once *within* a country, but it is the international sort of multiple taxation with which we are concerned here. As world society becomes more sophisticated and more interdependent, income will tend to become more and more subject to multiple taxation. This will require to be coped with by better and more wide-ranging double taxation treaties. If we recognise the significance of the trend of the character of the income itself, it becomes that little bit easier —though not easy—to spot a possible trend in the taxation of that income and in the probable reliefs intended to eliminate double or multiple taxation.

The fundamental problem is this. Which country has the right to tax income which is the property of a taxpayer who is not resident, or not solely resident, or which arises partly in one or more other countries? As national sovereignty is still a very touchy matter, despite our advanced state of civilisation, and taxation is one, if not the primary expression of that sovereignty, this whole question of multiple taxation and relief therefor has given rise, and will continue to give rise to profound problems. As almost every country in the world seems to be engaged in reforming its tax system, it follows that every existing double-tax treaty will have to be revised, probably several times over, in the next decade.

Avoidance

Avoidance of tax by the use of artificial international arrangements for individuals and companies is the despair of those interested in a fair incidence of tax between one taxpayer and another. While each country insists on going its own way taxwise, it is possible to exploit the national differences to mitigate or eliminate tax, sometimes by using one highly taxed country as a tax haven *vis-à-vis* another highly taxed country. This is, of course, all part of the game which is played by taxpayers against all national revenue departments which are so foolishly insular in a matter which does not permit of a parochial approach. This is natural cupidity versus national stupidity. In terms of multiple taxation the latter becomes international stupidity. But this is not the worst of it. There is evasion too. There are those who never tell the truth, who give false information, and who cut and run into and out of a national jurisdiction at will.

But, as is so often the case, hope arises from the despair and the frustration which can only be cured by international cooperation. Thus, the treaties which exist have a stated dual purpose, namely to eliminate (or alleviate) double taxation and to eliminate avoidance and evasion in the realms of international tax.

Present agreements

No country has a double taxation treaty with every other country, and even where agreements exist these are not always comprehensive, but simply deal with a few specific classes of income. There is, therefore, a good deal of double or multiple taxation about, although many countries give relief unilaterally where hardship would otherwise result.

There are a great number of double tax treaties, which are generally made between two sovereign states and, although individual treaties may cover dependent territories of the signatory countries, the usual arrangement is a bilateral agreement between two countries. There is a fairly complete network of agreements covering western European countries. But inconsistencies and anomalies still abound. There is much to do, and a great deal should happen in this area in the immediate future.

The bilateral procedure is now reckoned to be rather old-fashioned and cumbersome and, as the ideal arrangement is clearly a standard multinational agreement which each country can sign and thereby bind itself to every other signatory country, it would be reasonable to assume that some effort will be made to operate a standard multinational agreement, at least for selected groups of countries. The EEC is obviously a good example of such a group.

The multinational treaty

The EEC countries could reasonably work towards an umbrella-type standard agreement *re* multiple taxation arising on income within western Europe. The agreement could deal with the matter, not only within the Community but also in a uniform way as between individual member states and countries outwith the EEC.

There are a large number of countries (and several have dependent and associated territories, special arrangements with ex-colonial territories and even a few colonies) in western Europe and, as we have seen above, their tax systems are not standardised. In many cases they are not even similar. But a start could, and should be made within the enlarged EEC, even if only for specific classes of income. A standard double taxation treaty was produced by the OECD in 1963 which, although drawn up as a bilateral treaty, could have been adapted for a multilateral treaty, but this appears to have been lost sight of and is no doubt gathering multiple dust all over the place.

EEC and double taxation

There is no doubt that the enlarged EEC could provide a useful pilot scheme for a multilateral agreement. This would not only seem to be a fairly obvious exercise, but the abolition of double taxation is in fact required by the Treaty of Rome, and a committee appointed by the EEC (the Neumark Committee) to look at direct taxation recommended that all double taxation conventions should be standardised and eventually replaced by a multilateral agreement. This may seem strange, when direct taxation is not specifically mentioned in the Treaty of Rome, and the European Communities Bill—while accepting certain EEC legislation—reserves taxation matters to the U.K. It has to be remembered, however, that the EEC has extensive powers to put down anything which distorts trade or restricts the movement of capital, etc. within the Community, and it is in furtherance of these powers that an interest has been taken in direct taxation. The two areas in which the distortion apprehended is most liable to take place are the taxation of company dividends and the multiple taxation of international income arising within or without the EEC.

Developments

What, then, are the expected developments in this field? Most probably, they will be as follows:

1. A greater and ever growing awareness on the part of governments that the multiple taxation problem is a real one, bringing genuine hardships. This

will be brought about by the realisation that every problem of multiple taxation inevitably brings with it a problem of avoidance and evasion of tax, quite apart from the discouraging effect on foreign investment.

2. New double taxation arrangements on a bilateral basis but with a greater degree of standardisation.
3. The adoption eventually of a multilateral agreement by the member states of the enlarged EEC.

Overspill

A further development required in this field, albeit highly desirable, has little chance of being given attention by any government in the foreseeable future. This is the situation which is generally referred to as 'overspill', by which is meant the foreign tax which is denied full relief because the relieving country wishes to extract a certain minimum rate of tax.

Thus:

Income			
Net foreign income received			£50
Foreign tax deducted (at 50%)			50
Gross foreign income			£100
Tax and DTR			
Home tax @ 55%			£55
Less:	Relief for foreign tax	£50	
	Restricted to keep minimum of 20% in charge for home tax	35	35
	Excess tax (unrelieved)	£15	
Home tax due			£20

The net amount finally received by the taxpayer is £30 after tax of £70, i.e. foreign £50 plus home £20, an effective rate of 70%, which is manifestly far higher than the rate intended to apply in either the home country or the foreign country. Where there is excess foreign tax which arises solely because the resident in question is trading in a country which has a higher rate of tax than the home country, there can be no complaint, e.g.

Income	
Net foreign income received	£50
Foreign tax deducted (at 50%)	50
Gross foreign income	£100

Tax and DTR

Home tax @ 40%			£40
Less:	Relief for foreign tax	£50	
	Restricted to full home rate	40	
	Excess foreign tax (unrelieved)	£10	
Home tax due			£NIL

Relief from foreign country

This problem of overspill is bound up with, and is indeed part of a larger problem which takes in the whole question of excess foreign tax. What is the possibility of relief directly from the foreign government? The accepted principle is that, where income is taxed more than once, credit should be given such that the taxpayer finally pays the rate of tax which is the highest rate of all the countries through which the income passes, whether home or foreign. This appears to have become acceptable, not so much because it is fundamentally sound but rather as a matter of administrative convenience, and mainly because some relief for double taxation is better than none. But is it a sound principle? This is a large and little explored area, and it is unlikely that it will be explored very much because of the practical problems involved, but if rates and systems of tax were fully harmonised this problem would simply disappear.

Here again, western Europe can lead the way to achieve equity and to eliminate distortions. As the EEC is in fact required to do this, we have yet another reason to assume that direct taxation systems within the EEC will become just as much in step, just as harmonised, as indirect taxation.

Summary

Looking back on the preceding pages of this paper one may find it difficult to spot any trend at all. Certainly there *exists* a state of flux. Tax reform is the great cry—as these very words were written the news came of the French Prime Minister's dismissal and the fall of his Government (5 July 1972), one of the main reasons being the allegation of blatant tax avoidance by those responsible for making the tax laws—and every country is determined to show how independent it can remain fiscally and financially, despite being, or becoming, a member of the EEC. Trend, as has already been observed, is more than a mere tendency; it suggests something that goes on happening, gradually perhaps, but not wavering. If this definition were applied very strictly, one could hardly argue that there were any trends in taxation in western Europe, except perhaps in the general desire for tax reform of one kind or another. If, however, one looks a little more closely at the situation described, and if one can tolerate a little stop-go and a few modest digressions, it is possible to discern something of the general direction in which we are going, i.e. the underlying trends.

Reform and harmonisation

These general processes have gone on, and will go on, hand in hand, affecting and stimulating each other to an ever-increasing degree. It may be said with some firmness that there is a trend of reform and harmonisation in European taxation.

Indirect taxation

It seems reasonably certain that VAT will gradually be accepted, not only in western Europe but throughout most of the world, as the principal source of revenue from indirect taxation. There are bound to be modifications to the existing VAT systems, which differ from each other, and there will always be additional fund raisers—Chancellors always seem to be looking for that little extra revenue—such as stamp duties, customs and excise duties, etc. But basically VAT will stay and will spread over the Continent, and it will become more and more the principal means of raising revenue *via* indirect taxation. It may also be used progressively, in line with progressive direct taxation. There is also likely to be an increase in the *number* of 'special' indirect taxes, e.g. pollution and environmental levies.

Direct taxation: individuals

So far as taxes on income are concerned, there is already a fair degree of alignment. Differences are of detail, of sophistication, of personal reliefs and allowances. In the field of capital taxation, however, there is a great deal of difference at present, not only in the tax systems but in rates of tax which, while modest in total, can in individual cases vary from the very light to the penal. As regards capital gains tax, there is a trend towards acceptance of capital gains as a taxable base, just as much as income. When we turn to the corpus of personal wealth, a trend is visible, but it has hardly started and its course is not clear. The principle that personal wealth should be assessed to tax is now well accepted, but how to do it is not clear and will not be clear until governments make up their minds why personal capital should be taxed and what is to be done with the money. Pending the solution of this problem, the apparent trend is towards an inheritance tax, but the real trend, it is suggested, is towards a combined estate duty/gifts tax, although some features of the inheritance tax will be adopted, e.g. consanguinity reliefs. This will not work properly, however, until there is a harmonised system throughout the whole of the EEC, and until a permanent change of residence is treated as a gift or taxable transfer of capital.

Taxation of business profits

Like taxes on income, this is a fairly settled field where changes in detail rather than in principle can be expected. There may be some degree of harmonisation of allowable expenses in general and of depreciation allowances and stock valuation in particular. The biggest change, however, is likely to be in the greater encouragement to non-residents (in other EEC countries) to set up branches and subsidiary companies, mainly by taxing the profits no higher than applies in the case of resident traders.

Company taxation

Great changes are going on in this field, but the underlying trend seems to be towards the single entity concept of companies and their shareholders, and the particular form which is emerging is the imputation system. This appears to be the case despite the recommendation in the van den Tempel Report that the dual entity concept, in particular the classical system, should be adopted. One hesitates to disagree with the conclusion of such a brilliant and painstaking research paper, but to my mind the single entity concept reflects the true situation of companies better and is fairer in its incidence.

Double taxation relief

While there is a lot of confusion here, there are trends which are discernible. Firstly, the principle that relief for double and multiple taxation is not only equitable but is essential for healthy international trade is becoming more and more firmly established. Secondly, the double tax relief offered is of two main kinds:

(a) tax payable in one country only, with exemption in the other, or
(b) taxable in both countries but with a credit for tax paid in one against tax due in the other.

Exemption is given broadly where the capital and enterprise are in one country only. Credit applies where capital and enterprise are represented in both. This general line of reasoning is becoming more firmly established. One area of real difficulty is the taxation of the reward for capital and invention in the form of royalties, interest and dividends, but there seems to be some degree of recognition that, if these belong to capital and to ingenuity which is not indigenous, the taxing authority should not ask for tax thereon, but should allow for full 'border adjustment'.

There is, too, a noticeable trend towards standardisation of double-tax agreements, which ought to lead to a multilateral agreement, at least within the EEC.

Origin and destination

It was only after I had finished this paper that I appreciated how often the word 'origin' had appeared, and how consistently it seemed to be, or about to be, replacing 'destination' in relation to the place where tax becomes due. Here is a further trend 'across the board' of taxation.

Conclusion

There are trends in European taxation. They appear to be as set out above. On the whole the trends are towards better systems which will encourage trade and discourage avoidance. But there is a long way to go and a great deal to do. If this modest review assists this process by stimulating thought and discussion, even if not solving any problems itself, in relation to a subject which is absolutely vital to all of us, it will have been well worth the work involved in its compilation.

Appendix 11A

Comparative Yield of Death Duties in U.K. and other Countries, 1969

	Death Duties as Percentage of					
	Total taxes		Total taxes and Social Security contributions		Direct taxes	GNP
	Central and local government	Central government	Central and local government	Central government	Central government	
U.K.	2·5	2·8	2·2	2·5	5·9	0·82
Belgium	1·4	1·5	1·0	1·0	3·5	0·34
France	0·9	1·0	0·5	0·6	3·6	0·20
Germany	0·3	0·3	0·2	0·2	0·7	0·07
Italy	1·1	1·2	0·7	0·7	4·2	0·22
Luxembourg	0·8	1·0	0·6	0·7	1·8	0·19
Netherlands	1·0	1·0	0·6	0·6	1·7	0·25
Denmark		0·8		0·7	1·9	0·19
Norway	0·2		0·2			0·08
Republic of Ireland[2]	2·2	2·5	2·0	2·3	7·1	0·59
U.S.A.	1·8[1]	2·3	1·5[1]	1·7	2.6	0·48[1]
Australia[2]	3·2[1]	1·3	3·2[1]	1·3	2·0	0·59[1]
New Zealand	2·0	2·2	2·0	2·2	3·2	0·67
South Africa[2]		1·2		1·2	1·8	0·14

Death duties include gifts taxes which are small for most countries but substantial for the Netherlands.

[1] Including State death duties. [2] 1968 figures.

Reproduced, by kind permission of H.M. Stationery Office, from the Green Paper, 'Taxation of Capital on Death: A Possible Inheritance Tax in Place of Estate Duty', H.M.S.O., Cmnd. 4930, p. 11.

Appendix 11B

Company tax systems with an indication of national rate

Belgium

There is an imputation system for residents, with an additional withholding tax (20%) on distributions to non-residents, which is modified for residents of countries with which Belgium has double taxation agreements. The basic rate of company tax is low, at 35% (30% for smaller companies), but there is a temporary surcharge of 10% and an additional surcharge of 6%. The effective rate is more than 40%—basically a single entity, imputation system. It is interesting to note, however, that until two years ago certain dividends (5% on new capital) were allowed as a charge for tax purposes, thus giving a real touch of the nil-rate (dual entity) system.

Denmark

There is a basic company tax, which varies according to the residency status of the company but is normally between 40 and 45%. There is no withholding tax, but personal tax is payable on distributions. This is an example of the dual entity, classical system.

Eire

This is still based on the pre-1965 U.K. system—another single entity case. The combined rate of income tax and corporation tax is about 50%, the latter tax having once again (Finance Bill, 1972) become deductible from the former.

France

Company profits are taxed at 50%, with a credit to resident shareholders of 25%. There is a withholding tax of 25% for non-residents, but this is modified, in some cases to nil, where there are relevant double taxation treaties—basically therefore, the imputation system, recognising the single entity concept. France adopted this system in 1965 when it abandoned the classical system.

Germany

There are two rates of tax, one on retained profits at 51%, and one for distributed profits at 15%. At present there is a small surcharge which increases these rates slightly. Resident shareholders pay full personal tax on distributions. Non-residents have to bear a 25% withholding tax, again subject to modification by way of double tax agreements. The system is basically a split-rate or two-rate system which, as already indicated, is not very different *in principle* from the imputation system and thus gives effect to the single entity concept. Like France, Germany abandoned the classical system (in 1953), and the author understands that neither country is keen to go back to it.

Italy

There is a complicated tax structure for companies, with rates charged at sliding scales up to about 40% but with a separate tax which is based on net worth and on excess income over a standard based on net worth. The total tax usually exceeds 50% and can get up almost to 60%. There is no tax on dividends, except the equivalent of U.K. surtax, but non-residents are charged to a fairly steep withholding tax which is, however, very much reduced, often to nil, under double taxation agreements. The basic concept is one entity, and the system resembles the pre-1965 U.K. system—income-tax plus profits tax. Tax reform is very much expected but it seems to be impossible to find out what kind of reform will take place.

Luxembourg

Companies, other than very small companies, pay tax at about 50%, a flat rate of 40% plus a special municipal levy. There is a withholding tax of 25% on distributions to residents and to non-residents alike, but the latter may be entitled to some double tax relief. Basically the system tends towards the classical or double rate system, i.e. the dual entity concept, with individual company rates of tax running from under 50% to just on 60%.

Norway

The rate of tax on company profits can reach about 60%, but the allowances and reliefs which can be claimed are extremely generous, so that the effective rate is probably no higher than the 'norm' of 50%. There is a state income-tax and a communal tax plus a small equalisation levy. The communal tax is more important than the state tax. Municipalities have always had the right to tax. Dividends which are subjected to a withholding tax of 25% are allowed as a charge against the state tax but not the communal tax. A difficult tax system to fathom properly, but it seems to be half classical and half split-rate, both single and dual entity concepts being recognised.

The Netherlands

There is a basic rate plus surcharge, to give a combined rate of company tax of about 47%. There is no withholding tax on distributions to resident shareholders, but no imputation or other credit is allowed towards their personal liability. The withholding tax on non-residents (25%) is modified by double taxation treaties. This is a form of the classical system, the company and the shareholders being regarded as virtually unrelated. It is believed that the Dutch strongly favour the classical system and, although theirs is the voice of a small country, it is a voice which rightly carries tremendous weight in taxation matters.

United Kingdom

The classical system operates at present, giving corporation tax rates varying from 40 to 63.25%. This is to be changed, thus recognising the single entity concept, to the imputation system in April 1973, with a flat rate (no withholding tax) expected to be 50% (40% for smaller companies). The three largest members of the enlarged EEC—Britain, France, and Germany—appear to be firmly in favour of imputation, and all three have had practical experience of the classical system and found it wanting. It is perhaps interesting to note that the proposed U.K. system is not so far removed from its pre-1965 system, that Germany appears to like it, that Eire still retains it, and that the Canadian Royal Commission on Taxation (Carter Commission, 1967) recommended it for Canada.

Notes

1 First published in *The Accountant's Magazine*, September 1972.
2 The views and opinions expressed in this paper are the personal views and opinions of the author, who is alone responsible for them and who offers them in all humility, appreciating that the area of enquiry has not been fully explored and that acknowledged experts have expressed contrary views on some points.

As regards facts and general background information given in the paper, these are not authoritative. They are set down on the basis of the author's general understanding of the European tax situation and not as the result of a special research project. That is why, with one or two exceptions where the source is made clear, direct reference is not made to specific books etc., but the author gratefully acknowledges the information he has been able to acquire over the last few years from many different sources.
3 T. D. Lynch: 'Harmonising Taxes in the Common Market', *The Accountant's Magazine*, October 1967, page 495.
4 A. J. van den Tempel, *Corporation Tax and Individual Income Tax in the European Communities*, Office for Official Publications of the European Communities, Luxembourg.

Bibliography

CARR S. SHOUP (ed.), *Fiscal Harmonization in Common Markets*, Columbia University Press, 1967, 2 vols.

EDMUND S. PHELPS, *Fiscal Neutrality Toward Economic Growth*, McGraw-Hill, 1965.

SÉAN RÉAMONN, *The Philosophy of the Corporate Tax*, Institute of Public Administration, 1970.

ARTHUR DALE *Tax Harmonization in Europe*, Taxation Publishing Co, Ltd, 1963.

Income Taxes outside the United Kingdom, 1970, H.M.S.O., 1972. 8 vols.

Bulletin of The International Bureau of Fiscal Documentation, International Bureau of Fiscal Documentation, Muiderpoort, 124 Sarphatistraat, Amsterdam.

Journal UEC, Verlagsbuchhandlung des Instituts der Wirtschaftsprüfer GmbH, 4 Düsseldorf, Postfach 10226.

European Taxation, International Bureau of Fiscal Documentation.

12 Business Finance in Europe

by A. T. McLEAN

Difference exists within the European Community between nations, customs, laws and currency; to name but a few. The European Economic Community programme for the harmonisation of many of the differences is well documented and embraces the equalisation of diverse commercial laws, among other things, to facilitate the economic union of the signatories to the treaty. One of the greatest of the many differences existing between Britain and the founder member states is in the financing of business enterprise. The British providers of finance—the investors or savers—have different characteristics compared with their European counterparts. The users of finance—corporate industrial and commercial enterprises—make use of it in such ways as to create a distinction between British and European companies. The type of finance used in Britain typically differs from that of Europe, and the agencies linking the providers with the users—the stock exchanges—probably provide the greatest contrast of all. One aspect of business finance, however, is common to all countries and that is a form of currency known as the eurodollar.

Euro-currencies

The European Economic Community does not have a unified capital market or a federal currency. The Treaty of Rome which set up the Common Market is noticeably reticent about a subject which raises acute questions of sovereignty. Article 67 of the treaty restricts itself to mentioning only the movement of funds:

> Member states shall, in the course of the transitional period and to the extent necessary for the proper functioning of the Common Market, progressively abolish as between themselves restrictions on the movement of capital belonging to persons resident in member states and also any discriminatory treatment based on the nationality or place of residence of the parties or on the place in which such capital is invested.

Despite the abolition of exchange control for personal investment in 1968, which enables citizens of the founder member states to invest across national borders, including extra-Community investments, the Community has as yet been unable to create its own capital market and currency. This could be regarded as an example of chauvinism at its worst, but on the other hand an examination of the political and economic disasters which befell the currencies of most European countries in the first half of the twentieth century leads one to an appreciation of the reluctance of member states to yield control of their respective monetary policies. Economic planning, the fight against inflation, and strict control of individual capital markets are still a prerogative of individual member states.

Since the latter half of the 1950s, however, a new type of European currency and capital market appeared and grew, to the surprise of both bankers and governments alike. This currency is the euro-dollar, which is not a physical thing but merely a claim for a dollar existing outwith the United States. That is to say an American dollar banked outside the United States can be renegotiated on a commercial basis—which makes it the nearest thing yet to an international currency. Strangely, the Russians are given credit for giving the currency impetus and a name: Russian holdings of U.S. dollars were not unnaturally banked outwith the United States in the Moscow-Narodny Bank in London which then re-lent to other banks in Europe. The name euro-dollar is said to have stemmed from the telegraphic address, euro-bank, of the Moscow-Narodny bank in Paris. In the early years there was no real incentive to repatriate these euro-dollars as America sank into deficit, and companies responsible for earning substantial amounts of dollars were in no great hurry to convert them into their respective national currencies. Thus a cross-frontier currency grew in Europe. It was estimated that 15 billion euro-dollars were in existence in 1968: in 1972 at least 50 billion dollars were circulating. Only when euro-dollars are converted into pounds, marks, or francs do they disappear from the euro-dollar market.

A later development, the euro-bond market, provides Europe with an unofficial supranational capital market centred in London. The issue of euro-bonds is now a major method of financing industries, institutions, countries, cities, and even the European Coal and Steel Community. Euro-bonds are basically bonds in bearer form, denominated in dollars or other European currencies, interest being payable without deduction of a withholding tax. As securities, euro-bonds are readily absorbed by European investors; they inevitably have good coupon rates, interest is paid gross, and purchases are not reported to central authorities. It has been said that a large number of private fortunes have been buried in euro-bond issues, which pay higher rates of interest than do Swiss banks.

In addition to euro-dollars there exists a euro-currency market worth about 10 billion dollars and comprised mainly of Euro-Deutsche Marks, Euro-Francs Suisses, and surprisingly Euro-Yen. The Euro-Deutsche Mark is by far the most important of these and provides a strong market for short-term deposits. This brief appraisal of 'Euro-monies' would not be complete without mention of the Community's *unité de compte* or unit of account. The U/A is not a currency but a complexity, having a gold value of 0.888671 grams of fine gold, and a former relationship with the 17 currencies of the sometime European Payments Union. As from 1 January 1973 the U/A is linked to the currencies of the enlarged Community of nine member states. The complex nature of the U/A arises from its relationship with real currencies and its use in floating bond issues in times of international monetary uncertainty—the aim being to protect investors from devaluation losses, though profit can be made from revaluations. Generally, the U/A can be regarded as equivalent to the U.S. dollar, and is the financial unit of the Community.

It is of interest to note that the communiqué issued by the Heads of State of the nine member states of the enlarged Community following the summit conference in Paris in October 1972 included a declaration to institute before 1 April 1973, a European monetary cooperation fund which will be administered by the Committee of Governors of Central Banks within the context of general guidelines on economic policy laid down by the Council of Ministers. In an initial phase the fund will operate on bases which include the following:

Concerted action among the central banks for the purposes of narrowing the margins of fluctuations between their currencies.

The multilateralisation of positions resulting from interventions in Community currencies and the multilateralisation of intra-Community settlements.

The use for this purpose of a European monetary unit of account.

The administration of short-term monetary support among the central banks.

Company finance

Sources of long-term business finance available to the archetypal commercial or industrial company are basically classed as internal or external. Internal finance is available from a retention of profits earned from previous operations, and external finance is available by issue of shares, either equity or preference, or loan or debenture stock, or by some form of hybrid security such as a convertible bond. At the theoretical level the actual source of finance will depend on an appraisal of the company's optimal capital structure, dividend policy, the costs of the respective types of capital, the nature of the market and the firm's ability to take profitable advantage of investment opportunities. At the pragmatic level the source of finance to be tapped tends to be based on traditional national attitudes to finance, and will be related to the capital market of the country within which the company is based, or on the nature of the international bond market at any time. At the pragmatic level, therefore, no surprise should be expressed at the differences which arise in the long-term financing of companies in the Community, the U.K., the U.S.A., and Japan.

Internal sources

Statistics are difficult to obtain in respect of the degree of retention of profits by companies in the major trading nations. In its memorandum to the Council,[1] the Commission noted, from an analysis of material obtained from various sources roughly covering the period from 1960/66, that companies in certain countries used internal financing in the following proportions:

United States and Germany	65%
Netherlands, United Kingdom, Belgium, and France	55–60%
Italy	45%
Japan	25–30%

Meaningful conclusions are difficult to draw from this data. Italy and Japan, with fairly low rates of internal financing, are two countries that enjoyed the highest industrial growth during the period under consideration, whereas the U.K. enjoyed a very moderate rate of production growth. Italy and Japan, however, self-financed only 60–70% of gross capital investment whereas the U.S., the U.K., and the Netherlands financed approximately 100%. Of greater significance would be the type of external finance used in these countries.

One interesting aspect about self-financing becomes clear from an appraisal of the method of growth of some of the relatively large industrial concerns in the Community. Many large private companies without access to the capital markets exist in the founder member states—Germany and France in particular—and are financed either internally or from the dominant commercial banking system, or by a combination of these. These firms, however, by the very nature of their privacy, tend to have a greater opportunity to utilise their earning power internally. A classic example is the German firm Henkel.

Henkel,[2] noted for soap powders, such as 'Persil', and other household products is the fourth largest washing and cleaning products manufacturer in Europe, preceded only by Unilever, Procter and Gamble, and Colgate-Palmolive. The company, which is also a force to be reckoned with in the field of chemicals, had more than 8,000 different product lines in 1971, with a gross turnover exceeding one billion dollars and an annual growth rate of 10%. No shares are quoted in any stock exchange, the total equity being held by 41 members of the Henkel family. Significantly, until recently, the company has never sought any form of external capital and has no long-term debt in its balance sheet. Apart from normal short-term financing the company has grown internally—an astonishing feat by British and American standards.

External sources

Again statistics are not easily available, and many appear to be of extremely dubious validity, including those referred to by the Commission in its report to the Council. It would appear, however, that European firms have obtained sufficient amounts of external finance, most of which has come from banks and other credit institutions. The reason for this method of financing, unique to European countries, is to be found not only in the way in which the European finance market operates, but also in the fact that a considerable number of European firms are too small to have direct access to the capital markets.

In noting a European trend towards bond issues as opposed to share issues, the Commission remarked, with some anxiety, that the relative degree of high gearing in many European companies might not be to their advantage in times of economic regression. The observation was made that European companies did not particularly favour equity issues, and only had recourse to this method in many cases, in order to restore a proper balance between their resources and liabilities, or for reasons of prestige *vis-à-vis* rival firms, or again to meet the requirements of a credit institution. The weaknesses of stock exchanges in some countries tended to favour financing by capital loans or equity participation by the banking system rather than by new share issues. At the same time European investors tended to be discouraged from investing in equities, because of poor buoyancy of prices aggravated by sudden sharp upward and downward fluctuations, which is typical of inefficient markets.

One method of correcting the imbalance between risk capital and loan capital would be to make use of the popular American hybrid security—the convertible bond. Investors would suffer less risk than when buying shares, while preserving the chance of appreciation. Convertible bonds should also be acceptable to companies, who could thus issue shares indirectly at a price close to that of their shares on the stock exchange at the time of issue, which is not the case with new share issues in the Community. Curiously, convertible stocks in the Community are not classed for taxation purposes as loan stocks, but as shares. At present, convertibles have not developed to any great extent in the Community.

Another problem concerns the taxing of dividends and interest. Payment of interest on bonds is deductible from the tax profits of companies paying the interest but ordinary dividends are liable to profit tax payable by the distributing company and to income tax payable by the shareholders. The Commission noted that, at the time, companies with a profit basis of 100 can pay approximately:

	To resident *shareholders*	To resident *bond holders*
Germany	57	100
France	50	75
Italy	47.5	69
The Netherlands	42.5	100
Belgium	56	80
Luxembourg	51	95

The above data is subject, of course, to differences in personal income-tax payable by residents. The Commission concluded that the capital market was geared to a form of financing which limited the spreading of risk, profit, and control, and was not adjusted to the requirements of rapidly expanding firms.

A proposal to abolish deduction at source in respect of interest on bonds has already been made by the Commission on the basis that:

> ... in so far as deduction at source on interest on bonds is reflected in the rate of interest paid, its abolition would help to check the rise in interest rates and reduce the cost to European firms of financing their investments, an aim which is common to all member states,
>
> ... abolition would restore equality between national money markets and the Euro-bond market where there is no deduction at source, since issues are made on markets where non-residents are exempt from such tax,
>
> ... the introduction of deduction at source in countries which do not apply it might encourage a drain of international capital, not to say Community capital, towards third countries.

Having stated its attitude to deduction of tax at source *vis-à-vis* bond interest the Commission also advised that the same principle should apply to dividends on shares. Increase in tax evasion over and above the accepted continental European levels is not envisaged as a result of these proposals!

The creation of a pan-European capital market is also viewed as a necessary prerequisite in the over-all movement of company financing from the banking system to the stock market system. The Commission does not actually suggest that the banks have a money monopoly but nevertheless it envisages a movement away from inefficient national markets to investment on a supranational scale as increasing the financial institutions' efficiency through increased competition. In this respect monetary union in the Community is particularly important, but the thin end of the wedge would be established by companies applying to more stock exchanges for a quotation. The London Stock Exchange is an obvious market if such a proposal is going to succeed. However, for a variety of reasons, most of which are nationalistic, reaction has always existed against London as an European capital market, and typically, no more than a score of European companies are quoted on the London market. Most of these are Dutch; Akzo, Philips, Royal Dutch, and Unilever being the most familiar from over a half-dozen enjoying the privilege of the most efficient European market with, among others, the Belgian Wagons-Lits, the German Commerzbank and August Thyssen-Hütte, and the French Compagnie Financière de Paris et des Pays-Bas.

The question of quotation, on the London market for instance, involves problems of financial disclosure and auditing standards which immediately demonstrates further substantial differences between Europe and Britain. Undoubtedly, many European companies have been reluctant to comply with the British disclosure requirements, and an interesting development to watch for will be the trend, if any, of European companies seeking the benefit of multiple quotation on the London market.

External finance available to European companies is supplied in large quantities by the commercial banking system in the form of long and medium-term loans and equity holdings. The power and influence of many continental banks is enormous. Not only are they the financiers of industry, they now appear to be the controllers as well. The 'big three' German banks—the Deutsche Bank, the Dresdner Bank, and the Commerzbank—have an impressive network of holdings. It has been estimated that at least 25% of the equity of some 150 major German companies is held by the banks. Naturally the banks are represented on the boards of such companies, and in many cases have substantial authority. In Germany, for example, little dialogue exists between shareholders and management. The banks, as major shareholders, dominate management, and by using the proxy votes of their clients—which causes some controversy—have voting rights to an estimated 60% of all quoted shares in Germany. Not only do the banks act as clearing-houses, they also act as issuing houses and stockbrokers. The Dresdner Bank, for example, emphasises its role as a broker, supplying investment advice on domestic and foreign securities to national and overseas clients, and executing orders for any type of security. They also do substantial business as investment managers, and act as underwriters for new issues.

Conflict can arise in the continental banking system, however. Banks acting both as shareholders and as lenders may well have differing interests in a particular company. Similarly, as managers and supervisors of companies, banks obtain vital and confidential information which can then filter through to their broking and investment divisions. Sitting on both sides of the fence, as European banks are in the habit of doing, creates an economic and monetary atmosphere which is rather less than desirable or efficient. Steps are, however, being taken to regularise the situation.

Financing small and medium-sized business

The classic British 'Macmillan Gap',[3] observed in the 1920s and 1930s and essential closed by the 1950s, in the opinion of the Radcliffe Committee,[4] had its counterpart in Europe. Small and medium-sized firms by virtue of their size or legal structure suffered the usual problems of restricted access to the European markets, or to medium or long-term bank credit. In plugging the gap existing in the capital market structure between the commercial banking system and the Stock Exchanges, the British created special finance institutions such as the Finance Corporation for Industry Ltd and the Industrial and Commercial Finance Corporation Ltd. The purpose of the former company, which was established by the Bank of England in collaboration with the joint-stock banks and a number of insurance companies and investment trusts, is to provide temporary or longer-period finance for industrial businesses, more of which were medium sized (and even large) than small, the minimum amount lent being at least £250,000. The latter company, also created by the Bank of England and the English and Scottish banks, specifically assists smaller companies requiring long-term loan or share capital which cannot be raised by way of banking facilities or public issue. Other institutions were later set up to provide a variety of specified financial services.

The European authorities assist small or medium-sized firms in a variety of ways, either by:

> ... setting up public or semi-public bodies specialising in medium and long-term loans at preferential rates of interest, accompanied by a more flexible system of guarantees than that of banks, or by
> ... granting of credit on preferential terms through banks at subsidised interest rates, or by
> ... provision of security by specially created bodies, e.g. cooperative credit institutes, to enable firms to avail themselves of bank credit, or by
> ... creating public or semi-public bodies whose function is to take up shares in companies.

The European Commission, however, noted with dissatisfaction, that rapidly growing smaller businesses were in general unable to obtain necessary and sufficient funds to sustain their rates of growth. Similarly, new or relatively new enterprises suffer from the so-called 'appraisal gap' where finance institutions have difficulty in appraising the risks inherent in new ventures and are, therefore, unwilling to provide essential risk capital.

In the U.K. this gap has largely been met by financial institutions and merchant banks providing development or venture capital for such enterprises. Capital for development and expansion is available from specialist industrial development companies to the smaller type of business which finds bank financing sufficient only for limited growth. Venture capital is available to the relatively new proposition which has little or no 'track record'. In this case the inherent risk and potential rewards are higher. In both cases funds will be provided through a minority equity participation with possible back-up finance being provided by preference or loan capital. In both cases managerial support at board level would usually be provided. The real rewards to the institutions would be realised by the eventual public flotation of their investments—assuming that the economic goals of the developing companies are being achieved.

The British have apparently been quicker than the Europeans to appreciate the importance of providing risk capital to small enterprises who would otherwise be unable to obtain finance for development and innovation. The contribution of the small and medium-sized business enterprise to a nation's economy should not be underestimated, especially as all the founder member states have in general much smaller business establishments than have the United States or the U.K. Similarly, small companies in the United States, followed by U.K. firms, were quicker to recognise and take advantage of relatively new financing methods such a leasing and factoring. Leasing appears to be growing rapidly more popular in the Community but factoring has still to achieve financial recognition. From the evidence available it would appear that a 'euro-expansion gap' has still to be adequately plugged.

The stock exchanges

An efficient market has been defined as: A market where there are large numbers of rational profit maximisers (and large numbers of shares) actively competing, with each trying to predict future market values of individual securities and where important current information is almost freely available to all participants.

European stock markets hardly fit the above definition. The New York Stock Exchange, which is regarded as an efficient market by 'random walkers',[5] has a total market capitalisation of 780 billion dollars, 23% of which is accredited to the top ten companies.[6] The Netherlands national market has a total capitalisation of 13 billion dollars, 75% of which is accredited to the top ten companies. Although both examples are at extreme ends of a scale, the American data typify a healthy market position where it is difficult for a few stocks to dominate the others, unlike the much weaker situation in the small Dutch market. European markets tend to be small in total market capitalisation, with a relatively small number of stocks dominating the rest. The only exception is the French market, with only 24% of a total capitalisation of 27 billion dollars held by the top ten stocks. This compares with the U.K. market, which is the second largest in the world, where only 22% of a total capitalisation of 122 billion dollars is held by the top ten. France, however, only quotes about 900 securities, some of which are moribund, whereas about 3,000 are quoted on the U.K. market.

The European exchanges also have different types of trading procedure compared with that of the London Stock Exchange which operates the unique jobbing system. The two main systems in use in Europe are the call-over system and the trading-post system. Stock exchanges using the call-over system meet twice a day, when an exchange official, possibly the chairman, lists the securities dealt in at the exchange, with their relative prices. Clearly this method is suitable only for small exchanges. Bids and offers are made by brokers as each security is called, and bargains between buyers and sellers are struck. Prices which differ from the call-over price affect the succeeding call-over price. Brokers deal among themselves between the two fixed call-over times.

The trading-post system, which is preferred by large exchanges, including New York and Sydney, but not the U.K., involves the trading floor of an exchange being split into compartments where specified securities may be dealt in. At these specified points or 'trading posts', where current market price is indicated, brokers will conduct transactions with each other on an auctioneering basis. If clients' orders cannot be executed because of imposed quantity or price limitations, these may be passed for later execution to specialists who deal in specific securities at each post. Specialists trade, also, on their own account, and in so doing increase the 'efficiency' of the market. Individual exchanges normally oversee specialist dealing to prevent market rigging.

Both these methods of operating in European exchanges are in contrast to the singular London jobbing system by which jobbers, acting as principals on specific securities, buy and sell on their own account in dealing with brokers who act only as agents on behalf of clients. The jobber's 'turn' on the difference between buying and selling should represent his profit, brokers being rewarded by commissions on clients' orders, but due to the volume of dealing, and often rapid change of price, the jobber's profit or loss arises through changes in the price of personal holdings of securities.

Control over market operations and dealing demonstrates further difference between the British and European systems. Although neither has an exact equivalent to the United States' Securities and Exchange Commission (SEC), the relatively strong British Companies Acts, together with the Stock Exchange Rules and Regulations, have provided reasonably sufficient protection to investors. Shareholder protection relative to merger activity, which is much more pronounced than on the continent, was strengthened from the late 1960s by the City's voluntary and extra statutory City Code on Takeovers and Mergers. Despite demands for extra financial disclosure by companies the only real problem causing some concern in the U.K. markets is that of 'insider trading'. In contrast, European exchanges and company legislation generally offer less shareholder protection, though there clearly has been a raising of standards in the last few years, especially in the Netherlands, Germany, and France. Some euro-markets, however, have outside supervisory organisations which, though less effective than SEC, do exercise some control. Possibly the strongest of these is Belgium's Commission Bancaire, which has legal authority over new issues and take over bids. This is perhaps the nearest equivalent to SEC, but unlike SEC treats information as private. France set up the Commission des Opérations de Bourse in 1967, to improve control and regulate the activities of the French market. The Dutch and the Germans have also created bodies which take some interest in such stock market matters as mergers and financial disclosure.

A comparison of the European stock exchanges with that of London would be misleading without an appraisal of the market system in each of the founder member states. Each country has its own interesting characteristics:

Belgium

The principal exchange is in Brussels, with subsidiary exchanges at Antwerp, Ghent, and Liège. About 600 Belgium stocks and 400 bonds and foreign securities are quoted. The call-over system is used, and only registered brokers (*agents de change*) are authorised to deal. Banks, which supply most of the business, cannot become members, and must pass their orders to brokers. Dealing is mainly by cash settlement but dealing for the account is generally permitted for the largest companies. A number of securities, mainly foreign, without a quotation are traded by banks and financial institutions and at monthly public sales.

France

France has stock exchanges at Paris—the principal one—Bordeaux, Lille, Lyons, Marseilles, Nancy, Nantes, and Toulouse. About 900 shares are quoted on a market which has been criticised as being rather narrow. The call-over system is used, with some specialist dealing for some securities which have little marketability. Dealing is by accredited *agents de change* but most business from the public is via the banks. Settlement is for cash except in the case of the top 250 foreign and domestic securities, which may be dealt in for the account. A large amount of unofficial dealing takes place outwith market hours.

Germany

The German stock exchanges are based in Frankfurt am Main—the largest—and Düsseldorf, Hamburg, Bremen, Munich, Hanover, and Stuttgart. The Frankfurt and Düsseldorf exchanges have about 300 shares and 1,200 bonds registered in their quotation lists. The trading-post system is used and dealing is effected mainly by the banks, though each province appoints a *Kursmakler*, a special broker who fixes rates of securities. The official market – 'Amtlicher Market' – is under State control but a semi-official market – 'Geregelter Freivorkehr' – has less rigorous admission regulations. A substantial amount of transactions are effected outwith the Stock Exchange. All transactions are for cash.

Italy

The Italian stock exchanges are in Milan—the main centre—Genoa, Naples, Rome, Turin, Trieste, and Venice. Only about 150 shares are quoted on this small market. The Milan exchange has an unusual operating system, with collective pricing at the opening and closing of each session; a restricted list of high turnover securities is called at the commencement of each session, and new prices are set depending on the volume of trading; each session is closed by a similar calling procedure. Only members of the stock exchange – 'Agents di Cambio' – and their representatives are authorised to deal and most transactions are for the account. The market appears to suffer from some disorganisation which in itself tends to make investment in other countries more attractive. Even stockbrokers have gone on strike.

The Netherlands

Stock exchanges are in Amsterdam, Rotterdam, and The Hague, most business being done at Amsterdam. About 400 shares are quoted, with a small number of major companies dominating the market. An auction market system is operated by members of the 'Vereeniging Voor den Effectenhandel' (Association for Trade in Securities) who deal with the public, passing on orders to members, – 'hoeklieden' – who have no direct contact with the public and who, rather like the London jobbers, specialise in specific security groups. Most shares are in bearer form and settlement is for cash.

As can be seen, not only does continental stock exchange procedure differ from that of the U.K., it differs substantially among member states. The Dutch are well regulated but the Germans have a system which could do with thorough revision, and indeed, steps have been taken to reduce the banking influence on the stock exchanges. A major step towards harmonisation of stock exchange practice and control has been taken by the European Commission in proposing a pan-European prospectus for companies seeking a stock exchange quotation.

The European prospectus

In September 1972 the Commission delivered to the Council of Ministers —for their consideration as well as that of Parliament, the Economic and Social Committee and others—a proposed directive concerning the contents, supervision, and circulation of prospectuses when securities are admitted for official quotation on the stock exchanges of member states.[7] The proposal would make it compulsory for companies to follow common rules in publishing prospectuses, which must comply with specific rules concerning information content. Provision is made for adaption of these rules to allow for different types of issuer, e.g. financial institutions or public enterprises as opposed to the normal type of limited company, and different types of security. Chapter 5 of Appendix A of the proposed directive sets out the general rules concerning financial information and makes interesting comparison with its British equivalent contained in the Fourth Schedule to the Companies Act 1948 and Appendix 34 of the Stock Exchange Rules and Regulations. In brief, the following information is required:

(a) A comparative tabulation summarising the essential elements of the annual accounts of the last five years.
(b) The annual accounts as approved in general meeting for the last two years. If more than nine months have elapsed since the last financial year end an interim statement is required, though this need not be audited.
(c) If the annual accounts do not provide sufficiently detailed information in accordance with the Commission's directive (presumably referring to the information required by the proposed fourth directive) then additional notes and comments are required, with explicit corrections and modifications to the published accounts.
(d) The above provisions also apply if consolidated accounts are published by the company.

The above can be compared with the U.K. requirements, i.e. a five-year profit record demanded by the Companies Act, 1948—10 years by the Stock Exchange—and statement of assets and liabilities as at the last balance sheet date.

Where a company has interests in other companies, the proposal is much more explicit and demanding than the U.K. requirements.

(e) Where a company holds at least 10% of the capital of another it must state, preferably in tabular form, its name, headquarters, proportion of capital held, subscribed capital, reserves, and last financial results, unless they already figure in the annual accounts annexed to the prospectus.
(f) Where a company is deemed to have some control over the operations of

another, by holding at least 25% of the capital of that company, or where the investment is at least 10% of the subscribed capital of the investing company, or where the earnings of the 'associate'[8] company contribute at least 10% to the company's total earnings, then more detailed information is required about the 'associate' company, namely the field of activity, book value of stocks or shares held, amount remaining to be paid up on the stocks or shares, net amount of turnover[9] realised in the last financial year, amount of dividends received during the last financial year, intercompany balances between both companies, and amount of guarantees or surety given by the company in respect of the activities of the 'associate'.

(g) All the above information requirements of investments where at least 10% of the capital is held should be grouped in such a way as to distinguish between companies of the same member state as the publishing company, companies in other member states, and companies of third countries.

(h) Where consolidated accounts are published, detailed information is required in respect of principles and methods of consolidation, including details of consolidation adjustments and minority interests. The requirements in this case are particularly rigorous.

(i) In addition to the historical financial requirements of Chapter 5, Chapter 7 of Appendix A to the proposal requires a general indication to be given about the company's performance since its last financial year-end; this indication will refer in detail to turnover, trends in production and inventory, trends in costs and selling prices, and the state of the order book.

A financial forecast may also be made in the prospectus, provided that it is distinguished as a forecast and is based on sound commercial assumptions which should be identified in the forecast statement. Indication should also be given, if possible, as to the company's dividend and reserve policies.

The above description of the financial requirements of the proposed directive is necessarily brief and covers only a fraction of the Commission's requirements. It should, however, indicate that British prospectus standards may well require considerable revision.

These Community standards proposed by the Commission should improve the information available to investors in all member states, and in this respect it is fair to comment that many of the founder member states will be much more affected by the proposal than will the U.K. Furthermore, the equivalence of standards will facilitate interprenetration of capital markets by improving the quality and comparability of information published on securities quoted on Community stock exchanges.

Which brings us back to where we started—differences must be harmonised if we are to progress as one Community.

Notes

1 *Industrial Policy in the Community*, Brussels, 1970.

2 See *Fortune*, August 1972.

3 *Report of the Macmillan Committee on Finance and Industry* (Cmnd 3897) 1931 HMSO. London.

4 *Report of the Radcliffe Committee on the working of the Monetary System* (Cmnd 827) HMSO London 1958

5 The random walk hypothesis demands an efficient market.

6 See *Vision*, June 1972; data quoted mid-March 1972.

7 'Proposition de directive et projet de recommandation du Conseil concernant Le Prospectus D'Admission En Bourse de Valeurs Mobilières', *Supplement 8/72, Bulletin des Communautés Européennes.*

8 Terminology of the author.

9 A literal translation of *montant net du chiffre d'affaires.*

Bibliography

Small Firms and the Common Market, 1972. Confederation of British Industry.

Paul Ferris, *Men and Money – Financial Europe To-day*, Pelican, 1970.

The Institute of Chartered Accountants of Scotland. *Company Prospectuses: The Accountant's Role*, 1970.

Anthony Sampson, *The New Europeans*, Panther. 1971.

Investment Guide to Western Europe, Parkland Research Europe SA. 1972.

Industrial Policy in the Community, Commission of the European Communities. 1970.

Le Prospectus D'Admission En Bourse De Valeurs Mobilières, Commission of the European Communities. 1972.

Index